FRACTURING RESEMBLANCES

EASA Series
Published in Association with the European Association
of Social-Anthropologists (EASA)

FRACTURING RESEMBLANCES

Identity and Mimetic Conflict
in Melanesia and the West

Simon Harrison

Berghahn Books
New York • Oxford

First published in 2006 by

Berghahn Books

www.berghahnbooks.com

© 2006 Simon Harrison

Library of Congress Cataloging-in-Publication Data

Harrison, Simon, 1952–
    Fracturing resemblances : identity and mimetic conflict in Melanesia
and the West / Simon Harrison
        p. cm. -- (EASA monographs ; v. 1)
    Includes bibliographical references and index.
    ISBN 1-57181-680-1
    1. Group identity. 2. Social groups. 3. Social conflict. 4. Resemblance
(Philosophy) 5. Cognition and culture. 6. Social psychology. 7. Group
identity--Melanesia. 8. Social conflict--Melanesia. I. Title. II. Series.

HM753.H37 2005
3036.'08--dc22
                                    2005040615

British Library Cataloguing in Publication Data

A catalogue record for this book is available from the British Library.

Printed in the United States on acid-free paper

ISBN 1-57181-680-1 Hardback

Contents

Acknowledgements

My greatest and most immediate debt is to the British Academy and Leverhulme Trust, whose award of a Senior Research Fellowship for the 2001–2 academic year enabled me to write this book. I began some early work on the book while a Visiting Fellow in the Department of Anthropology of the Research School of Pacific and Asian Studies at the Australian National University, during the northern summer of 1994. Members of the social anthropology seminar there and at Queen's University, Belfast, Manchester University, the London School of Economics, and L.S.B. College, Dublin (now Dublin Business School), as well as my colleagues at the University of Ulster – particularly Nick Dodge, Max Koch, Joe McCormack and Andrew Sanders – have all given helpful comments on the papers which helped form some of chapters of this book. Glenn Bowman called my attention to the works of Girard and to Freud's writings on the narcissism of minor differences, Richard Ekins gave me bibliographical assistance on the works of Freud and Dominic Bryan drew to my notice the case of St Patrick. I thank Dr Rosanne Cecil for preparing the index. Finally, I would like to thank the journals *Anthropology Today*, *Comparative Studies in Society and History*, *Journal of the Royal Anthropological Institute* and *Social Anthropology*, for allowing me to use materials from articles I have published with them.

Introduction:
Order, Conflict and 'Difference'

Perspectives on Order and Conflict

Two contrasting perspectives seem to underlie much of Western thought concerning the problem of social order. One of them (the dominant paradigm historically) problematises, above all, the formation of commonalities among people. Its central aim is to understand how human beings manage to join together into collectivities within which they have a common good and share a common identity. This perspective often invokes visions of an opposite state of presocial, or asocial, existence in which people lack such bonds and are thus potentially or actually in endless conflict. Durkheim (1964 [1893]) was perhaps the classical social theorist most closely associated with this view. For him, social cohesion arises ultimately out of a certain kind of homogeneity. Even in the most advanced societies, with much social diversity and a complex division of labour, order depends in the end on the majority of people subscribing to the same fundamental values and beliefs.

But there is another, I think unjustly neglected, tradition of thought in the social sciences, represented by theorists, such as Simmel (1955: 42–45) and Coser (1956: 67–72), to whom it seemed that the deepest and most destructive antagonisms often occur in the closest relationships and between those who have the most in common. Simmel argued that the more completely and intimately people are involved with one another – the more their ties encompass what he called the totality of their being – so their conflicts too, when they arise, tend to be all the more total and all-consuming. And to people who are very much alike, the smallest differences can appear major and seriously divisive. Hence, for instance, the bitterest and most violent controversies in religion have tended to occur between confessions whose doctrines were most similar (Simmel 1955: 43; see also Enloe 1996: 199).

Freud, too, can be placed in this tradition, because he argued that even people in intimate relationships and having very much in common are also inevitably hostile to one another at times and can experience their commonalities as a threat to their identities. In this respect, so he felt, people were like those porcupines described in a simile by the philosopher Schopenhauer: the creatures crowded together for warmth, only to find that their spines drove them apart, until they settled at a distance at which they could exist together with the least pain and discomfort. This mixture of attraction and aversion is inherent in relations, not only between individuals, but between social groups as well:

> Every time two families become connected by a marriage, each of them thinks itself superior to or of better birth than the other. Of two neighbouring towns each is the other's most jealous rival; every little canton looks down upon the others with contempt. Closely related races keep one another at arm's length; the South German cannot endure the North German, the Englishman casts every kind of aspersion upon the Scot, the Spaniard despises the Portuguese. (Freud 1945: 101)

Freud called this phenomenon, when it occurs among peoples or states, the 'narcissism of minor differences'. Neighbouring groups tend to exaggerate their distinctiveness from each other, attach a disproportionate significance to those few features that differentiate them and jealously – even violently – seek to protect their real or imagined collective idiosyncrasies (Freud 1930: 114; 1945: 101; 1957: 199; 1964: 91).

In this tradition of social thought, certain kinds of conflict – indeed, especially destructive kinds – can arise when people are too close, or insufficiently distinct from one another. The emergence of order therefore requires social actors to disaggregate themselves, reduce their commonalities, and achieve a modicum of mutual distance. Of course, even Durkheim himself argued that commonalities among people do not create cohesion necessarily, but do so only under certain conditions: most notably under those conditions of low social 'density' which he envisaged as typical of early societies. As population size and density increase, homogeneity tends increasingly to bring people into competition with one another, into an ever more acute 'struggle for existence' (see Durkheim 1964 [1893]: 266–82). Hence, as the scale of society grows, so people must diversify to avoid conflict, 'speciating' into functionally interdependent groups, their overall integration coming to rest increasingly – though never completely – on their differences.

The realisation that being alike can generate conflict – evident, if inconspicuously, even in the work of Durkheim – has perhaps been developed most overtly and powerfully in the works of the literary critic René Girard (1977; 1978), in his theory of imitative, or 'mimetic', desire. Desires, Girard argues, are not innate or naturally given, but are acquired by imitation. They are contagious; we catch our desires, like illnesses, from other people. Hence desire is not a relation between a desiring subject and an object, as is naïvely supposed. It is an inherently triangular relationship, between a desiring subject, an object and what Girard (1965) calls a model or 'mediator' – a real or imagined Other from whom the desire was copied. If this third party is a living contemporary, that person may represent not just a model, but an actual rival as well, a subject in his or her own right whose own desires have the same mimetic structure. One then has two opponents who imitate each other, and whose mutually mimetic desires for their shared object feed upon each other:

> We find ourselves reverting to an ancient notion – mimesis – one whose conflictual implications have always been misunderstood. We must understand that desire itself is essentially mimetic ... Two desires converging on the same object are bound to clash. Thus, mimesis coupled with desire leads automatically to conflict. However, men always seem half blind to this conjunction, unable to perceive it as a cause of rivalry. In human relationships words like *sameness* and *similarity* evoke an image of harmony. If we have the same tastes and like the same things, surely we are bound to get along. But what will happen when we share the same desires? Only the major dramatists and novelists have partially understood and explored this form of rivalry. (Girard 1977: 146; italics in original)

More recently, Blok (1998) has drawn upon the insights of Simmel, Freud and Girard, marshalling an impressive range of evidence to argue that it is minor differences, rather than major ones, that tend to be most closely associated with violent social conflicts. Violence, in these situations, is the antagonists' reaction specifically to the threatening lack of differentiation between them. Indeed, I would suggest that Girard's argument implies even more than this: namely, that conflict is itself an inherently imitative process, tending to generate similarities at the same time as it is generated by them. In this respect, the processes of mimetic rivalry discussed by Girard are very much like the patterns of mutually amplifying interactions which Bateson (1958: 175–97) called schizmogenesis. Bateson developed this concept as a way to understand certain forms of dualism in the thought and social organisation of the Iatmul, a people whom he had studied in New Guinea as an anthropologist. But he expanded the idea into a general framework for understanding progressive change in social relationships (at the time he was formulating these notions, in the 1930s, the prevailing models of society in social anthropology emphasised stability and homoeostasis). Schizmogenesis is a process in which two or more protagonists react to one another, and react to one another's reactions, in a circular, escalating pattern. Bateson envisaged schizmogenesis as taking two alternative forms. In one, the actors' mutually reinforcing behaviour patterns are the complements of each other: for instance, the assertiveness of one partner in a relationship may evoke, and be evoked by, submissiveness on the part of the other. In the second pattern, which Bateson called symmetrical schizmogenesis, the escalating behaviour patterns are identical, as happens when two rival states, for instance, elicit mutually intensifying hostility from one another in an arms race.

In symmetrical schizmogenesis, as in the patterns of 'conflictual mimesis' described by Girard (1978: xii), opponents are locked in a rivalry generated by their similarity, a rivalry generating further reciprocal imitation – and escalating rivalry. To Bateson and Girard alike, this is a relation of interdependence as well as competition, in which the identities of the antagonists are, to some extent at least, shaped by their very rivalry itself and owe their continued existence to it. Girard, in particular, explores at length the ways in which such 'mimetic rivalry' (1978: xii) can entangle the opponents in strange bonds, in which enmity mixes with mutual fascination, even mutual need. Bateson (1958: 238–40) and Girard (1977: 56) both observe that an understanding of resemblance as a competitive or conflictual relationship seems much more fully and openly developed in some other societies than it is in the modern West.

There is, in short, a strand of thought in the social sciences and some related disciplines, according to which certain intense kinds of conflict can arise out of a background of similarity – indeed because of similarity – and may perhaps even generate further resemblance between the antagonists, causing them to grow yet more alike. In this tradition of thought, an ordered collective existence requires that social actors preserve a certain degree of disconnectedness from one another. Undifferentiation and sameness do not necessarily constitute a state of moral consensus and cohesion, as Durkheim imagined. Instead, they can give rise to the destructive and conflictual entanglement of identities that Girard (1978: 81) called the warring confusion of the doubles. This paradigm thus problematises, above all, processes of differentiation and dissociation among people: it views the central problem of social order as one of understanding how people come to be different, or to view themselves as different, and so minimise the conflicts that inevitably arise when they perceive others to be trespassing on their private domains of identity.

Symbolic Practices as Inalienable Possessions

In this book, I hope to show that the perspective I have just outlined, broadly shared by Simmel, Freud, Bateson, Girard and Blok, can help shed some useful new light on the nature of social identity – in particular, on the meaning of a type of conflict in which the antagonists confront one other as what I shall call proprietary identities. By this term, I refer to social identities whose outward symbols or markers are treated as property, and may be disputed as property. In conflicts of this sort, the opponents' perceptions of each other are not so much those of difference or otherness, but of mutually hostile resemblance.

In exploring the significance which situations of this kind have for an understanding of social identity, I shall draw also upon a further work, one which seems at first sight rather far removed from my topic. This study – *Inalienable Possessions*, by Annette Weiner (1992) – arose out of fieldwork in Melanesia, and is an important contribution to economic anthropology and to the understanding of the symbolism of exchange. Weiner's book is a critique of the long-standing tendency of anthropological studies of economic behaviour to give primacy to a norm of reciprocity. This tradition, whose main exponents are Mauss (1925) and Lévi-Strauss (1969), assumes that the motivating force of practices such as gift transactions or marriage alliance is the moral obligation to repay debts; we give because we expect others to make return for what they receive.

Weiner argues, against this tradition, that all such apparently 'reciprocal' practices are more profitably viewed as surface manifestations of much deeper strategies: strategies aimed at withholding assets of an important, indeed fundamental, type. These goods, which she calls inalienable possessions, are those felt to represent the identities of the transactors themselves. Everywhere, people own objects so deeply imbued with their identities that they make every effort to keep these symbolically vital assets out of circulation, resisting all attempts by outsiders to acquire them. These precious goods may, for instance, be heirlooms whose possession confers political office, or insignia that define their owners' rank and status. One's enemies may try to capture or destroy such goods; one's trading partners may make insistent demands for their surrender; through lack of heirs to claim them, they may be lost to strangers. Constant effort and strategic ingenuity are therefore needed to protect these irreplaceable, identity-defining objects from loss and withstand the pressures to relinquish, exchange or sell them. For only by such resistance can social actors construct identities that endure across time, particularly generational time. If they cannot keep the goods which define their identities from being drawn away into the trading and exchange systems and dispersed, they must at least work to secure their eventual return.

Identities that continue over time are therefore never more than provisional constructions which social actors preserve with effort and difficulty, and only for so long as they remain able to evade, counteract and subvert their obligations to transact or exchange with others. Keeping one's goods out of the exchange circuits, or manipulating the circuits so as to reacquire the same valuables repeatedly, is in fact an important demonstration of power. In Weiner's view, much apparent 'reciprocity' is actually just the outward, visible manifestation of these deep strategies of retention, which she called 'keeping-while-giving'.

What interests me in Weiner's argument is an implication that makes it very different from the views of Mauss (1925) and Lévi-Strauss (1969), for whom the circulation of goods had a positive and socially constructive significance. Her thesis suggests quite the opposite: that exchange can represent, at least from the situated perspectives of social actors themselves, a force of entropy that they must work as much against as with. There are certain classes of goods whose movement, when free and unrestrained, can erode social identities and dissolve social distinctions. The preservation of differences among people requires that they must in some way inhibit, restrict or control the circulation of those goods that symbolise important aspects of their identities. Property, then, is deeply involved in the constitution of identity, and vice versa.

I shall try in this book to extend Weiner's insights into the potentially corrosive and entropic effects of flows of goods a little further than she herself might have wholly approved: first, in regard to the types of phenomena I wish to consider as inalienable possessions. In thinking of such possessions, Weiner clearly had primarily in mind physical objects, such as the crown jewels, Hawaiian feather cloaks, the Australian Aboriginal sacred objects known as *tchuringa* and the shell valuables circulated in the ceremonial gift-exchange systems of Melanesia. She seems to have viewed material objects such as these as particularly well suited for use as inalienable goods, on the grounds of their physical durability. Land, for instance, is one form of inalienable wealth which she felt to be often particularly important. I, though, shall try to extend her thesis to the understanding of phenomena which seem a little distant from her own focal conceptions of inalienable possessions.

The phenomena I shall be concerned with are symbolic practices by means of which people represent their identities as members of social groups and categories. I am thinking, for example, of the way that collectivities such as ethnic groups, social classes, gender categories and youth subcultures may define themselves through the display of distinctive consumption practices and tastes, styles of dress, speech habits, religious practices or other forms of symbolism (Bourdieu 1986; Eriksen 1993; Hebdige 1979). At a much more concrete level, institutions as diverse as schools, political parties, business corporations, sports teams and army regiments may employ distinctive flags, emblems, logos, songs, uniforms or regalia (Firth 1973; Jacobson-Widding 1983c). In clan-based societies, descent groups may distinguish themselves from one another by means of those animal, bird, plant and other sorts of emblems which anthropologists have called totems. These kinds of symbolic practices may seem very diverse; but I suggest that they can all be considered as belonging to a single functional category in that they are all means by which social identity is more or less self-consciously constructed and expressed. I shall borrow from Spicer (1971: 798) the term 'identity symbols' to refer to objects and practices used to represent aspects of social identity. The first way, then, in which my argument departs from Weiner's is that I focus upon the use of practices, rather than objects, as identity symbols.

My second extension of Weiner's argument is that many of the types of the identity symbols I discuss do not figure as goods in systems of exchange, and, indeed, are not necessarily even economic assets in any obvious sense. But the point I want to emphasise is that all symbolic practices are capable of being copied, either with or without the consent and cooperation of those from whom they are borrowed. In the cases I shall discuss in this book, we will see social actors treating certain kinds of identity symbols as though these were vulnerable to appropriation and loss, in very much the same way as the inalienable possessions discussed by Weiner; the difference is that the symbols in which I am especially interested are not objects needing to be kept out of circulation – although, as we shall see, they can be closely associated with such objects. Rather, they are practices needing to be protected from unauthorised copying or reproduction. From this point of view, social actors may view imitation of themselves by others, or at least unrestricted imitation of themselves, as a potential threat to their identities in very much the same way that Weiner suggests is the case with the unrestricted circulation of goods. For reasons which will be clear, I shall often adopt the viewpoint of the patients rather than the agents of these processes of appropriation, and refer to the improper reproduction of symbolic practices as piracy. Those carrying out such acts are, of course, most unlikely to represent them as theft of some kind, but will see them as the rightful exercise of an entitlement.

That these symbolic practices are, as we shall see, often closely connected with much more concrete sorts of inalienable possessions suggests strongly that Weiner's argument has a relevance beyond the understanding of economic behaviour (where her primary interest lay), and can shed light upon an important area in the study of identity politics: namely, contexts in which social actors come into conflict over the use or possession of symbols of collective identity (see Harrison 1992, 1995a, 2002; Kertzer 1988: 43; Mills 1970: 86–87; Root 1995; Ziff and Rao 1997).

Main Point

My approach to such situations draws on Weiner's view of the role of inalienable possessions in the construction of identity – collective identity in particular – and in its reproduction across time. Weiner drew attention to the way that the maintenance of identity often depends on maintaining an exclusive association with a distinctive set of symbolic objects, and preventing rivals and others from acquiring them. Extending her argument, I want to explore the ways in which it can rest also on preserving an exclusive association with a distinctive set of symbolic practices, and thus, crucially, on the power to prevent those defined as outsiders from reproducing these markers of identity.

Identities and 'Differences'

A very fundamental advance in the understanding of social identity has been the realisation of its deeply relational nature. Social groups and categories are rarely, if ever, self-defined monads of some kind, but exist in and through their connections and interactions with others (Duara 1996; Eriksen 1993: 9–12, 111; Schwartz 1975: 107–8). Of course, to regard social identity as a relational phenomenon is merely to pose the question of the nature of the relationship. The prevailing view is that the relation is to be understood, broadly, as one of 'difference': in short, that identity is inherently contrastive. This perspective has been taken to its most radical extreme in studies influenced by poststructuralism. Here, the notion of difference carries a sense given it by Derrida (1978), suggesting that categories are constructed negatively and have no intrinsic content. In this vein Handler (1988), for instance, astutely portrays Quebec nationalism as grounded upon a contrast between Quebec and what he calls 'not-Quebec' (principally, the external world of anglophone North America). The nationalists' Quebec is, in reality, not so much a positive entity as a doubly negated one: it is simply everything that is, so to speak, not not-Quebec. R. Cohen, discussing British national identity, argues similarly that 'one only knows who one is by who one is not' (1994: 198; see also Hall 1989). From this type of perspective, groups depend for their reality on processes of exclusion that produce marginalised 'Others'. These subaltern categories, in turn, can form a basis from which oppositional identities emerge, mobilising themselves through resistance (Hall and du Gay 1996; Wilmsen and McAllister 1996).

To put this differently, the central processes in the construction of identity are boundary processes, as Barth (1969) argued in his classic essay on ethnicity. To understand how identities are created and maintained is to understand the ways that separations between the collective Self and Other, between the in-group and the out-group, between Us and Them, are posited, contested, defended, effaced and so forth. In short, identities are defined at, or by, their boundaries (Barth 1969; A.P. Cohen 1985). From this perspective, boundary processes are fundamental, irreducible social phenomena. Social groups and categories, in contrast, are merely their epiphenomena. They are just the visible effects of successful acts of differentiation.

In a number of senses, then, difference, or felt difference, is widely understood to lie at the heart of social identity. The important insight that all perspectives of this kind share is that human collectivities exist only by having outsiders, and by having boundaries to keep them out. In this, albeit perverse, respect groups rely on one another for their existence. Each can sustain a sense of separate identity only in the context of relationships with others, however much these relationships may be conflict-ridden and unequal (A.P. Cohen 1985; Collier 2000; Fabian 1983; Gupta and Ferguson 1992; Marcus and Fischer 1986; Said 1978; Thomas 1992; Wolf 1982).

An ethnic group, for example, is defined by the dissimilarities (of culture, history, mentality, physical appearance and so forth) imagined or perceived to exist between itself and others (Roosens 1989: 12, 16–18; Smith 1986: 22). Barth (1969) was the first to develop this perspective, viewing ethnicity as the use of signs of cultural difference to mark social boundaries and structure interactions across these boundaries. Such signs include the different modes of dress, of livelihood, language, cuisine, music, ritual, religious belief, historical memories and other symbolic content conceived as distinguishing groups from one another:

> In brief, the ethnic identity of a group consists of its *subjective, symbolic,* or *emblematic* use of any aspect of a culture, or a perceived separate origin and continuity in order to differentiate themselves from other groups. In time, these emblems can be imposed from outside or embraced from within. Ethnic features such as language, clothing, or food can become emblems, for they show others who one is and to what group one's loyalty belongs. (De Vos 1995: 24; italics in original)

Such groups, then, are social entities attributed, by their own members, by outsiders or by both, with what Kopytoff (1986: 73) calls 'symbolic inventories' of particular practices and attributes conceived as differentiating them from each other expressively. These repertoires may bear only a loose relationship to the actual distribution of cultural attributes – so far as this can even be known – among populations on the ground. As Eriksen (1993) and others remind us, what are significant in this context are not so much the objective similarities and differences of culture between groups, but rather people's perceptions, representations and theories about such similarities and differences. Often, particularly in situations of conflict, culturally very similar communities may exaggerate or hypercognise their differences. Conversely, groups may downplay cultural dissimilarities between them in the interests of good relations.

Ethnicity thus belongs to the 'self-reflexive' component of culture, as Schwartz (1975: 108) calls it: it expresses people's folk theories about their own cultural commonalities and differences. For this reason (and as much of this book will illustrate) cultural identity is often a focus of conflict in a wide range of ways, both within groups and between them. Unlike cultures in the anthropological sense, which are endlessly forward-moving processes, braided streams of human activity, the self-aware 'cultures' that figure in the discourses of ethnicity and ethnonationalism tend to assume the form of bounded entities: static, closed, thing-like and discrete (Handler 1988).

But, in viewing perceptions of difference as central to identity, current perspectives may themselves also sometimes reflect, and even reinforce, certain everyday folk assumptions. I am thinking of those apparently commonsensical sorts of everyday wisdom that tell us it is 'natural' for people to prefer the company of 'their own kind'. Such seemingly self-evident conceptions are often employed powerfully in contemporary political discourse. In Europe, for instance, they are invoked by those writings of the New Right which argue that some degree of cultural xenophobia is normal, beneficial and healthy (for examples, see R. Cohen 1994: 178, 202–3, 209). Indeed, Blommaert and Verschueren suggest that all contemporary European nationalisms, even in their most benign and liberal forms, share an essentially similar underlying ideology of 'homogeneism', according to which '[a] homogeneous society – implicitly defined in terms of the vague and largely imaginary feature cluster of history, descent, ethnicity, religion, language, and territory – is seen as the norm and as a condition for social harmony, yielding "natural groups" with a self-evident right to self-determination' (1996: 109). Accordingly, significant cultural diversity within the same society is assumed to be abnormal, a form of social fragmentation (Blommaert and Verschueren 1996: 114; see also Stolke 1995). Assertions of cultural difference certainly do seem almost inevitably to accompany ethnic animosities. We do not hear of ethnic conflicts in which a key issue for the antagonists is that they conceive themselves to be too similar, even though – as I shall argue in this book – this can in fact be a key issue. On the contrary, they are likely to claim to be culturally (even biologically) incompatible and alien to each other, though it may be obvious to outsiders that they are very much alike (Cole and Wolf 1974). Eriksen (1993: 38–39), for instance, notes how the Croats and Serbs came to magnify their cultural differences when the civil war in Yugoslavia began in 1991. The main distinctions between these two peoples relate to religion and the writing scripts they employ. But with the outbreak of war they came increasingly to claim to possess cultures so deeply and irreconcilably different as to make it impossible for them to coexist.

Groups may claim in this way that it is their inherent cultural differences that give rise to conflict. Of course, this is not so much an explanation of their conflict, but rather a kind of rationalisation of it – indeed, part of the justificatory rhetoric accompanying it, in which the opposing sides may ideologically discount and deny even their most self-evident similarities. Nevertheless, such folk ideas do seem to have influenced academic theory, for ethnic and other sorts of social categorisations tend to be explicitly understood in scholarly discourse, as they are implicitly in everyday discourse, as having to do specifically with perceptions or imputations of otherness. Thus ethnopolitics is often understood as a politics of difference, in which minority groups are categorised as 'other' and marginalised or excluded on the basis of traits attributed to them by the majority (e.g. Sibley 1995; Wilmsen and McAllister 1996). As a corollary, it is often assumed in the social sciences – just as in the folk 'homogeneism' discussed by Blommaert and Verschueren – that powerful forms of social cohesion are manifested in common values, shared background and allegiance to the same symbols, or are generated by these cultural commonalities. Hammell, for instance, reflecting on the civil war in Yugoslavia, suggests optimistically that the diffusion of 'cultural and symbolic systems across social groups' (1997: 7) can help to soften the hard edges of ethnic boundaries and reduce social divisions:

> Especially under the homogenizing influence of the much maligned mass media, ethnic groups in many countries share large parts of major symbolic systems. The sports and entertainment industries are cases in point. Football and baseball in the U.S., soccer in other countrie basketball in many, the cinema, and musical forms such as jazz and rock are great unifiers and diminishers of cultural distance. (Hammell 1997: 7–8)

From this very widely shared point of view, it appears self-evident that cultural commonalities promote powerful forms of social cohesion. While cultural differences divide people, shared culture, it seems, must unite them.

The Subversion of Resemblances

But certain aspects of social identity do seem puzzling from perspectives of this sort. First, identities ostensibly 'different' from one another are often remarkably similar. Dissimilarities are often overdrawn by social actors themselves, and in many cases these assertions of difference seem to conceal or deny very real commonalities. For example, Schnieder, researching

American family life in the 1960s, was told by his Irish-American respondents that the key to understanding their identity lay in understanding the special role of the 'Irish mother':

> The interesting point, however, is that the assertion about the crucial role of the mother was repeated for group after group. You could not understand Jewish family life unless you understood the Jewish mother, similarly with Italian, similarly with Polish, and so on ... [T]here seems to be a striking uniformity with respect to focusing on the mother as the symbolic guardian of the ethnic identity. (Parsons 1975: 65–66)

The respondents all viewed their ethnicities as distinctive and ascribed this distinctiveness to the peculiar role of their mothers. Yet in sharing this notion they were indistinguishable. Such a pronounced disjunction between imagined difference and objective similarity calls for explanation. One wonders, for a start, by what process these groups came to acquire the same self-constructs. It was as though American society shared, in spite of its appearance of ethnic diversity, a single generic schema of 'the ethnic minority family', a single template for conceptualising any ethnic group and the 'distinctive' attributes it ought to have.

Simmel (1955: 42–47) pointed out that resemblances of this kind can exist even between mutually hostile groups. Indeed, following the lead of Girard, I would go even further: it is not just that similarities may give rise to destructive conflicts, but that the similarities themselves seem sometimes to be generated or deepened in the course of such conflicts. A case in point is the symbolism of political identity in Northern Ireland. Here, particularly since the social conflicts beginning in the 1960s, Catholic and Protestant working-class communities have evolved a rich visual symbolism for demarcating territory in the politics of urban space. Yet these emblems of identity are strikingly similar in their style, iconography and expressive conventions. The most visible include prominently displayed national and paramilitary flags, kerbstones and lampposts painted in the Irish or British national colours and large painted murals depicting a variety of historical and political themes (Buckley 1998: 6–7; Jarman 1998). Through mostly unacknowledged mutual emulation, these communities have together developed a unique shared genre of political folk art. Although in conflict, they are united in one respect at least: by a common visual language for expressing their differences.

This situation, like those resemblances found by Schnieder among ethnic minorities in the United States, is obviously more complex than a case of groups simply portraying themselves as distinctive from one another. Rather, one needs to try to understand why they have come to share the same ways of portraying themselves as distinctive and what these commonalities reveal about the nature of their identities.

Certainly, cases such as this, and many other similar ones which I discuss in this book, remind us that people of purportedly 'different' cultural backgrounds can in reality have much of their culture in common. They remind us too that borrowing and emulation can occur across even the most formidable social boundaries. But more importantly, they call into question the assumption – in both its social scientific and folk forms – that shared culture, or affiliation to shared cultural symbols, has an inherently unifying effect, and that ethnic divisions are always associated specifically with perceptions of difference. They suggest, on the contrary, that cultural similarity, or rather perceptions or attributions of similarity, may contribute to creating and maintaining social oppositions and boundaries in a way that has not been properly recognised. They point to the possibility that cultural commonalities may play a role in the creation and maintenance of the boundaries themselves, and that imitation and identification with the Other might be deeply involved in some way in the construction of apparent 'differences'.

Main Point

My principal concern in this book is with actors' perceptions of their cultural similarities and differences, and much of the book will therefore focus on ethnic and national identity and on the forms of social conflict to which these collective identities can give rise. My aim in examining this evidence is to extract from it the outlines of a certain widespread way of thinking about the nature of social identity. The book is not intended as a study of ethnicity and nationalism; nor, I believe, is it written in a way which specialists in those fields would find acceptable. Rather, it is an argument about the nature of social identity, which draws, somewhat eclectically and idiosyncratically, on the rich literature on national and ethnic identity for its evidence – as well as on a variety of other sources – with the aim of explaining why conflicts and social divisions seem often to be associated with fraught perceptions of mutually hostile resemblance.

MP

Thus, if my argument happens to shed any light on aspects of nationalism and ethnicity, it does so only as part of a broader argument concerned with collective social identity in general. In short, I am interested in situations in which social actors conceive themselves to be in conflict not so much because they have irreconcilably different identities, but rather because they share important aspects of their identities in common, or have irreconcilable claims or aspirations to the same identities. They are competing to occupy the same regions, or overlapping regions, of that dimension of social existence Friedman (1992: 837) has called identity space. In effect, the protagonists in these situations are opposed because – though they may not acknowledge it openly – they perceive themselves in certain respects as too alike. In these contexts, it is the perceived similarities of the Other that are experienced as threatening, rather than the differences. The construction and negotiation of social boundaries and identities seems to involve not only a politics of difference, but also an (albeit sometimes more veiled and covert) politics of resemblance. A fully adequate theory of nationalism and ethnicity, for example, therefore needs to be able to account not only for circumstances in which group identity and cohesion are defined in terms of common attributes of culture, history and so forth. It must also be able to explain those other, perhaps less well understood situations, in which, as I shall try to show, these cultural and historical commonalities are a focus of conflict, and group boundaries and divisions are defined through the contested sharing of attributes of identity.

This book will suggest that situations such as these are best explained if collective identities, such as those exemplified by ethnicity and nationalism, are conceptualised as arising from relationships, not of difference or perceived difference, but of denied or disguised resemblance. In other words, these identities are most adequately understood as emerging through processes in which certain kinds of felt similarities, and other, shared features of identity are disavowed, censored or systematically forgotten. Understanding the nature of social groups, then, involves understanding the ways in which they are constructed, in part at least, from devices for the elision and undoing of resemblances.

From this perspective, the members of any collectivity will tend to represent themselves, not simply as distinct from others, but as distinct in regular, and quite specific ways that imply some form of identification with those others. Their identities are, then, relational ones indeed, but the relationship is an ambivalent one in which constructs of difference and of shared identity always exist together. Groups define themselves through contrasts, not just with any others at random, but with specific others with whom they represent themselves as having certain features of their identities in common. For it is only when people identify with one another that a felt need can arise to differentiate themselves. Paradoxically, it is the commonalities between groups that create the conditions that make distinctions between them necessary – indeed, that make them possible. What appear at one level as cultural 'differences' may be, at another level, more or less elaborate and effortful attempts by social actors to forget, subvert, deny or obscure certain of their resemblances.

I argue, then, that representations of cultural difference, such as those so central to ethnicity, are bound closely to perceptions of alikeness and are elaborated in antithesis to certain kinds of felt commonalities. This perspective implies, among other things, that the most elaborate and extreme forms of ethnic 'othering' are more likely to occur within relationships that are in some sense close, rather than in distant ones. The more intensely people identify with each other, and the greater their felt commonalities, so the more radical are the measures needed to counter these connections. More generally, my perspective suggests that social identities are created, above all, by the imposition of constraints on imitation and resemblance (even, as we will see, on the perception of resemblances). This is the proposition which theorists as diverse as Girard in literary criticism, and Weiner in economic anthropology, have argued in their different ways: in the sphere of social identity, resemblance and imitation are ontologically primary. Differences are secondary effects produced by the regulation, control, suppression or denial of similarities.

1

Proprietary Identities

The standard view [of imitation], derived from Plato's *mimesis* via Aristotle's *Poetics*, has always excluded one essential human behavior from the types subject to imitation – namely, desire and, more fundamentally still, appropriation. If one individual imitates another when the latter appropriates some object, the result cannot fail to be rivalry or conflict ... In human beings, the process rapidly tends toward interminable revenge, which should be defined in mimetic or imitative terms.

Not only in philosophy but also in psychology, sociology, and literary criticism a mutilated version of imitation has always prevailed. The divisive and conflictual dimension of mimesis can still be sensed in Plato, where it remains unexplained. After Plato it disappears completely, and mimesis, esthetic and educational, becomes entirely positive. No philosopher or social scientist has ever challenged this strangely one-sided definition of the concept. (Girard 1978: vii; see also xi)

Impostures, Counterfeits and Stolen Gods

Doubles and identical twins are a recurring theme in literature and in myth. Significantly, they tend to figure, at least implicitly, as opponents (Girard 1978: 41–43; Hamerton-Kelly 1987: 123; Rank 1971; Rogers 1970: 61–62). The nineteenth-century writer De Quincey once argued that if he were to encounter his double he would be entitled to kill him, out of jealousy:

> Nature does not repeat herself ... Any of us would be jealous of his own duplicate; and, if I had a *doppel-ganger* who went about personating me, copying me, and pirating me, philosopher as I am I might (if the Court of Chancery would not grant an injunction against him) be so far carried away by jealousy as to attempt the crime of murder upon his carcass; and no great matter as regards HIM. But it would be a sad thing for *me* to find myself hanged; and for what, I beseech you? for murdering a sham, that was either nobody at all, or oneself repeated once too often. (De Quincey 1897: 460–61; quoted in Coates 1988: 37)

The scenario pictured here is not entirely fanciful. There have been societies in which it was quite possible for one's name and social persona to be appropriated by very much the sort of hostile doppelganger imagined by De Quincey. It was common in lowland Melanesia, for example, for men to take possession of their victims' names when they killed in warfare (Harrison 1993b: 129–30). The clans of the Abelam people owned their own hereditary stocks of personal names, but a man could acquire a name belonging to another clan by killing the name's bearer (Forge 1972). In Iatmul society, too, killers took possession of the names of their head-hunting victims, and here the names became part of the hereditary name stock of the killer's clan. The names not only served thereafter as personal names for the clan's members, but were also given to tracts of land and served in this way as title-deeds to clan territory (Bragge 1990: 43). Similarly, the main motive of the Marind-Anim people for mounting head-hunting expeditions was the need to obtain fresh supplies of names to give their children (van Baal 1966: 676).

In some of these Melanesian societies the killers appear to have appropriated not merely the names of their victims but at least part of their actual social identities as well. The Asmat people gave the name of each head-hunting victim to a boy during his initiation ceremony, and the boy thereby acquired the powers of growth and vitality contained in the head. Afterwards, the victim's kin treated the initiate as the incarnation of their relative. Whenever they encountered him they called him by the dead man's name, performed songs and dances for him, and gave him gifts. If Asmat men planning a head-hunting raid did not know the names of their intended victims, they had to discover them first, perhaps by a ruse. They might invite the victims to their village on some pretext, and ask their names so that they could be honoured in a song. Only once the victims had disclosed their names could they be killed (Zegwaard 1968: 430, 443).

The people of Tanna, in the Melanesian nation of Vanuatu, had a comparable practice, in which a group which took over the territory of another in war acquired both the land rights and the personal names of the former owners. To gain legitimate ownership of the land, the victors had, as it were, to assume the social identities of the losers, whose names and identities seem to have been conceived as bound inextricably to the land itself. The Tannese also used the same principle in the settlement of feuds. If someone was killed in fighting, the killer's group gave the victim's family an individual to replace him. In many cases this was the killer himself. He henceforth lived under the name and social identity of the dead person (Lindstrom 1985: 35, 37).

In these societies, everyone was vulnerable to the violent theft of their name and kinship position, along with their soul-substance, life-force or vital principle. The new possessor of these personal attributes does not seem to have been viewed as some sort of 'impersonator' or counterfeit of an 'original'. Personal identity appears to have been conceived as transferable in a sense in which it is not in Western societies – where it can perhaps be imitated or counterfeited but not actually alienated or reassigned. But in some Melanesian societies it was as though a person were imagined as a kind of miniature corporation sole (see Fortes 1969: 303), like that office of priest in the sacred grove at Nemi – made famous by Frazer's classic of Victorian anthropology, *The Golden Bough* (1967[1911]) – capable of being bodily occupied by a series of position-holders, each replaced in turn by his killer. Who was the 'real' person so-and-so was simply not an issue. Each had simply succeeded, albeit by violence, to the social identity of his predecessor. Clearly, what brought people into conflict in these societies was not so much that they were different from one another but, rather, that they were, or sought to be, identical. A killer and his victim were enemies because they both wished, in a sense, to be the same person.

Transactions of Collective Identity

There were similar conceptions of collective identity, as well as personal identity, in Melanesian societies. Groups often showed a pronounced possessiveness towards their cultural forms, a strong concern with protecting them from what they viewed as misappropriation by outsiders. The Ngaing and other peoples of the Rai coast, for instance, treated their deities and the myths and rituals relating to them as precious assets in this way, as stores of wealth they needed constantly to safeguard from misappropriation by covetous outsiders: 'Rights to deities had to be established by genealogy or purchase. Otherwise, they were invariably withheld from outsiders who, it was believed, would exploit them to their own advantage and so impoverish the original owners' (Lawrence 1964: 30). Many Melanesian societies treated their cultural practices, especially their religious and ritual systems, in a similar way: namely, as valuable property which they had definite rights to withhold. They might sometimes disclose their cultural practices to outsiders, but this could not be done lightly because it was understood to benefit and empower the recipients and created an important bond of trust and indebtedness, as Suwa (2001) has shown for the inter-village trafficking in dances still current in the Madang area of Papua New Guinea. Hence, too, in some parts of precolonial Melanesia, rights in rituals, religious sacra or other important cultural property were bestowed or exchanged to seal political alliances between groups (see, for instance, Bowden 1983: 67; Gewertz 1983: 109).

Schwartz (1975) illustrates this attitude in his discussion of 'cultural totemism' among the ethnic groups of the Admiralty Islands (part of modern-day Papua New Guinea). Before European contact, the societies of the Admiralties formed a single area-wide sociocultural system, all of whose peoples interacted regularly with each other in trade, warfare and intermarriage and shared many basic features of culture in common. One especially prominent shared feature was a deep preoccupation with their differences in language, ritual, art, architectural styles, craft specialisms and so forth. Although these diacritical features might seem minor to an outside observer, they were intensely significant to the islanders as markers of identity. Each group treated its emblematic practices as precious monopolies it jealously had to safeguard from outsiders; and it sought constantly, not just to preserve, but to accentuate, its distinctiveness. Paradoxical though it may seem, these cultures were unified above all by a shared concern with maintaining their differences.

Ambitious men, competing with one another for followers, often sought to introduce new cultural practices and so establish new group identities under their leadership: 'Such innovations may be minor, perhaps a change in the design of the men's house or of canoe prows, or they may involve a major block of culture, such as a new form of ceremonial in affinal exchange with associated paraphernalia and perhaps a mythological rationale' (Schwartz 1975: 112). Over time, the effect of cultural totemism in the Admiralties was to generate and amplify ethnic diversity. It produced a pattern of small, fragmented and yet interdependent social groups (at the time of Schwartz's study there were some twenty ethnic groups in Admiralties, some of them tiny) each claiming its own special identity and uniqueness.

These groups seem to have had much the same relationship with their 'cultures' as medieval craft guilds had with their trade secrets or as business corporations have with their brand names and trademarks: namely, they treated them as intangible but vital assets needing protection from piracy. An ethnic group 'owned' its culture as a kind of patented possession, its patent consisting fundamentally in the right to control its culture's diffusion. No group allowed outsiders to copy its special distinguishing practices 'without securing the right to them through kinship, marriage, or some form of purchase or licensing' (Schwartz 1975: 117).

Clearly, ethnic groups in the Admiralties were highly conscious of their cultural differences. These processes of cultural self-objectification seemed to focus on the felt need to protect oneself against outsiders imagined as eager to usurp or appropriate elements of one's identity. The prime concern of each group was with restricting the access of outsiders to its culture, reified as a valuable – albeit partly intangible – possession.

Such intangible goods often functioned as valuables within, as well as between, Melanesian societies. They were not simply transmitted from one generation to the next, but had to be transacted in often complex exchanges in which the balance of material wealth went from juniors to seniors, from heirs to their legators or from neophytes to their initiators (see, for instance, Bateson 1958: 57; Errington 1974; Jolly 1991; Malinowski 1922: 185; Rubinstein 1981).

In lowland Melanesia, one type of incorporeal property that seems often to have been treated as an important form of wealth in this way consists of magical spells (see Harrison 1990). Kahn describes magic as 'the most valued form of traditional wealth' among the Wamira, and Malinowski speaks of magic in the Trobriands as one of the most valued and valuable possessions (Kahn 1986: 96; Malinowski 1922: 178). Spells are among the most important parts of a Trobriand man's inheritance, and he must solicit his mother's brother with several very substantial payments in order to obtain them (Malinowski 1922: 185). Weiner has shown these payments to consist of prestige goods such as polished stone axe blades, and she also notes the purchase of spells from other islands (1977: 152–53, 180).

In some areas of Melanesia, copyrights in religious iconography seem similarly to be treated as wealth. An example is the Malanggan statuary of New Ireland. These sculptures are carved and displayed at mortuary ceremonies, in which the rights to their designs are transacted between descent groups in exchange for shell valuables and nowadays also money (Küchler 1988: 631, 635). The designs are the media of an exchange system in which, Küchler writes, 'not objects, but the images they embody are circulated in transactions' (1988: 626; see also Küchler 1987; Wilkinson 1978). In the Tumbuan cult of the Duke of York Islands, indigenous leaders (called 'Big Men' in Melanesian pidgin) operate by sponsoring mortuary feasts, at which masked figures impersonate spirit beings. These leaders own the copyrights to particular mask patterns, as well as owning the ritual knowledge associated with them and the rights to sponsor their construction and display, and aspiring Big Men must acquire these artistic and ritual copyrights from them in return for shell currency (Errington 1974: 79–121).

Schwartz points out in his discussion of the Admiralty Islands that when intangible goods such as ritual knowledge are trafficked in the trade and exchange systems, they 'are treated as negotiable hardware; that is, as if they were material' (1973: 160). The islanders of Tanna, likewise, regarded knowledge as: 'a thing ... a possessed commodity. In this regard, as is common throughout Melanesia, people sell to others medical and magical recipes, spells, dance steps, artistic motifs, ritual practices, and new songs. A person can possess knowledge, exchange it, and consume it' (Lindstrom 1990: 44). The wealth objects involved in these kinds of exchanges in Melanesian societies were often equated symbolically with the parts and substances of their transactors' bodies: with breast milk, semen, bone, blood and so forth (see, for instance, Wagner 1967). The transmission of ritual knowledge was often portrayed in the same way, using the same metaphors of sustenance and procreation. Among the many obligations that Manambu men had towards their sisters' sons, for example, was the obligation to teach them myth, ritual and magic. They were understood to nurture the sisters' sons with knowledge in this way, just as they were expected to nurture them with food; the two forms of nurture were equated, both alike being spoken of as 'giving mother's milk' (Harrison 1990). The cultural elaboration of these sorts of transactions in Melanesian societies gave rise to an equivalent cultural elaboration of a conception of persons as immanent in their relations and transactions with each other. For wealth items, whether material or intangible, were not conceived merely as inanimate 'things'. They represented parts of their transactors' selves – often indeed parts of their bodies – carrying aspects of human identity with them as they circulated (see M. Strathern 1988).

Cultural practices tended, then, to be equated with material valuables in certain respects. Both sorts of goods could move in the same exchange circuits and they were often not only semantically equivalent as components of personal identity but also convertible into each other. It would have appeared to actors quite natural to regard, let us say, a myth or magical spell as thing-like, equivalent perhaps to a valuable pearl-shell or boar's tusk not just in worth but, as it were, ontologically. Indeed, the two types of goods were often so closely linked that they were often combined together as unitary valuables in the same exchanges. Physical objects such as ritual sacra were sometimes important symbols of group identity in Melanesia, and might move between groups in various ways, being traded, exchanged in peace treaties, captured in war and so forth. But it was often not just objects that were transferred in transactions of this sort; more importantly from the participants' point of view, the entitlements to replicate the objects were transmitted as well (Forge 1990; Harrison 1993a; Mead 1938: 333–35). In other words, it was not simply the artefacts but also the practices of making and using the artefacts that could be 'owned' and transacted as cultural property.

When a European colonial presence began establishing itself in the late nineteenth century in parts of coastal and island Melanesia, Melanesians tended to treat mission Christianity in a very similar way: as a powerful new cultic ritual or system of magic that had to be acquired by means of the proper conventional transactions. Consider Otto's account of a man of Baluan island in the Admiralties describing how his ancestor brought the Seventh Day Adventist (SDA) mission, or *lotu*, to his island:

> He accepted the SDA and sent it to Baluan. It came straight to [the village of] Patangkon [and thence to the village of Pungap]. When it arrived the village Pungap had already accepted the Catholic Church. All right, Pungap is the village of the mother of my father. When they [i.e. the missionaries] arrived, an old man called Lima told them: I have already a *lotu*, I cannot accept this one. My father was in the bush. When he came back he heard about it. He went and talked with the people of his mother's village. He said: if you have already this church, that is all right, it is for all of us. Keep it. And the *lotu* that has come to you now, give that one to me. And I will take it to [the village of] Perelik, because Perelik has not got a *lotu* yet. (Otto 1991: 116, footnote omitted, and parentheses mine)

The narrator speaks of the *lotu* here as a sort of entity or object: after it 'came' or 'arrived', people could 'give', 'send', 'take', 'keep', 'have' it, and so forth, as though it were a material thing. Otto points out that on Baluan, cultural forms such as the *lotu* 'are considered property just like material goods and may be requested and given within the appropriate relationships'; affinal relationships, in particular, are important channels for these transactions of new forms, as the passage above illustrates, because affines have an important exchange relationship and cannot easily refuse each other's requests (1991: 112, 116).

Otto shows that it was vital for a community to be able to demonstrate that it had acquired the Christianity legitimately in this way in order to be considered a rightful co-owner of it (1991: 116, 144). The Tolai people initially treated the Catholic *lotu* likewise as a powerful new system of magic; and, as with any magical complex, legitimate possession of it could only be acquired in exchange for wealth. In the case of the Catholic mission, the payments of shell money were presented, not to other Tolai communities already possessing the *lotu*, but directly to the mission itself (Neumann 1992: 90–91; see also pp. 131, 186, 222).

Mission Christianity was introduced to the Wiru people, in the Southern Highlands of Papua New Guinea, in the 1960s. The Wiru eagerly accepted Christianity as a new equivalent of the fertility cults which they regularly used to import from neighbouring peoples in precolonial times. Like these earlier cults, Christianity was accepted because it was perceived to promise a new, and perhaps more powerful, source of prosperity. The Wiru acquired it in the same way they had acquired other cults in the past; that is, in exchange for wealth. When conversions took place, the Wiru killed pigs and offered meat as payment to the missionaries for having bestowed on them this new source of power and well-being (Clark 1985: 154–89).

Melanesians did not envisage the traffic in culture between themselves and Europeans during the colonial period as one-way. Rohatynskyi (1997) has described how the Ömie people of Papua New Guinea, among whom she first carried out anthropological research during the 1970s shortly before the nation gained independence, viewed themselves as bestowing on her a valuable gift by imparting knowledge of their culture. In revealing their cultural practices to her and, as they perceived it, to the colonial government through her, they were performing a powerful act of self-disclosure which created a bond of trust and indebtedness, and in their view was a vital way of demonstrating to the government a worth equal to that of other Papua New Guinea peoples. The Ömie at that time perceived that recognition by the colonial authorities as a distinct ethnic group depended on having a 'culture' to disclose to outsiders, and that in this situation the measure of such a group's political strength and autonomy was its power to retain or disclose the secrets of its culture. As Rohatynskyi points out (1997: 452), it is significant in this respect that the Tolai, now one of the most wealthy and powerful ethnic groups in modern Papua New Guinea, employ as an important icon of their identity the Tubuan, a secret initiatory cult into which non-Tolai are admitted only as an exceptional privilege.

Ritual Knowledge as a Limited Good

Practices such as these seem to rest upon a particular set of assumptions about the nature of culture, or at least of cultural knowledge. Many Melanesian peoples had terms in their languages to denote 'customs' or habitual practices perceived to distinguish social groups (see, for instance, Otto 1991: 23, 144). But they seemed to conceive such customs as having been acquired, rather than created, by the groups that observed them. The members of a community represented 'their' customary practices as theirs on the grounds, not that they created them but that they were given them – by external donors such as ancestors, culture heroes, or neighbouring peoples, typically imagined as in some sense superior and powerful. Even genuine innovations – novel art motifs, newly composed songs and so forth – were usually represented as having been imparted to their human originators in dreams by ancestors or spirits. In short, culture was not imagined as a human invention (see Lawrence 1964: 30–33; Strathern 1988: 322–24; Wagner 1975), but as something acquired in exchanges or interactions of some sort. People might claim ownership of their cultural practices, but not authorship (see Strathern 1988). On the contrary, they were more likely to deny authorship emphatically. Such practices could be transacted among human beings, but not created by them. Except in minor matters the peoples of the southern Madang area: 'dismissed the principle of human intellectual discovery … All the valued parts of their culture were stated to have been invented by the deities … Even when a man composed a new melody or dance, he had to authenticate it by claiming that it came from a deity rather than out of his own head' (Lawrence 1964: 30). Lindstrom, similarly, shows how the people of Tanna in Vanuatu regard knowledge as valid only if it is has been obtained from some authoritative source. For them, the production of knowledge is governed by an 'authority-principle' rather than an 'author-principle' (Lindstrom 1990: 74):

> Knowledge is revealed, not individually created. It is passed down, not made up (see Lawrence and Meggitt 1965: 215–18) … People do not explain the production of knowledge in terms of a knower's individual talent, genius, or creativity. Local epistemology seeks authorities and not individual authors. Individual creativity, in fact, is devalued vis-à-vis external inspiration. One's own ideas are never as good as information externally received. (Lindstrom 1990: 43–44)

An important corollary of these conceptions was a view of cultural knowledge, and especially valuable knowledge such as religious and ritual lore, as static, fixed and finite in quantity – at least from the point of view of human actors. Such knowledge: 'came into the world ready made and ready to use, and could be augmented not by human intellectual experiment but only by further revelation by new or old deities' (Lawrence 1964: 33). Barth (1975) describes how the Baktaman people regard knowledge in very much this way, as a precious finite resource. To them, the more widely an item of information is disseminated, the lower its value becomes, almost as if they conceive it as a physical substance or thing, which must inevitably be diminished by being shared (see Harrison 1995b). Hence perhaps the widespread idea in Melanesia, noted by Brunton (1989), that rituals gradually lose their efficacy over time and need eventually to be replaced by new ones. Hence also the strong tendency to treat ritual knowledge, in particular, as a closely guarded value, protected by devices such as secrecy, as well as by physical and supernatural sanctions. It is as if there were an assumption that one's cultural practices could somehow be devalued, their potency depleted, their efficacy lost, if they were exposed, or too widely copied or shared.

Often, these sorts of proprietary claims were so jealously defended that their infringement or the 'piracy' by one group of a ritual belonging to another could lead to feuding and bloodshed. The peoples of Humboldt Bay, on the coast of West New Guinea, provide an example. They had male initiation cults similar to those in many other parts of New Guinea, in which the principal sacred objects were bamboo flutes. The existence of the flutes was in principle a secret known only to initiated men, and boys were shown the flutes and taught to play them as part of their initiation into adulthood. In the Humboldt Bay villages, women and non-initiates were told that flute music was produced by a spirit, identified with the cassowary, which devoured the boys during their initiation and then restored them to life as adult men (Kooijman 1959: 21–22).

These coastal villages had important trading relationships with their inland neighbours (who differed from them in language and culture), and especially with the villages on the nearby eastern shores of Lake Sentani. They gave the lake-dwellers dugout canoes and sea-fish in return for pigs and sago flour. In particular, the coastal villages supplied coloured beads, which were used as valuables in prestige transactions such as marriage payments (Kooijman 1959: 14–15).

Around the beginning of the twentieth century, the men of the coastal village of Nafri taught the ritual to a man called Asareu, the chief of the lake village of Ayafo, apparently in the expectation of receiving from him some particularly valuable beads. Asareu managed to make a set of working flutes after some trial and error, and then staged the ritual in his own village, shortly afterwards organising the building of a men's house there so as to institute the cult permanently:

> The men of Nafri, however, looked upon this imitation as theft, and the resultant tension between the two villages led to fights and murders. The strife only ended when Asareu did what he should have done in the beginning – he paid. For the sum of ten ancient beads, a glass ring and several old drums Ayafo acquired legal ownership of the sacred flutes and their secret. (Kooijman 1959: 15)

The chiefs of two other eastern Lake Sentani villages, presumably wishing not to be outdone by Asareu, soon followed his example and acquired the cult from their coastal trade partners in exchange for valuables, though the cult spread no further along the lake. Significantly, in acquiring the cult these three villages acquired certain other cultural practices of the coastal peoples: the architectural style of their cult houses, with distinctive pyramidal roofs; the prohibition, imposed on initiated men, of killing or eating cassowaries; and, in the 1920s, the coastal styles of male and female coiffure (Kooijman 1959: 21–22). To a degree, these three Lake Sentani villages 'became' coastal ones at the level of culture, acquiring a portion of their trading partners' identities.

This seems to have been a common pattern with the diffusion of rituals and other important cultural forms in Melanesia: the donors did not usually surrender their title to the ritual, losing the title themselves, but rather extended to the recipients rights to perform the ritual. That is to say, these transactions typically took the form of a kind of franchise, the practice in Western commercial law by which a business licenses another to trade under its name and identity. In Melanesia, the donors sold or formally conferred the rights to reproduce certain aspects of their culture. To reproduce them without making proper payment was treated as a serious offence. In the Admiralty Islands, there were cases in which the infringement of a group's exclusive rights in its cultural practices – its right, for instance, to ornament the prows of its canoes in a particular way – resulted in warfare (Schwartz 1975: 117).

Neumann describes a situation of this sort among the Tolai of New Britain during the introduction of Christianity to their region. The first Methodist missionary among the Tolai arrived in August 1875, bringing the *lotu*, or mission Christianity, to a community called Molot:

> From Molot the *lotu* went to Matalau ...
> From Matalau the *lotu* went to Matupit.
> From Matupit the *lotu* went to Raluana.
> From Raluana the *lotu* went to Vunamami ... And so forth.
> The *lotu* often 'went' as an item purchased from people of one place by people of another place. The usual price was five fathoms of *tabu*. The item was not actually the lotu. It became the lotu after it had been in use for a while at the purchaser's place. The item that was purchased was a *malira*, a magical charm, or at most the *letu*, as the Tolai initially called the novelty. The purchase was sealed by the dispatch of instructors who were to initiate the purchasing party into the *letu*. They were in the beginning Fijians, Samoans or Tongans. Later the instructors could be Tolai. (Neumann 1992: 81–82)

To be legitimate, the expansion of the Methodist mission from one community to the next had to be accompanied by transactions of wealth. If the process was not ratified by the villagers in this way, the consequences for the mission could be disastrous: four missionaries were killed in 1878 when they sought to establish a mission unilaterally, without first waiting for the appropriate donor and recipient communities to complete the necessary transactions (Neumann 1992: 82).

Warfare

In some societies, aspects of collective identity can be legitimately reassigned or transferred from one group to another by force or violence. One thinks, for instance, of the raiding among the tribes of the Kwakiutl, and other peoples of the American north-west coast, aimed at acquiring the ownership of rituals, songs and dances in the Winter Ceremonial (Goldman 1975). This ceremonial was a complex ritual common in its broad outline to all the north-west coast tribes. Its central and most prestigious role was that of the Man Eater spirit, which transformed the dancer into a ritual cannibal. This dance was a prerogative of men of the highest rank and could be acquired in only two ways: either by marriage alliance with a chiefly family or by killing a holder of the prerogative in another tribe and taking his masks and other ceremonial trappings. The powers of the role were greater if the role was acquired by homicide. Boas (1921: 1017) recounts how the men of one Kwakiutl tribe attacked another village at night, burned it and killed a number of its men including its chief (see Goldman 1975: 176). They took away with them some heads as trophies, as well as a box of Winter Ceremonial regalia and a woman as a slave. The attackers' chief thereby assumed all the dead chief's entitlements in the Winter Ceremonial, including his Man Eater spirit. That winter, he danced as this spirit, having made the slave instruct him in the manner of dancing and the songs. At the climax of the dance, the slave was killed and he ate her, taking a fresh name to mark the full assumption of his new powers (Goldman 1975: 20, 110, 176, 244).

The Kwakiutl obtained one of their most important ceremonies from the Bella Bella tribe in this way by killing the original owners in a head-hunting attack (Boas 1966: 258–59; Codere 1961: 440; Rohner and Rohner 1970: 88), and Codere in fact speaks of Kwakiutl warfare as having had as one of its functions the acquisition of the ceremonial practices of neighbouring tribes. It seems that these foreign ceremonies were sometimes known already in full to the killers; but, as Benedict (1935: 151) points out, what were in every case gained by the act of killing were the formal titles to the ceremonies as property. These ritual entitlements functioned as a kind of intangible regional currency shared by many different tribal groups, but they were a currency that could be circulated in violent transactions as well as in peaceful ones. There was consensus over the value of these entitlements, but often lethal conflict over their social distribution.

The capture of religious symbols in warfare was by no means restricted to the American north-west coast. There was a comparable practice in the early Roman republic, in which the Romans used to take over the tutelary gods of cities which they conquered, thereby acquiring control of the key symbols legitimising these cities' statehood and political independence. Roman battles were not just military events but were symbolic, ritual contests as well. When two cities fought, their armies carried their tutelary deities in effigy into combat with them and a battle was a trial of strength not just between two human armies but, at the same time, between the two sides' gods (Fustel de Coulanges 1963: 146–55, 205–10). Roman generals prepared for battle by promising their gods festivals, sacrifices, and spoils if they ensured victory (Fustel de Coulanges 1963: 205–6).

In war, the goal of each side was not only to demonstrate, through victory, the superior powers of its own gods, but also to appropriate the gods of the enemy. Before going into battle, Roman generals carried out ceremonies intended to suborn the enemy deities with prayers and promises of extravagant sacrifices, tempting them to defect to the Roman side. In the early republic, for instance, the general Camillus laid siege to the Etruscan city of Veii, at that time the habitation of the goddess Juno, a powerful protective deity. An integral part of his siege was the performance of ceremonies invoking her, aimed at tempting the god to defect to his side and become a Roman god (Fustel de Coulanges 1963: 215). For this reason, the Romans kept the real name of their own guardian deity a close secret: 'lest the enemies of the republic might lure him away, even as the Romans themselves had induced many gods to desert, like rats, the falling fortunes of cities that had sheltered them in happier days' (Frazer 1967 [1911]: 345). Proof of the enemy gods' desertion was, of course, victory itself. The loser's gods, having fled to the side that promised them more, formed part of the spoils of battle and became the property of the winners. A battle was simultaneously a contest to determine the relative powers of the two sides' gods and a struggle for their possession. The winning side was the one that emerged from the battle possessing both sides' gods.

The Romans acquired many foreign gods in this way and took possession of their cults. Between the eighth and fourth centuries, Rome 'obtained possession of a Juno from Veii, a Jupiter from Praeneste, a Minerva from Falerii, a Juno from Lanuvium, a Venus from the Samnites, and many others that we do not know' (Fustel de Coulanges 1963: 366). Some of the gods were given to specific Roman descent groups, and others were incorporated into the state pantheon of the republic. It would be absurd to suggest that a desire to appropriate enemy gods motivated their warfare; my point is that these appropriations were an institutionalised feature of warfare and a completely integral part of the process of conquest.

For defeated cities were required to make a special vow, called the *deditio*, in which they formally surrendered up 'their persons, their walls, their lands, their waters, their houses, their temples, and their gods' (Fustel de Coulanges 1963: 375; see also pp. 207, 215, 381). 'From this moment', Fustel de Coulanges writes, 'the gods, the temples, the houses, the lands, and the people belonged to the victors' (1963: 207). A city's gods and its religion seem to have been regarded simply as part of its total state assets, like its land, its treasury and public buildings, and they were expropriated by its conquerors in just the same way as these other assets were. The difference was that the city's gods were in effect, assets whose primary function was symbolic. What they symbolised, of course, were the city's political identity and independence; once a city surrendered up its gods, Fustel de Coulanges writes, the city itself might well remain standing but as a state it had vanished (1963: 376). The Romans and their neighbours would surely have agreed with Durkheim's fundamental observation that every religion belongs by definition to a particular social group or community: but it was precisely because these religions *were* conceived as the property of groups that their ownership could be disputed by these groups, and could be changed forcibly in warfare along with many other property relations.

As with Kwakiutl warfare, these practices need to be understood in the context of a framework of religious ideas and assumptions common to all the antagonists. Rome and the other cities seem to have shared much the same religious conceptions: each had its own state cult or cults, but the gods and rituals were essentially similar, interchangeable and transferable. In that sense, one can perhaps speak of these cities as the components of a regional ritual system, analogous to the region-wide ceremonial interdependencies among the clans of the Tallensi of Ghana (Fortes 1987) or the Australian Aborigines, in which each clan has a specific role within a larger, shared system of ritual and cosmology. But in the Roman case, this mutual intelligibility in religion constituted, not so much a universe of shared moral values, but rather a regional economy of politico-religious symbols in which ownership claims were often violently contested. In this system, the victors in war always installed themselves in the symbolic appurtenances of the losers' identities. By investing themselves with the key religious symbols of the losers' legitimacy and prestige, the winners could transform might into right.

In some societies, then, the violent transfer of power can be made legitimate by the device of transforming oneself, so to speak, into the person from whom one seized it. Thus, when the Persians under Cyrus conquered Babylon in 539 BC, Cyrus did not seek to destroy his defeated enemies' state religion (Kuhrt 1987). On the contrary, he fostered and encouraged it, especially the cult of the city's patron deity Marduk, clearly thereby seeking legitimacy for himself and his dynasty as Babylon's new ruler. In fact, these rituals seem to have sufficiently impressed Cyrus for him to appropriate some of them for the Persian kingship, incorporating Babylonian rites into the Persians' very different system of state ceremonial. As Cannadine (1987: 8) puts it, the Persian armies may have conquered the Babylonians, but the Babylonian rituals conquered the Persians. In a rather similar way, the Germanic tribes that settled in the territory of the later Roman empire adopted the Latin language and Christianity in the process (Renan 1996 [1882]: 42). Sometimes, it seems, it is not so much the victors who appropriate the identities of the losers. Rather, the losers' identities absorb and appropriate the victors.

2

A Phenomenology of Trademark Ownership

Trademarks and Magical Theft

As one can see, there have been societies in which honouring the same gods, or respecting the same religious symbols, could constitute a violently conflictual and divisive relationship in some circumstances. This may seem odd from a Durkheimian perspective, in which such symbols always appear as expressions – perhaps, indeed, paramount expressions – of social solidarity and moral consensus. But in some cultures and historical periods, people clearly recognised that shared religious affiliations could both unite them, and divide them and turn them into enemies – fundamentally because they conceived these affiliations as involving claims to religious symbols as forms of property.

Such practices may seem alien to modern religious sensibilities. But they have a close analogue in an unexpected area of contemporary life: namely, in the law of commercial trademarks. In this chapter, I want to identify some key underlying similarities between the practices of warfare and exchange which I have described, and disputes relating to trademark ownership. Later, I shall suggest that both can shed light on the nature of cultural identity.

The trail-blazing work of Coombe (1998) has revealed just how vital a role trademarks and other forms of intellectual property play in contemporary culture, and in consumers' constructions of identity (see also Baudrillard 1988). But relatively little seems to be known as yet about the role played by trademarks in the identity constructions of their holders, or would-be holders, and in the social relationships of these commercial actors. This is the topic on which I would like to make some – unavoidably tentative – observations, and on which I hope the ethnography of premodern warfare may shed some useful light.

My starting-point is the sociology of Georg Simmel. In his analysis of the phenomena of tact and discretion, Simmel described social life as conducted as though there were around each person a sphere of 'intellectual private property', as he termed it, regarding that person's 'affairs and characteristics'. To intrude into someone's domain of psychological privacy is, he wrote, to violate the personality:

> Just as material property is, so to speak, an extension of the ego, and any interference with our property is, for this reason, felt to be a violation of the person, there also is an intellectual private property, whose violation effects a lesion of the ego in its very center. Discretion is nothing but the feeling that there exists a right in regard to the sphere of the immediate life contents. (Simmel 1950: 322)

The radii of these personal spheres vary, according to Simmel, depending on a range of situational and other factors, but among these is people's relative 'significance': in other words, their power and status. One shows greater respect and deference to someone by 'keeping one's distance', allowing that person a larger sphere of psychological privacy.

Simmel was thinking primarily of the privacy of personal information. This broad theme – the essential role played by secrecy, reserve, obliqueness and miscommunication in the maintenance of personal identity – has recently been explored in an important collection of essays (Hendry and Watson 2001). But I want to develop Simmel's insight in a slightly different direction, because there are other intangibles, besides information concerning themselves, that people may treat, or attempt to treat, in a very similar way. They may define their names, or visual images of themselves, as extensions of their identity, as part of that exclusive proprietary sphere of which Simmel wrote. In discussing these sorts of behaviour, I shall draw in particular on Simmel's insight that differences in power and status between people are reflected in the differing extent of their personal spheres of intellectual property.

Adopting this perspective, there appears to be no absolute distinction between the commercial, or corporate, forms of identity that trademarks signify and simple human, personal identity. This is evident, for instance, in certain occupations in which affliction by doubles and impersonators can be a very frequent and unwelcome hazard. A few years ago, some famous performing artists in the United States began a campaign in Congress to outlaw the hundreds of impostors who hold concerts and perform their songs under their identities.

> By amending the 1947 Lanham Act, introduced to protect durable goods rather than intellectual property, the artists want to establish a Famous Names Registry administered by the US Copyright Office. Only registered artists could then use the names for commercial purposes ... 'On any given night you can find 30 or 40 counterfeit groups working in the country,' said Joe Terry, of Danny and the Juniors, a group from the early American bandstand generation. 'These impostor groups perpetrate a fraud on the public and a terrible injustice on the artists who created the original works.' ... So bad has the problem become in the United States that the Great Pretenders, as they are nicknamed by their real counterparts, are able to fool even the most illustrious of audiences. Bill Clinton, when Governor of

Arkansas, apparently shook hands with Sam Moore's double at a Sam and Dave day in Little Rock. 'That wasn't me down there', Mr Moore said ... Moore, who with his wife has founded the Artists and Others Against Impersonators organisation, claimed that counterfeit bands had played at the 1992 and 1996 presidential inauguration celebrations. (Rhodes 1998)

These performers sought to have their own names and identities protected as their intellectual property in the same way as the trademarks of business corporations. Someone's name, face or signature, protected by law as a trademark, is not essentially different from the logo of a multinational corporation.

The ostensible purpose of trademarks is to enable consumers to identify the sources of goods and so make rational choices between the goods of different producers or suppliers. A corporation's trademarks and the consumer 'goodwill' they embody are valuable assets which competitors may try to purloin. Famous brand names attract various kinds of imitations, ranging from outright forgeries and counterfeits, to so-called 'look-alike' goods, packaged in such a way as to resemble top brands and subtly mislead consumers (Walker 1995). The Lanham Act – the American legislation appealed to by the Artists and Others Against Impersonators organisation – is intended to protect firms against 'passing off': the selling of counterfeit goods under their trademarks, the impersonation of their identities in the market-place.

Interestingly, some business corporations maintain collections of counterfeits and imitations of their own products. The beer manufacturer Bass, for instance, keeps albums containing thousands of examples of forgeries of its own labels (Stiling 1980: 9). The question arises why a corporation should maintain a rogues' gallery of this sort, publicising the passing off and trademark infringement it has suffered over the years. The reason, presumably, is that it is an advertisement of corporate success, kept for the same reasons that warriors keep as trophies the skulls of those who tried unsuccessfully to appropriate their names and identities. Of course, when pirates trade falsely under a firm's brand names, they are seeking to profit at its expense. But in doing so they pay it a perverse form of homage. The quantity of imitation which a corporation attracts is an index – perhaps in some ways more reliable than its share price – of the prestige and commercial value of its trademarks. Its share price indicates its worth principally in the formal economy. Its pirates and imitators, on the other hand, presumably attest also to its worth in the black or grey economy – to the 'street value', as it were, of its name. Indeed, they can surely provide evidence of real, untapped market share, of reservoirs of unsatisfied demand for its products in the actual economy. If this is so, a curious kind of symbiosis occurs here between a business enterprise and its pirates, an invisible partnership, a covert exchange of market esteem from which both sides benefit.

Certainly, the holders of a trademark will try to stop imitators and counterfeiters. But also, I suggest, they are likely to want to be seen to attract them. It is this conspicuous, simultaneous and vigorous attraction-and-repulsion of imitators that adds to the firm's reputation. Perhaps it is for this reason that a certain world-famous manufacturer of shoe polish 'is constantly engaged in tracing and preventing imitations', and has sought and found imitators of its famous trademark in 'Finland, India, Vietnam, Singapore, Korea, Japan, Indonesia, Mainland China, Israel, and Egypt' (Stiling 1980: 29). It is perhaps for similar reasons that some corporations seem to interpret 'imitation' of their names very broadly, and try to bar any commercial use of names resembling their own:

> The company most vigilant in defence of its name is probably Harrods. Targets of its disapproval over the years have included an outfit in Eccles (Café Arrods, run by a Mrs Rowbotham, who had also considered calling the place Fortnum and Bacon); a discount furniture shop in East London (initially, Herrods; they later renamed it 'Errods'); and several businesses in New Zealand, some run by people called Harrod. In retaliation for that, the Otorohanga Business Association announced that most shops in the town would be putting up Harrods signs, and the town itself would from now on be calling itself Harrods. (*Guardian* 1996)

The sacred power, or *mana*, of a Polynesian chief is measured in the range and extensiveness of the taboos surrounding his person. Simmel, as we saw, suggested in a rather similar way that someone's status and power are measured by the range of acts that count as trespasses against their private sphere. The protectiveness of high-status corporations such as Harrods towards their trademarks seems to reflect much the same sort of logic. The policy of Harrods seems to be that not only its own trademark, but all trademarks resembling it, are representations of itself, or references to itself, and fall within its proprietary sphere. The businesses that bore the names Herrods, Harrod, Café Arrods and so forth were quite obviously not competitors stealing its business by passing off, and in that respect they posed no threat to its commercial interests. Rather, it is as though the holders of high-prestige trademarks deem their marks able to suffer damage through the mere use or possession of similar marks by other, lower-status firms. The apparent reference to a renowned name by an Eccles tea shop, or some obscure small-town businesses in New Zealand is enough to detract from the name's prestige. The more famous and valuable a trademark is, the more vulnerable it appears to its holders to be to the signifying acts of others, and the longer the chains of association through which it can be tarnished or given detrimental connotations.

There is evidence that these sorts of claims by trademark holders are often acknowledged and upheld by the courts. Coombe argues that the more prestigious and valuable a mark is, the more strongly the law tends to protect it – and vice versa. In other words, the law can do more than merely protect the commercial value of a trademark; in doing so, it can enhance its value:

> [T]he more famous the mark, the more likely judges are to extend it protection against 'dilutions' of its commercial aura. The more valuable the mark becomes, the

more legal protection it receives, which of course means that it accrues even more value because it is granted further immunity from scrutiny, competition, or denigration. Protected because it is valuable, it is valuable because it is protected. (Coombe 1998: 71)

Coombe shows that corporations try to employ trademark law for a much wider range of purposes than merely protecting themselves from passing off (1998: 67–73). They may seek to stop satirical and parodic treatments of their brand names, logos and so forth, or to censor other uses of their marks that might give these marks undesirable associations in the minds of consumers. Trademark law can sometimes be used, in effect, to curtail freedom of expression because it regulates an area of life where the protection of commercial interests is so closely intertwined with the protection of reputation, good name and public image. In 1991, the Pink Panther Patrol, a group of homosexual vigilantes based in Greenwich Village in New York, were sued by MGM-Pathe for trademark infringement:

MGM-Pathe argues that its wholesome image is at risk from the self-defence tactics of the vigilantes. 'The Pink Panther motion pictures were created and promoted in the spirit of light-hearted, non-controversial family fun and entertainment, a purpose not in keeping with the issues the Pink Panther patrol faces,' says the lawsuit filed in Manhattan's Federal Court which seeks at least $100,000 damages (£58,000) ... 'The use of the designation "Pink Panther Patrol" and a stylised paw-print to identify a gay rights self-help group and their activities, services and goods, has and will continue to diminish the identity and reputation of the trademark, and reduce their value.' (Walker 1991; see also Coombe 1998: 354)

Clearly, trademarks are in practice ranked in more than just their commercial value, and the law protects trademarks in other respects besides their monetary worth. Rather, trademark holders – the more powerful of them at least – seem to conceive marks as ranked also in a hierarchy of prestige and moral valuation, in which the highest-ranking ones are distinguished by the range and stringency of the taboos and prohibitions – even conceptions of purity and defilement – with which they are protected, with the law's support. Hence some intellectual property disputes and trademark infringement litigation have the character of 'tournaments of value', to borrow Appadurai's (1986: 21, 50) term, expressive contests in which commercial interests are inextricably fused with matters of prestige, morality, honour and even revenge.

Some years ago, the late Alan Clark, a wealthy Conservative member of the British Parliament, tried to register his name as a trademark, in an attempt to stop it being used in a lampoon. If his action had been successful, it would presumably have turned all his namesakes into potential trespassers on his proprietary rights, and converted their names into mere counterfeit copies of his own.

Alan Clark is taking steps to ensure he remains a one-off [and] is attempting to register his name as a trademark with the European Union. He began registering his name before he successfully took a local newspaper in London to court to prevent it from publishing the *Not Alan Clark's Diary* column, its spoof of his own chronicle.

But Clark will have to wait until mid-June before he finds out if the EU will prevent such imitations. Until then, any other Alan Clark who feels that the owner of Saltwood Castle should not enjoy exclusive rights to the use of the name can lodge a formal appeal.

There is, of course, my old friend, the Right Rev Alan Clark, the erstwhile Bishop of East Anglia, and Alan Clark, formerly of HM Diplomatic Service. 'If Mr Clark encroaches on my right to use my name, I would be very cross,' the latter tells me. 'It's not as if he's Elvis Presley. There are tens of thousands of Alan Clarks.' (*The Times* Diary 1999)

To seek a monopoly of one's name is not quite as egregiously self-aggrandising as it might seem. There is currently much debate concerning the ways in which a wide variety of attributes of personal identity might be owned as trademarks or other forms of intellectual property, and thus become commoditised. It has been proposed that athletes could hold copyright over all visual images of key moments in their sporting careers, or have patent or trademark rights over any sports 'moves' they invent – their individual styles of performing high jumps, rugby kicks, and so forth (Ford 1996; Rush and Reeve 2000). In 1998, the Diana, Princess of Wales, Memorial Fund tried to register images of the late Princess as trademarks.

The face of Diana, Princess of Wales should belong to the world instead of becoming the property of her memorial fund, the Patent Office has decided after a seven-month investigation.

The attempt by the Diana, Princess of Wales Memorial Fund to turn her image into a trademark has provoked objections from civil servants who fear it would allow celebrities to stop anybody using pictures of them.

The trustees sent 26 photographs of the late Princess in various fashions and hairstyles to the Patent Office in December to register the images as intellectual property. The fund could have made millions of pounds for charity by licensing her face on tea towels and mugs sold as souvenirs the world over. It would also have had the power to stop her image being used in bad taste. Its application has been watched by pop and sports stars.

To secure maximum power over the use of the Princess's image, the memorial fund applied for copyright in a huge variety of classes of goods, from kitchen utensils to Christmas tree decorations. The list included items such as yeasts, fire extinguishers, salad dressings, advertising, clothing and games.

The copyright examiner who has studied the application has objected on the ground that the Princess's face was not distinctively linked with the origin of goods, as the law requires. [Her face] has no obvious connection with a saucepan, a rug or a typewriter, all classes of goods where the fund wanted to register her image as a trademark. (McGrory and Kennedy 1998)

What is at issue in cases such as this is the propriety of creating private property rights over public symbols and commoditising valued public icons. As in the case of Alan Clark's attempts to register his personal name, to create or extend such rights must inevitably restrict or diminish the proprietary spheres of some other parties, and may appear to them as wrongful appropriation. There have been cases in which business corporations have used images of public figures without their consent in advertising campaigns, to suggest misleadingly that these figures endorse the firm's products.

> [T]he plundering of a person's physiognomy is not proscribed under any theft act.
>
> The latest incident in a long line of 'borrowing' personalities to plug products brings something approximating to disgrace on the marketing department of Rank Xerox. Two months ago they launched a campaign featuring three famous people … used for the campaign completely without their knowledge or permission.
>
> [One of them wrote to Rank via solicitors] looking for damages and an instant stop to the campaign. The response to this request was an offer 'of a derisory sum' but with the condition that the US office equipment company could continue using his picture. 'That was absolutely not what we wanted,' he says, 'but it was a bit shocking to find Rank Xerox maintain that they had bought the rights to my photo from a library and could therefore use it without my permission.' …
>
> What is perhaps most surprising is that there is no statute in civil law which expressly forbids using people's photographs without their permission … Chris Parkinson, … a specialist in trademark law, says that recent relaxation of rules governing the trademark register might make it worth while for personalities to register their faces: 'There are an amazing number of things that have been successfully registered in the past, so it's probably worth a crack.' (Bell 1995)

A corporation's power may be measured by its ability not only to protect its own commercial identity against infringements, but also to encroach on, or capture, the identities of others, to appropriate valued images of other people and make them appear to speak in its favour, attach them in some way to its own identity, or turn them into symbols of its identity. What is interesting here is the idea that someone thus involuntarily made to appear to 'speak' on some corporation's behalf can be considered to have been wronged or harmed. I do not wish to deny that a person's interests can be harmed in this way. Rather, what I find significant is the method of harm: namely, the use of something that signifies a person, such as a photograph. There seems to be a basic formula governing the world of trademarks and other similar forms of intellectual property: namely, that the greater the commercial value and prestige of a person's identity (I include here the identities of corporations) the more such a person will appear to be vulnerable to being wronged or injured through the medium of their representations. The more extensively that attributes of personal identity become commoditised, or acquire some sort of potential market value, the more that representations of persons become porous channels through which others can extract value from them, any unwarranted extraction of value from persons via their representations constituting a form of harm, from which they deserve the protection of law. Someone whose identity is used or appropriated in this way may thus be advised to have recourse to trademark legislation, as in the case above. Firms, of course, expect to receive legal protection for their marks in any case. But we should be clear about what it is that commercial actors thus wronged are seeking from the law. Quite simply, they want to stop images of themselves from being used to injure them or benefit others at their expense. The greater the commercially exploitable value of some identity, the more exposed it is to this kind of appropriation. Consequently, the greater the protection it appears to require – and so we find the law of intellectual property serving conceptions increasingly similar to those of sympathetic magic.

Mimetic Conflict and Disputed Icons

My interest here is in the constructs of personal identity – including the identity of corporations as legally constituted persons – on which the commercial value of trademarks rests. No doubt, trademark law is a requirement for the rational operation of large-scale, impersonal markets. But in practice, trademark ownership and use are grounded in an ontology of personhood which seems both highly enchanted and also implicit in other, apparently quite unrelated, forms of social identity, including (so I hope to show) ethnic and national identity. This ontology is reflected in the language in which debates over issues of trademark ownership are, as one can see, described in the media: a language in which people's faces, for instance, are vulnerable to 'theft' or 'plunder', or can become the 'property' of someone else or be deemed to 'belong to the world', and so forth. The phenomenology of trademarks seems to share a fundamental idea in common with the world of sorcery beliefs and magic, and with the world of lowland New Guinea warfare, with its violent appropriations of heads, souls and names: namely, that persons are coterminous with their images and representations. Anything that stands for someone is also a part of that person, and people are 'in' everything that signifies them.

In these conceptions, which I call proprietary identity, it appears perfectly possible to appropriate the parts-cum-representations of someone and so acquire some attributes of theirs, some qualities of value which that person embodies: the powers of growth and vitality contained in an enemy's head, the cachet of a celebrity's photograph appearing to endorse one's products, the prestige of a renowned brand name on which one's own counterfeit goods illicitly capitalise, the extra saleability of fire extinguishers and salad-dressings that carry as their trademark the image of a famous princess. One's own identity and its representations can appear, in turn, as values needing to be protected from similar encroachments, capture or appropriation by others.

Taussig's (1993) discussion of mimesis may help elucidate these conceptions. By mimesis, Taussig suggests a basic human capacity to imitate, and to experience this as an intense, sensuous, even magically efficacious, connection to and participation in the originals which one copies. To Taussig, the significance of mimesis is that it is the means by which people relate to alterity; it is a gateway from the Self to the Other. But, surely, it also involves an equally intense capacity for involvement with simulacra of oneself. People may identify powerfully not just with images of otherness, but with their own images or with things they conceive to represent themselves. Taussig's paradigm case of mimesis is the ritualist manipulating his magical effigies and dolls. But those persons at whom these actions are directed may surely also identify with these representations of themselves just as deeply and intensely as the ritualist himself, and in some ways perhaps even more so. Like head-hunting victims, firms plagued by piracy and passing off or celebrities whose photographs are used without consent, they may experience these mimetic actions as the appropriation, alienation and unwarranted circulation of aspects of their own identities. In short, social actors are likely to be intensely concerned with mimetic behaviour directed at them and to seek some kind of control over representations of themselves.

Taussig describes mimesis as a 'faculty'. But perhaps it is more useful, for the reasons I have just given, to view it as a type of social relationship or social process, in which one actor imitates another, or is perceived by the other to do so. To one party in the relationship, that copy is a representation of the Other; to the other party it is a representation of the Self. But both parties, from their different perspectives, identify with this copy with that same intensely participatory embodied involvement so well evoked by Taussig. It is simply that through this copy one party engages with Otherness, while the other confronts an image of sameness, or purported sameness – perhaps that hostile and threatening sameness envisaged by De Quincey when he imagined encountering his doppelganger, counterfeit or rival *alter ego*.

The two sides in a mimetic relationship may, of course, be unequally placed in regard to power, and the relationship can be a highly contested and conflictual one. In the case of the famous newsreader's photograph used in the advertising campaign, the issue was whether the office equipment corporation had the right to use an image of his widely known face without his consent. That it was a picture of him was not in dispute. But a mimetic conflict can occur also when someone merely claims that someone else is representing their identity: as, for example, when Harrods seeks to portray the names of certain unrelated businesses in Eccles or New Zealand as infringing its trademark. In these sorts of cases, it is the very meaning of some signifier that is in dispute: is the name 'Cafe Arrods' really a sly reference to the famous London department store or not? As I have tried to suggest, power in this context includes the power to define what counts as an imitation or representation of oneself, and to enlarge the sphere of things deemed by others to be one's semblances.

Conclusion: Mimesis and Exchange

These, then, are the kinds of mimetic relationships that pervade the experiential world of trademark holders, a world in which it is possible to have one's identity absorbed or assimilated by others through the medium of representations of one's identity and thereby suffer harm and even social extinction. As we saw, similar constructs seem to be shared by Melanesian warriors fighting to capture souls and names, and they also occur in literature in the theme of antagonistic twins and doubles. To all these actors, identity has an essential proprietary dimension, because it is fused so inextricably and contagiously with its outward symbols that it appears always at risk, needing protection from harm and loss (see also Dittmar 1992; Weiner 1992). In these conceptions, social relationships between those who share elements of their identities in common can be highly conflictual and contested, joining them together, not in cohesion, but in what might be called conflictual resemblance, fraught likeness or disunity in similarity.

Earlier, in the Introduction to this book, I pointed to what I consider an unjustly neglected tradition in social thought and to some of the key figures associated with it. Despite their differences in other respects, Freud, Simmel, Bateson, Blok and, in particular, Girard all recognised the deeply ambivalent nature of relations of resembl.... They were aware of the existence of a vital dimension of social identity which can be threatened by similarity and can experience the mimetic acts of others as injuries. They recognised too that such mimetic acts need not necessarily have any harmful intent; merely being resembled can in itself be experienced as actually or potentially damaging.

To Girard and Simmel especially, the role of mimesis in social life seems very much like that which Weiner, in her theory of inalienable possessions, envisaged exchange as playing in the economic sphere. The circulation of practices by means of mimesis and the circulation of goods by means of exchange are alike in that both can appear to social actors in certain contexts as placing their identities at risk of misappropriation and loss. Practices, as well as objects, can in this sense be inalienable, identity-defining possessions.

I have tried to apply these writers' insights to the understanding of certain ritual practices connected with exchange and warfare in some societies. I then compared these practices with disputes in contemporary society over the ownership and use of commercial trademarks. My reason for discussing the symbolic aspects of premodern warfare and the phenomenology of commercial trademark disputes is that these are both paradigmatic cases of a form of conflict in which identities are alienated or appropriated and opponents come to embody contested parts of each other. They exemplify with particular clarity the phenomenon of proprietary identity, which can be defined as that aspect of social identity capable of suffering mimetic injury.

In the following chapters, I want to explore in more detail the ways in which mimetic conflicts of these kinds can figure in the negotiation of group identity (see also Harrison 1992, 1995a, 1999a, 1999b, 2002, 2003). As we shall see, between people who share, or appear to each other to share, aspects of their identities, a special type of conflict can arise over these shared characteristics – a type of competition in which icons of group affiliation assume the forms of contested possessions (see also Kertzer 1988: 43; Mills 1970: 86–87). The conceptions of proprietary identity that inform these conflicts are, ultimately, also those that give rise to disputes over the ownership of trademarks or to wars that can entail the capture and loss of the combatants' souls or gods.

3

Mimesis and Identity

Difference as Superiority

In the Introduction, I referred to a key leitmotif in contemporary social science: namely, the conception of social identities as relational phenomena, constructed through acts of division. According to this view, an identity is never in some sense self-sufficient, but is always linked to an Other – real or imagined, overt or covert – against which it is defined. This Other, so central to the constitution of the Self, may, for instance, comprise images of an exoticised East (Said 1978) or representations of the 'primitive' against which the West has counterposed itself historically as 'civilised' (Fabian 1983; Kuper 1988). It may be one's own community imagined at an earlier period in history, as Hastrup has shown for contemporary Icelanders (1995: 107–17). To Atatürk and his fellow Turkish modernisers, the Ottoman past which they sought to disown as backward had a similar significance (Yoruk 1997).

The first step in understanding such acts of differentiation or imputations of difference is to recognise that they are never neutral. They are evaluations, differences of value and esteem. They constitute judgements about the Other's inferiority, superiority or equality in relation to the Self. These valuations may be made of social groups or categories as totalities. This is the case, for instance, in ethnically stratified societies: each group is ranked in relation to the others in a hierarchy of worth or status. Of course, people may also view any given cultural Other as differing from themselves in several attributes, valorising certain of these positively and others negatively.

There are, therefore, three logically distinguishable relations which the Other may present to the Self, either separately or in combination. The Other may embody, first, what I will call difference-as-inferiority. The term 'difference' has tended in practice to be used in much of the literature on social identity to refer, above all, to these attributions of lesser worth. But there are two other relationships which also need to be included in the construction of difference. I will call these difference-as-superiority and difference-as-equality.

Taking conceptions of cultural 'difference' involved in ethnicity and nationalism as my principal test case, I examine in this chapter and the next the role played by these three abstract modes of defining Self and Other. As we shall see, they seem to share a fundamental feature in common: they are all patterns of ideologically muted identification with the Other, assertions of distinctiveness that serve to disguise underlying commonalities. The 'differences' they appear to evidence arise from the concealment or denial of resemblances.

Mimetic Identities in Melanesia

I begin, then, by discussing difference-as-superiority, by which term I refer to processes of valorising other groups positively and attributing certain kinds of superiority to the culturally foreign (Harrison 1992, 1995b, 1999a, 1999b, 2002, 2003). This form of identification with the Other is connected closely with those processes which Taussig (1993) refers to as mimesis. I want to consider this pattern in some detail, because its role in the construction of ethnic and national identities is the least adequately recognised. Indeed, in order to understand the key role played by processes of imitation here, it is most useful to start with societies in which these processes are more openly acknowledged than they tend to be in the West. For this reason, I want to return first to Melanesia, a region many of whose peoples have been described as culturally highly acquisitive, actively seeking exotic and novel items of culture as valued and prestigious enhancements of the group or person (Allen 1981; Harrison 1993a; Jolly 1992; Mead 1938; Tuzin 1990: 365).

The reader will recall that cultural forms seem to have been objectified in many of these societies as prestige goods, valuables or transactable wealth objects of some sort. They entered readily into the prestige economies and systems of trade characteristic of these societies, in which power and status depend on the ability to acquire politically strategic goods and control their circulation. Characteristically, it was aspiring or established leaders who took the initiative in these processes, seeking out and introducing these cultural innovations in pursuit of influence and prestige, in exactly the same way that they sought out famous valuables and prestige goods from their foreign trading-partners (Allen 1981; Otto 1991: 144; Schwartz 1973: 159, 1975).

In many of these societies, political leadership tended not to be hereditary, or entirely ascribed by birth. It was, to a significant extent, an achieved status, won by becoming successful in the trafficking of prestige goods and in the manipulation of credit and debt. The prestige economies – for instance, the Kula, the ceremonial gift-exchange system of the Trobriand Islanders and neighbouring groups, described by Malinowski (1922) – were the key political institutions. To put this differently, the basic sources of political authority tended not to be groups, so much as the relations between them or across their boundaries (Feil 1984; Lederman 1986; Strathern 1971). It was through these relations that power was established and legitimised, rather than by ancestry or by appeal to an immutable past. Aspiring leaders had to build relationships with their contemporaries by making them indebted in trade and gift transactions. Power came from controlling the circulation of goods, including goods such as rights in rituals, and from using opportunities these systems could offer for converting between intangible and material forms of political capital. The driving force of many Melanesian prestige economies was rivalry between men of the same group; it was their struggles for status that spurred them to seek valuables from partners in other groups (Feil 1984; Uberoi 1962). It seems to have been these same struggles that also drove men to seek to acquire foreign ritual forms (see for instance Allen 1981). It was not simply out of a fascination with novelty and strangeness for their own sake (see Brunton 1989: 94). It was because transactions in such forms, like transactions in any other prestige goods, was a measure of the scale of their power.

Often, these cultural goods were conceived as having been acquired originally, as we saw, from neighbouring peoples, ancestors, deities or other outsiders in transactions such as purchase, gift exchange or formal bestowal, in this way affirming important social relationships between their possessors and these outsiders. Hence many Melanesian societies claimed to have obtained their present-day rituals from other peoples, and rituals so acquired often retained their associations with their original donors for a long time. Far from being concerned to suppress these associations, the recipients tended to memorialise their relationship with the donors. The foreign provenance of an imported item of culture tended to be preserved for a long time and overtly stressed by the recipients, rather than suppressed (Harrison 1993a; Jolly 1992), precisely because this quality of foreignness enhanced the prestige of the person or faction that introduced it. Williams (1940: 396–99), for instance, describes descent groups among the Orokolo disputing which of them had imported, several generations earlier, key episodes of the Hevehe ritual, the main ceremonial cycle of the Orokolo. It conferred high status to be credited with having introduced these foreign ritual forms, in much the same way that a Trobriand chief could enhance his renown by bringing home famous valuables from an overseas Kula expedition.

Hence the Kaluli people, for instance, happily admitted that most of their dance ceremonies were foreign imports (Knauft 1985b: 328; Schieffelin 1976: 225–29). The Kunimaipa also: 'acknowledge that their major ceremonies came from neighbouring ethnic groups, not from a creator, and they readily accept modifications and innovations' (McArthur 1971: 189). One of their cultural acquisitions was a ritual which McArthur calls the dance village ceremony, in which a local group held funerary rites for its dead members, killed large numbers of pigs and distributed the meat to guests. The Kunimaipa said that they had acquired this ceremony from a being called Matere, whom they invoked in spells to promote the growth of pigs. Some Kunimaipa regarded Matere as a spirit, but others claimed he was an important leader from a certain nearby ethnic group. The first Kunimaipa to witness this ceremony did so as guests of this people after Matere's death, when his kin performed it to celebrate the funerary rites over his skull. After the ceremony, these guests: 'asked for the skull so that they, too, might organise a ceremony back in their parish. In turn they handed both the skull and the knowledge of the ceremony on to their neighbours, who in due course continued the process. Gradually all the Kunimaipa-speaking peoples learned the custom' (McArthur 1971: 173).

In some societies a sequence of performances such as this, by a series of local groups in turn, was the normal way in which certain rituals were staged. Modjeska (1991) describes a cult called the Kiria, a male cult with a series of initiatory grades, among the Duna of the Papua New Guinea Highlands. According to myth, the cult was established by two sisters who had travelled across Duna territory. Certain stones and other ritual objects, used in the Kiria, had materialised at each spot where the sisters slept, and every Kiria cult house stood on one of these sacred sites. Performances of the Kiria were staged in sequence by the local groups along these ancestral routes, re-enacting the sisters' travels (Modjeska 1991: 246–48).

Modjeska argues that this system of enchained performances foreshadowed, in a symbolic or 'enchanted' form, the systems of enchained ceremonial exchanges such as the Moka or the Tee, found in some other New Guinea Highland societies. In these exchange systems, prestige goods such as pigs are transacted in large-scale gift-giving ceremonies along a chain of local groups, with each group making a prestation to the next. At the end of the sequence, return gifts are passed along the chain in reverse order (Feil 1984, 1987; Strathern 1971). These systems represented the most highly evolved indigenous political economies of the Highland societies, and were capable of integrating large populations politically over wide areas, but they were quite lacking among the Duna. Yet it is as though the Duna had imagined, in the form of the Kiria cult, the possibility of such a system, and were: 'ritually acting out principles of organisation still beyond society's capacity to envisage and operationalise in real terms as practical political economy' (Modjeska 1991: 248). Moka exchange, and these sequential transfers of rituals from group to group, share similar principles and logic. In some societies, they in fact coexisted: rights in rituals were transacted in ways not only resembling, but closely interlinked with a prestige economy or system of ceremonial gift exchange.

In about 1949, some of the eastern clans of the Kyaka, another Highland people, purchased from their Melpa neighbours a ritual complex called the Goddess cult. It was believed to promote the health and fertility of any clan possessing it, as well as success in the Moka ceremonial exchange system and in warfare. The cult was spread from clan to clan by these groups' leaders ('Big Men' as they are called in Melanesian pidgin), who had been initiated into it by their affines and exchange partners in clans already possessing the cult (Allen 1967: 44; Bulmer 1965: 133, 136, 148, 158).

The whole cycle of rituals took at least five or six years to complete, and only two clans near the Melpa border had performed the full sequence by 1958, though others were part-way through. The final ceremony, which took a year or more to prepare, involved the construction of a series of enclosures containing a building in which were stored special stones representing the Goddess and other related powers. In this ceremony, the men of the clan killed their pigs and distributed the meat to exchange partners and other guests from surrounding groups. Women were excluded from the cult, except for the wives of important cult leaders, who were allowed to enter the enclosure and assist their husbands with the distribution of pork. In acquiring this cult, the Kyaka also adopted the Melpa practice of secluding women in special huts during menstruation and childbirth, for the Goddess was said to kill a menstruating woman who inadvertently polluted an initiate (Bulmer 1965: 148–50).

Once a clan had completed the cycle of ceremonies, it was entitled to pass the cult on to a further clan. The men of the clan receiving the cult were described as thereby 'marrying' the Goddess. The Goddess was not conceptualised as an ancestress, but as the clansmen's collective bride. She was an affine, and an affine moreover 'not to one group but, in sequence, to all participating in the cult' (Bulmer 1965: 151). The cult thus spread by means of a sequence of 'marriages' between the Goddess and the men of a chain of local groups, each clan bestowing this imaginary bride on the next. Again, we see ritual in Melanesia symbolising, not groups, but their relationships with each other. In this case, these were the intermarriages between clans and, in particular, the politically most significant of these marriage alliances: those between their respective leaders, under whose leadership the cult was in reality being spread from clan to clan.

It was, of course, these selfsame Big Men who also took the leading roles in the Moka, the system of inter-group exchanges of pigs and valuables. Big Men led factions of their clans, rather than genealogical segments of their clans, and Big Men of the same clan seem often to have been rivals for status. Bulmer argued that Big Men sought to acquire the cult in order to increase their own power and influence within their own clans, just as in the Moka exchanges they used their marriage ties and exchange partnerships with Big Men in other clans to enhance their status (1965: 151). He noted that the cult coordinated 'the activity of more people, both within the clan and outside it … than any other traditional institution with the exception of the Moka' (Bulmer 1965: 151). Indeed, I would suggest that the transmission of the Goddess cult from group to group was equivalent in its political effects to a chain of Moka transactions: the gift of the cult expressed and confirmed alliances, and particularly the mutually supportive alliances of Big Men, in the same way as did their gifts of pigs and other prestige goods in the Moka. In a sense, the Goddess cult *was* a prestige good: for a certain period in their history, it was one of the objects in the Kyaka prestige economy, albeit a complex symbolic object instead of a material one.

Peripatetic cults similar to this seem to have been common in the western Papua New Guinea Highlands, meandering across cultural boundaries through the trade and exchange systems. The Melpa, from whom the Kyaka adopted the Goddess cult, claim to have originally bought it themselves from the Enga people in about 1880; the Mendi bought a version of this cult from the Melpa area in about 1930 and purchased another similar cult, called Timp, from their southern neighbours around the same time, subsequently reselling it northwards up the Mendi valley from one local community to the next (Allen 1967: 43, 45–46; Ryan 1961; Vicedom and Tischner 1943–48).

Durkheim (1976 [1912]) regarded rituals as symbolising social groups. Mauss (1925) regarded gifts and prestations as symbolising the relations between groups. Societies such as the Kyaka and their neighbours seem to have fused these two principles together. That is to say, property rights in their cults were not tied exclusively to groups but, like the property in material valuables alongside which they were transferred through the channels of trade and exchange, they belonged to the prestige gift economy that interrelated these groups.

Western Comparisons

Historically, processes of purposive diffusion analogous to these seem often to have played an important role in the formation of ethnic and national identities in many Western societies. But, as we shall see, social actors here have seemed far more ambivalent about acknowledging these flows of culture than their counterparts in Melanesia. By way of illustration, let me begin with Armstrong's (1982: 297) discussion of the emergence of ethnically based monarchies in Europe during the Middle Ages. He suggests that this form of political organisation did not diffuse purely as an abstract idea or theory, but also, much more concretely, through the emulation of the identity symbolism and mythologies of particular nations, especially those of France. France represented a prestigious model for the growing national consciousness of élites in the peripheral polities such as Poland and Hungary, not just because it was powerful politically but because it had a potent and richly developed symbolism of national identity, focused on its status as a sacral monarchy legitimised by the Papacy. In short, the French were endowed with an ideologically powerful '*mythomoteur*' as Armstrong calls it, following Abadal i de Vinyals (1958; see also Smith 1986: 15, 16, 25, 57, 201–2), a driving or constitutive national myth. It was this identity myth in particular that nascent national élites elsewhere in Europe sought to borrow (see Armstrong 1982: 227, 287, 293–94, 296–97).

Their relationship with France seems to have involved, in other words, something of that intense identification with the Other – especially an Other conceived as a source of magically appropriable power – that Taussig (1993) terms mimesis: an imitation that seeks a merger with its model, overcoming the distinction between Self and Other. Of course, the aim was not to replicate French national identity exactly, to actually become French. It was to copy partly, to adapt the French national myth to 'their' particularities, so making that copy distinctively their own. If they wanted to relive the French past, they wanted to relive it in their own way, distinct from that of the French. In short, they sought to imitate France in such a way as to identify with France as a prestigious model and also set themselves apart from France. Borrowing of this sort is neither pure imitation, nor pure differentiation of Self from Other, but something in between. It is imitation intimately involved in the production of difference. It is a kind of mimetic appropriation, an attempt to re-enact the identity myths of others so deeply as to make them completely – and genuinely – one's own.

Gellner (1983) and Anderson both note how the strongly 'modular' character of nationalism made it readily 'pirated' (Anderson 1983: 67, 80–82) by new nationalist movements. As Handler points out, all nationalists participate by definition in a common culture that transcends national boundaries:

> [T]he 'culture' of cultural objectification is shared throughout the modern world of nation-states and ethnic groups. Indeed, one might almost believe nations and ethnic groups to be the naturally bounded units they claim to be – if only one were permitted to define them as that species of social system whose function is to produce and market their own specificities. Like a row of ethnic restaurants in any North American city … nations and ethnic groups participate in a common market to produce differences that make them all the same … [T]he desire to appropriate one's own culture, to secure a unique identity, places one in the mainstream of a modern, individualistic culture to which national boundaries are irrelevant. (Handler 1988: 195)

At an even more specific level too, the borrowing of other nations' particular ways of defining or individuating themselves does seem to be a widespread feature of nationalism. For example, let us take the use of language to symbolise national identity. Some states attach great symbolic significance to preserving the conceived 'purity' of their national language (Edwards 1985: 27–34, 161–2). A state may purge its language of supposed foreign 'adulterations' while standardising it, and legislate to protect it thereafter from external contamination. So, for example, the Turkish state under Atatürk, seeking to rid itself of the legacy of the Ottomans, acted to remove Persian and Arabic loanwords from the language (Mango 1999: 496–97; Robbins 1996: 68), echoing the measures taken earlier by the Greek nationalist movement to remove Turkish admixtures from Greek (Herzfeld 1987, 1995) – the Greeks themselves reiterating similar nationalist legislation in France and Germany aimed at ridding their respective languages of foreign impurities.

A standard language may well be a functional requirement of a nation state (Gellner 1983), but the excision of foreign loanwords is hardly necessary for language standardisation or for effective communication. It can, however, be a powerful symbolic device with which a state can portray itself as having achieved full cultural and political independence. Of course, by no means all nation states link their sovereignty and language in this way, and many are quite unconcerned with issues of language purity and contamination. The choice to follow the model of the Académie Française (see Ball et al. 1995) and employ this particular symbolism of national self-definition seems largely a matter of convention and historical accident. One wonders how common it might nowadays be for states to have laws to protect the purity of their musical or architectural traditions or of national dress or cuisine if the seventeenth-century French academicians had established this precedent.

For another example of a shared practice of generating and preserving national differences, let us take European nationalisms in the nineteenth century. Their close connection with the Romantic movement gave these nationalisms a strongly marked common set of themes: the search for the nation's historical roots in its rural folk culture, the idealisation of the nation's landscape, the imagining of its peasantry as the truest embodiment of the national character. The essence of a nation was to be found above all in its rural heartlands, uncontaminated by the kinds of modern, external influences to which – as Lash and Friedman (1992: 23) remind us – Romanticism itself of course belonged. The élites of one nation after another drew on the same ideas as they sought to define their separate national identities (Burke 1992; Nairn 1996 [1974]; Smith 1986: 172–208).

Obviously, the forms of discourse through which nations and ethnic groups define themselves and develop their constructions of collective selfhood tend to be widely shared. These groups may imitate each other's ways of 'othering' one another. They may construct symbolic boundaries between themselves and others in ways obtained at second-hand – from those others. Hence Morris-Suzuki (1998: 79–109) suggests that early twentieth-century Japanese nationalism drew on an imported discourse of racism (originally, in the nineteenth century, in the form of Social Darwinism) with which to distinguish themselves and claim superiority over other 'races', including the putative races from whom these ideologies had been acquired (see also Henshall 1999: 78).

Ethnic and nationalist movements may construct exclusionary and particularistic identities. But they do so, in part, using symbolic practices which they have appropriated mimetically, copying others with whom they identify or seek to be identified, outsiders to whom they attribute power and prestige and whom they value positively as exemplars. Some peoples are more a focus of mimesis than others. French national identity, for example, seems to have been highly attractive mimetically to many others since its emergence in the Middle Ages (De Vos and Romanucci-Ross 1995: 363). My point is not simply that élites collaborate and borrow from each other, as they clearly often do, in constructing their respective ethnic or national mythologies. It is that these types of mimetic relationships should be viewed as intrinsic to nationalism and ethnicity, because they are the channels along which many of the devices circulate with which actors constitute their own particular national or ethnic identities.

Mimetic Communities

It was fashionable among the European nations in the Middle Ages to trace their origins back to the sacking of Troy, claiming to have been founded, like ancient Rome, by a Trojan hero. In this way, the British were supposed to have stemmed from a figure called Brutus, the Franks from a Francion, the Turks from a Turcus, and so forth (Burke 1969: 8, 71–74; Smith 1986: 72, 205). There was a clear status rivalry driving the production of these national origin myths: first, one state claims a Trojan ancestor, then another fabricates a virtually identical Trojan founder equal in prestige and differing only in his name and particular exploits. We see similar processes in the status rivalries between the medieval universities, which seem to have preoccupied themselves with assertions of having been instituted by ancient kings: Oxford claimed King Alfred as its founder, Cambridge claimed King Arthur or his forebears, while Paris laid claim to Charlemagne (Burke 1969: 74–75).

These are processes of competitive emulation just as much as invention. The groups concerned are making claims to equality as well as to superiority, and are engaged in a process of mutual identification with each other as well as competitive differentiation from each other. It is true that these nations created these historical representations to differentiate themselves, each seeking to make itself singular and unique. But the differences between the myths of the different nations were small, even though these minor variations may have had the utmost importance to the actors themselves. The point is that the act of producing these representations was not only an assertion of an identity separate from other peoples; it was also an assertion of equality with them, and a newly created symbol of national identity had therefore to resemble the corresponding symbols of rival nations and belong to the same genre, as well as differing from them.

Hobsbawm (1983) shows that the thirty or forty years before the First World War were a period of intense creativity of very much this sort in the 'invention' of traditions throughout Europe, and that this period saw in particular an efflorescence of many nationalist symbolisms (1983: 263). Most of what we now regard as the typical symbolic appurtenances of nation statehood – flags, anthems, military uniforms and so forth – seem to have originated in France and Britain, and were then adopted by many other states during this period (Hobsbawm 1983: 266, 282). Cannadine (1983) discusses the elaboration which state ceremonial, especially royal ritual, underwent throughout Europe, and he relates these processes to the intense international rivalries and tensions of the time. It was at least in part the heightened competition for national prestige and power that drove these innovations, in a phenomenon which he calls competitive inventiveness (Cannadine 1983: 139, 145, 161–62).

These processes of innovation seem to me to occur along two distinguishable dimensions. On the one hand, the same symbolic form may be competitively elaborated in some way: an example of this is the rise in the scale and complexity of European coronation ceremonies during the late nineteenth century. The other dimension is the competitive creation of new categories of symbolic forms. An example of this is the creation of the custom of royal 'jubilees' or anniversary celebrations, invented by the British in 1887, an innovation which seems to have impressed other states because they later adopted it (Hobsbawm 1983: 281–82). Along one dimension one has the production of successively more elaborate versions of the 'same' symbolic object, along the other the proliferation of 'new' symbolic objects. In this way, there was a process of competitive escalation in the quantity and complexity of the competing groups' diacritical symbols.

Nowadays, an ideal-typical modern nation state might include among its inventory of symbols its own flag, anthem and military uniforms; distinctive state holidays, commemorations and ceremonials; a national museum and academy (Davis 1994); a tomb of the Unknown Soldier (Anderson 1983: 9; Laqueur 1994; Piehler 1994); a patron saint or some other sort of figure (Britannia, Germania, Marianne, John Bull, Uncle Sam, Deutsche Michel, Mehmetçik, and so forth) personifying the state or its people (Hobsbawm 1983: 272, 276, 278); and a quasi-totemic animal or plant emblem – the shamrock, thistle, bulldog, bald eagle and so on (see also Mach 1994: 61–62). A standard language is, of course, typically a central symbol of nationhood (Anderson 1983: 67–82). Even the seemingly most nonsymbolic attributes of a nation state – its own state airline (Firth 1973: 347) or banking system – can function as important symbols of national identity and prestige, in the same way that a national epic poem or a state religion might at one time have done.

My point is that there is a conventional symbolic form of the nation state. The convention clearly changes over history and has subvarieties. Some states also seem much richer than others in these symbolic assets. But there is, at any particular time, a more or less agreed minimal complex of symbols that a political entity should have in order to be understood as a nation state or, indeed, even to be understood as a political movement having aspirations to nation statehood. The diverse symbolic inventories of all the particular states appear as the many refractions of this abstract form, in much the same way that the foundation myths of the medieval universities were all versions of one myth or the Trojan progenitors of medieval European nations were all derivations of the same figure.

Thus, today, it would be wholly unsurprising to find some nation state possessing an anthem, or a cenotaph, or its own official holidays. Nor would anyone think it odd if it had its own national sport or traditional folk costumes. On the other hand, if it claimed descent from a Trojan warrior or possessed its own state pantheon or tutelary god, these would appear rather less normal differences. Such attributes belong to other, vanished, communities of conventions about how people should differ from one another intelligibly (see Harrison 1995a: 260–63).

The groups that individuate themselves within a community of this sort are connected to each other by shared principles of individuation. They are related and alike in the respects in which they create dissimilarities among themselves. Of course, shared conventions for the production and understanding of differences change over time, and are therefore inherently partial, provisional and contingent.

It is in this vein that Jackson (1995) has examined the production and objectification of 'traditional culture' among the indigenous Tukanoan peoples of Colombia. To gain official recognition by both government and non-government agencies, these communities are required to possess 'traditional Indian cultures', differentiating them from one another and from other cognate groups. This involves redefining their contemporary situation in Colombian society or allowing it to be redefined by external agencies in such a way as to accommodate these outsiders' expectations of authentic Colombian indigenous cultural diversity. The various objectified 'ethnic' traditions thereby (partly bureaucratically) produced closely resemble each other and belong to a single, historically specific genre.

The emergence of another such mimetic community, though on a much larger scale, can be seen in ethnopolitics in the Soviet Union during the 1920s and 1930s. The policy of the Soviet state at the time was to promote the ethnic cultures within its borders, and 'all officially recognized Soviet nationalities were supposed to have their own nationally defined "Great Traditions" that needed to be protected, perfected and, if need be, invented by specially trained professionals in specially designated institutions' (Slezkine 1996: 226). These constructed Great Traditions seem to have tended to take on a marked symmetry with each other. Slezkine describes the 1934 Congress of Soviet Writers:

> Pushkin, Tolstoy and other officially restored Russian icons were not the only national giants of international stature – all Soviet peoples possessed, or would shortly acquire, their own classics, their own founding fathers and their own folkloric riches. The Ukrainian delegate said that Taras Shevchenko was a 'genius' and a 'colossus' 'whose role in the creation of the Ukrainian literary language was no less important than Pushkin's role in the creation of the Russian literary language, and perhaps even greater.' ... The Azerbaijani delegate insisted that ... Mirza Fath Ali Akhundov was ... a 'great philosopher-playwright' whose 'characters [were] as colorful, diverse and realistic as the characters of Griboedov, Gogol and Ostrovskii.' (Slezkine 1996: 225; parenthesis in the original)

Similarly, the Armenian, Turkmen, Tajik and Georgian delegates all praised their own literary traditions in very similar terms. Each delegation in turn claimed to have literary giants equivalent to those of Russia and the world at large, in what Slezkine describes as a 'curiously solemn parade of old-fashioned romantic nationalisms' (1996: 225). What I find notable about this orchestrated celebration of unity-in-diversity is that the more these nations were presented as distinct and unique at one level, the more they seemed to become similar at another. By the end of the 1930s all the Union republics had 'their own writers' unions, theatres, opera companies and national academies that specialized in national history, literature and language' (Slezkine 1996:

226) and in these respects had in a curious way became clones of each other. They had become tokens of a single type, variants that all conformed to the same model of official culture. And the model to which they had all come to conform seems to have been, implicitly, Russian. To have one's own high culture, one's own literary Great Tradition, meant, it appeared, having above all one's own Pushkins, Tolstoys and Gogols, and being able to claim equality – and symmetry – with Russian high culture. Clearly, it did not mean possessing writers who could match Mirza Fath Ali Akhundov or the Turkmen poet Makhtum-Kuli (see Slezkine 1996: 225).

The processes of ethnonational identity formation that occurred during those decades involved, certainly, the promotion of ethnic differences. But they also involved the simultaneous development of a historically highly specific framework of commonalities within which to cultivate and exhibit this diversity. The Soviet ethnonations became, culturally, increasingly individuated at one level, and increasingly disindividuated at another. The delegates at the Soviet Writers' Conference, for instance, could not have prided themselves on having their 'own' Tolstoys and Pushkins unless – or until – they had much in common, including an esteem for Tolstoy and Pushkin, or at least an outward willingness to pay homage to them. In order for ethnic groups or any other entities to differ, they must resemble each other in some way, sharing some dimension on which they can be contrasted and compared (see Lévi-Strauss 1973; Radcliffe-Brown 1951). In this respect, differences always presuppose similarities and can exist only against a background of resemblance. To create diversity, one has to ensure the existence of the background similarities against which the differences can be made to appear.

The creation of differences in this way seems implicitly to summon into existence the shared background attributes which the differences presuppose. To claim to possess one's own Proust or Tolstoy is to assert both a difference and a resemblance. And if groups multiply these surface variations – generating, besides their own Prousts and Tolstoys, their own Beethovens, Einsteins, Platos and Shakespeares – in doing so they also multiply and deepen their resemblances. When actors differentiate themselves in these sorts of markedly constrained ways, they make the ﹍lves in certain other respects more closely alike.

Mimesis Hidden and Denied

A feature of ethnicity and nationalism, then, is mimetic communities, or networks, in which actors circulate among themselves – sometimes, perhaps, impose on one another – common practices and understandings about how to differ. Their identities are defined in ways acquired from each other, so that they do not just imagine themselves to be dissimilar, but imagine their dissimilarities in similar, more or less standardised terms. A mimetic community thus creates a kind of domesticated cultural diversity (see also Gellner 1983: 50–52). It enables a more or less bounded set of groups to differ from each other in structured and meaningful ways by generating a specially restricted form of cultural variation. It replaces mere random, uncoordinated heterogeneities with stable, normalised, socially significant relationships of difference.

An important aim of every nationalist movement, of course, is to make emphatically visible precisely these apparent 'differences'. On the other hand, it is less likely to have a goal of making visible the mimetic processes involved in producing these differences, or the close similarities between its own ways and other nations' ways of being different from each other. So, for example, the Soviet ethnonations differed culturally, and their representatives certainly understood them to differ. Each with its own Tolstoys, Pushkins, Gogols, state opera companies and national academies, they were all – from the point of view of their members – uniquely different. The fact that in regard to having their own Tolstoys, Pushkins, Gogols and so forth they were all highly symmetrical, and were furthermore all modelling themselves after the exemplar of a dominant Russian culture, was perhaps less likely to be acknowledged or celebrated.

If ethnicity and nationalism are a process of domesticating cultural diversity, its products are very conspicuous, but the process is less so. The mimetic dimension of ethnicity and nationalism tends to be, from the actors' point of view, under-acknowledged and at times denied.

Of course, there are historical instances of large-scale and quite open imitation of Western models. Japan in the Meiji period (Westney 1987) and Atatürk's Turkey are particularly notable cases in which modernisers imported Western practices and institutions as entirely deliberate and explicit state policy. To Atatürk, a modern mentality needed to be demonstrated outwardly by practices such as the adoption of modern Western attire. Hence his Hat Law of 1925, which outlawed the fez (symbol of Ottoman and Moslem orthodoxy) and made hats the compulsory national headgear for Turkish men (Kinross 1964: 411–17; Macfie 1994: 136, 140–41; Mango 1999: 433–38). Even before the Hat Law, the hat riots and the ensuing executions, a Moslem cleric had been hanged for publishing a tract decrying such 'imitation of the Franks' (Mango 1999: 436).

Evidently, there are situations in which the role of mimesis in the formation of ethnic and national identity is quite open. But I would suggest that it is perhaps more likely to be denied, or rapidly elided from national memory, the more markedly and overtly oppositional the borrowers' identities are towards those from whom they borrow. For example, Kiberd (1989), discussing the emergence of Irish nationalist 'traditions' in the nineteenth century, describes what he calls the 'device of national parallelism' through which these traditions seem to have been constructed in a kind of oppositional counterpoint to perceived English or British equivalents: 'For every English action, there must be an equal and opposite Irish reaction – for soccer, Gaelic football; for hockey, hurling; for trousers, a kilt' (Kiberd 1989:

320). For each perceived major icon of English identity, each attribute appearing to distinguish the English, it seems to have been important to the Irish nationalist movement to be able to reciprocate with an equivalent Irish icon of their own. Hence the emergence of Gaelic football as a 'traditional' national sport, an occurrence which Kiberd describes as a piece of 'instant archaeology' not known to the legendary Celtic hero Cuchulain (Kiberd 1989: 320). In this way, Kiberd seems to imply, the presence of England as Ireland's Other had an important formative influence on Irish national identity. To use poststructuralist terminology, England represented a key part of Irish nationalism's 'constitutive outside' (Hall 1996: 4). Irish identity came to reflect certain aspects of Irish perceptions of Englishness precisely to the extent that it was constructed as a counter-identity, devised to oppose and exclude its Other. To create a maximal 'difference' between the two nations required first contriving an isomorphism between them, maximising the points of contact between them where differences could be generated.

I referred earlier to a puzzling feature of ethnicity and ethnonationalism: namely, that groups can have strong mimetic attractions to those with whom they are in conflict or whom they oppose in some way, and can imitate them. Hence, nineteenth-century Irish nationalism replicated aspects of its coloniser's cultural identity, as it saw it, in the process of establishing an identity of its own. At least part of the explanation of this seems to lie in the need to first put similarities in place in order to be able to generate differences. The initial problem faced by a group that seeks to make itself dissimilar to another is to find a particular way of resembling it, or perhaps of resembling it more closely. In a sense this is precisely what ethnicity and nationalism offer: ready-made ways of resembling others so as to be able to begin the process of becoming different from them.

One manifestation of this is the profound contradiction often faced by nationalist movements in Asia and other formerly colonised parts of the world: namely, that they claimed freedom from European domination using European forms of political thought:

> [E]ach new nation created by independence from colonial rule had in turn to create its own narrative of possessing an authentic precolonial past, suffering the rupture of colonial possession and reachieving authenticity through its struggle for freedom. The master narratives of nineteenth-century European nation-states were appropriated by the subjects of colonial rule and turned against the master narratives of imperial history. But in the process what has come to be realized is that although defined in opposition, the shape of that historical narrative is still that of the colonizer. (Rowlands 1994: 135)

The political philosopher Chatterjee (1986, 1993) shows that a very common way in which Asian and African nationalist thinkers have sought to resolve this dilemma is by arguing that 'their' nationalisms are 'different' from Western nationalisms, indeed superior, emphasising spiritual values as opposed to the materialistic nationalisms of their colonisers, or ex-colonisers (see also Eley and Suny 1996: 29). To these nationalists, the colonised needed to assimilate Western 'techniques of organising material life' before they could free themselves from Western domination:

> But this could not mean the imitation of the West in every aspect of life, for then the very distinction between the West and the East would vanish – the self-identity of national culture would itself be threatened. In fact, as Indian nationalists in the late nineteenth century argued, not only was it undesirable to imitate the West in anything other than the material aspects of life, it was even unnecessary to do so, because in the spiritual domain, the East was superior to the West. What was necessary was to cultivate the material techniques of modern Western civilization while retaining and strengthening the distinctive spiritual essence of the national culture. This completes the formulation of the nationalist project, and as an ideological justification for the selective appropriation of Western modernity, it continues to hold sway to this day. (Chatterjee 1993: 120)

In this way, Chatterjee argues, the 'imagined communities' (Anderson 1983) of anticolonial African and Asian nationalisms were predicated on the idea of a 'difference' from the West, representing themselves, in certain respects, as the diametrical opposites of those of Europe. The colonised could thereby claim to have developed a form of nationalism authentically their own, not a derivative one; they were not merely passive consumers of a Western modernity (Chatterjee 1993: 5).

4

Difference as Denied Resemblance

Orientalisms and the Other: Difference as Inferiority

Penrose observes how nationalist discourses often employ what he calls the 'foil of other': '[N]ationalist rhetoric frequently asserts the existence of a nation by documenting what it is *not* ... [F]or example, Canadians can assert that they are not loud and brash like the Americans; Bretagnes can insist that they are untouched by French snobbery; and Sami can argue that Finnish regimentation and reserve are alien to them' (1993: 33; see also p. 32). The particular stereotypes which people hold of other nationalities tell us much about the way they wish to define themselves. Indeed, such stereotypes of others – representations which I shall call difference-as-inferiority – are often important means by which people construct their own identities. De Vos and Wagatsuma, for instance, discuss the attitudes of the Japanese majority to the Burakumin (descendants of a feudal outcaste group), and compare these attitudes with white stereotypes of blacks in the American South. Outcastes, they suggest, whether black, Burakumin or any other kind, represent a type of scapegoat for the majority:

> The kind of scapegoat he or she is depends on the particular kind of behavior that the culture is most concerned to disavow and attribute to others who are less virtuous, in short, what is 'projected' out. Thus ... a predominant element in the southern white's stereotype of the 'Negro' was his *potent and primitive sexuality*. *Dirtiness* and *aggressiveness* were also components.
>
> Japanese stereotypes directed toward both Burakumin and Koreans contain the same basic components. In the case of the Burakumin, the relative emphasis on unacceptable sexuality and aggression found directed toward African-Americans is reversed. Concern with the aggressiveness and crudeness of the Burakumin or Korean is more intense than worry about their sexuality ... [I]t is the 'unclean' habits with reference to language and manners, as well as supposed tendencies to be inordinately violent and aggressive, that are emphasized. Within Japanese society sexual experience is more tolerated if exercised at the right time and place, but there is a great need to disavow the appearance of direct aggression in everyday relations and to emphasize specific rules of propriety. (De Vos and Wagatsuma 1995: 284–85)

A group's ethnic stereotypes, its representations of outsiders, tend to reflect and serve to emphasise its own cultural values by making non-members appear to embody those specific qualities which it denies and disparages in itself. These ethnic Others may be portrayed as negative embodiments of its own self-ideals, or indeed be made to reflect other disavowed aspects of the group's own identity. Leone, discussing the history of the Mormon Church in the United States, considers why the Mormons excluded blacks from their priesthood for many years until 1978. He suggests that through this policy of exclusion the Mormons were displacing or projecting onto blacks the low status which they themselves experienced within the wider American society. In this sense, they were seeking to deny their own felt exclusion:

> By excluding blacks, Mormons recapitulated and internalized their own subordinate, inferior position. They did unto others what was being done to them, and, when they did it to others, they masked the locus of reality, namely, their own true condition. Further, the doing was the becoming; by making others inferior, unacceptable, and unworthy, they acted out on others what they themselves were and so modelled their own condition. (Leone 1981: 84)

In a rather similar way, Morris-Suzuki (1998) suggests that certain strands of Japanese nationalist thought in the 1930s and 1940s attributed racism to foreigners in a way that was itself quite obviously racist. Some Japanese nationalist writers of the time claimed that the Japanese were superior to other races because they, unlike other races, had no sense of racial superiority. They argued that only other, inferior races, such as the Chinese and the Europeans, were racist. The distinctively Japanese lack of a sense of racial hierarchy, Japan's unique respect for equality and harmony among the races, became: 'the source of Japan's claim to global racial leadership. The argument, in short, is that we are superior because we do not consider ourselves superior' (Morris-Suzuki 1998: 94; see also pp. 101, 108).

The more one examines the kinds of perceptions I have called difference-as-inferiority, the less they seem to concern difference at all, and the more they appear as distorted and suppressed forms of perceived resemblance. Only superficially is difference-as-inferiority a disjunction between the Self and the disvalued Other. At a deeper and more covert level, it is a dichotomy between valued and disvalued aspects of the Self.

Many commentators have understood an idea of very much this sort to be implicit in Said's (1978) analysis of Orientalism (see Grossberg 1996: 91, 95–96): namely, that the 'Orient' of the European colonial imagination (exotic, sensual, cruel, decadent and so forth) was a kind of mirror, in which colonial society expressed preoccupations of its own in a disguised form, projecting onto the societies of the East attributes which it sought to deny in itself. Kuper makes a similar point explicitly, in his analysis of the way the idea of 'primitive society' was constructed in nineteenth-century anthropology:

The anthropologists took this primitive society as their special subject, but in practice primitive society proved to be their own society (as they understood it) seen in a distorting mirror. For them modern society was defined above all by the territorial state, the monogamous family and private property. Primitive society therefore must have been nomadic, ordered by blood ties, sexually promiscuous and communist. (1988: 5)

A construct such as 'primitive society' is an implicit self-portrait by its authors. Carrier (1995) argues that every Orientalism entails in this way a corresponding 'Occidentalism': stereotyped and essentialist representations of the cultural Other are linked inextricably to similarly distorted, tendentious and simplified representations of the cultural Self.

Such arguments suggest, then, that the cultural Others of colonial Europe came to embody censored and disowned aspects of the colonial society itself. The discourses of Orientalism (and its accompanying Occidentalism) ignored, denied or suppressed aspects of European society, and made them reappear in overt and extravagant forms in other societies. The cultural Other seemed to express precisely what was muted in the Self. In the very act of representing the Other as essentially different in this way, these discourses defined specific similarities or commonalities – but ones which they were unable to acknowledge – between the Other and certain dimensions of the Self.

Sax recognises this when he argues that all constructs of difference are inherently ambivalent. They do not simply valorise the Self positively, and negatively valorise the Other, but involve:

a double movement, where the Other is simultaneously emulated and repudiated, admired and despised, and the source of this ambivalence is the recognition of Self in Other. That is to say, the Other represents a kind of screen upon which both the despised and the desired aspects of the Self can be projected, so that the dialectics of sameness and difference is resolved into a kind of difference *in* sameness. (Sax 1998: 294)

This, to me, is the most interesting and potentially productive implication that may be drawn from a consideration of Said's *Orientalism*. It is not simply that the West fantasised the East as its Other, but that certain kinds of subterranean identifications with that imagined alterity were intrinsic to the fantasy and to reproducing it over time. Of course, the literature on ethnicity and nationalism is depressingly full of depictions of prejudice, xenophobia and racism. Some studies even seem to suggest that stereotyping at least some cultural others as inferior is intrinsic to the construction of national and ethnic identity (see, for example, R. Cohen 1994). My point is that to ascribe to outsiders attributes forbidden or unacceptable to one's own group is to define those outsiders, not as different, but as ambivalently different and alike. It is to make them assume the form of one's own group's anti-Self: alien indeed, but alien in such a way that they evince towards one's own group submerged and distorted likenesses.

The Narcissisms of Minor and Major Differences

A long-standing observation by social anthropologists concerning witchcraft beliefs and accusations seems applicable also to ethnic prejudices: namely, that a group's fantasies of radical Otherness – its culturally standardised nightmares, as Wilson called witchcraft beliefs – tend to reflect its cultural values. So, for example, witches are imagined as figures of insatiable greed in one culture, as figures of sexual excess in another, and so forth, according to each culture's particular conceptions of normality and morality (Wilson 1951; see also Mair 1976: 33–35).

Another common anthropological observation on witchcraft beliefs is that these fantasies of evil are directed, not only at remote strangers, but very frequently against relatives and neighbours (see for instance Barth 1975: 134–35; Knauft 1985a; Marwick 1964). People often project their most radical and powerfully divisive constructs of Otherness upon those to whom they conceive themselves to be – perhaps not willingly – most closely bound. They may demonise those with whom they most identify, and with whom their own self-concepts are most closely intertwined. And, of course, to disown some of one's kinsmen or neighbours as inhuman or satanic is to continue to depend on them for an important part of one's own sense of self. In this respect too, those representations I have called difference-as-inferiority have parallels with witchcraft beliefs and accusations: they are directed not just at groups in some way socially distant, but often at people very close to home. Nationalism has often been viewed as having close analogies with religion – indeed, even as being a kind of secular replacement for religion (see for instance, Kapferer 1988). Racism and ethnic prejudice seem to play much the same role in this secular cosmology as witchcraft beliefs and accusations do in religious cosmologies.

This brings me to a third and final pattern of identification with the Other that can underlie apparent 'differences'. This pattern – I have called it difference-as-equality – involves representations of similarity, parity and closeness between Self and Other. This, too, is a form of muted or denied resemblance involved in the production of difference: it is a type of negation, diminution or elision of resemblance that occurs when a nation or ethnic group differentiates itself, or is differentiated, against a background of commonalities shared with some other or others. One may think of it as a midway point between the two poles of difference-as-superiority and difference-as-inferiority, combining elements of both. Here, social actors share aspects of identities with their Others by virtue of identifying with them, or by being identified with them, at some higher level of inclusiveness.

Let me begin with the Australian nationalism analysed by Kapferer (1988). To these nationalists, the key characteristic of Australia is an egalitarianism differing deeply from what they conceive as the hierarchical and class-ridden nature of English society. This is an ideologically central contrast in Australian nationalism, but one that also implies a strong identification with the English:

Australia, or the nationalist egalitarian ideal, discovers its form in relation to its conceptualized opposite, that of inegalitarian, hierarchical, England. Historically and ideologically, many Australians understand their social world as having a strong identity with England but simultaneously as being its inverse. Australia, through its progress to independence, succeeded in effecting a transformation of the English scheme of things. While inequality, the ideals of aristocratic birth, the privileges of socially produced position, and so on are the unifying principles of England, equality metaphorized by the underclasses of England, constitutes the organizing principle of Australia. Ideologically, England and Australia are bound, together composing a unity of the strongest similarity and difference.

This conception of Australian nationalist thought extends an understanding of the reason many Australians express identity with England even as they assert a distinct Australian identity. The latter reproduces the former ... The sense of a historical identity with England is produced ideologically, as it is emotionally, in the very constitution of an Australian identity. (Kapferer 1988: 199–200; see also pp. 14, 167)

As one can see, this nationalism shares certain features with Orientalism. It defines itself in relation to an Other that inverts certain aspects of its collective Self. And England, as the arch-embodiment of class hierarchy, represents everything which Australian nationalism most seeks to mask and deny in Australian society itself. But it differs from Orientalism in one crucial way. Australian nationalism strongly and overtly identifies with its Other in certain respects. This is alterity, then, but within the context of an overarching relationship of commonality and shared cultural identity. The explicit connection with England is an essential component of this form of Australian nationalism, because, as Kapferer makes clear, it alone provides the felt common background (of history, culture, religion, language and so forth) on which 'differences' can be made to appear. This is why Australian nationalism defines itself by a contrast with the English and not with the Peruvians, Icelanders or other unrelated peoples. One can distinguish oneself only from those with whom there is a relationship in the first place.

A strongly felt background of shared history and culture can provide a context, then, from which strong claims to difference are able to emerge. Lowenthal (1994) suggests a similar process among ethnic groups in the United States. Ethnic minorities there often claim to possess their own unique cultural 'heritages', distinct from mainstream American culture and deserving the same esteem. But, as Lowenthal points out, these assertions of cultural difference are all couched within the same, culturally and historically quite specific, conceptions of 'heritage', and in this respect these groups are identical. For example, minorities may claim to have 'their own' Tolstoys, Prousts and other literary and artistic figures. Although these are meant as claims to have their 'own' cultures, equal to the dominant Euro-American tradition, Lowenthal argues that the claims implicitly conform to Western notions of the individuality of the creative artist (1994: 46). Far from representing an alternative to the dominant culture they replicate key aspects of it and, in this respect, are clearly part of it (see also Handler 1988: 157–58, 195). What these ethnic actors take to be manifestations of cultural dissimilarity, or even of a clash of incompatible cultures, are, at a deeper level, signs of a shared culture. The conceived differences are surface expressions of underlying commonalities.

Horowitz (1975) describes how ethnic groups in colonial India crystallised out of an earlier social context in which boundaries had been highly fluid and permeable:

> Even during the colonial period some groups were differentiating themselves from others who had earlier been regarded as members of the same group. In nineteenth century India, for example, one of the effects of religious revival movements was to sharpen the lines between Hindus and Muslims. A side-effect was to differentiate Sikhs from Hindus. The reformism of the Hindu Arya Samaj was not very different in content from the Sikhs' own movement, the Singh Sabha. But the Arya Samaj emphasized Hindi as the language of a revitalized Hindu culture, whereas the Sikhs were attached to the Punjabi language. Gradually, the Sikh movement sought to 'purify' Sikhism by excising Hindu influences, thereby creating a sense of a distinctive Sikh identity. This, it should be said, was a development that proceeded in the face of centuries of ritual and social interaction, as well as intermarriage and conversion, between Sikhs and Hindus. In short, the earlier boundary was exceedingly fluid, and now, for the first time, an ascriptive Sikh identity emerged. (1975: 135; footnotes omitted)

Here, ethnogenesis was clearly a process of mutual disengagement among communities once deeply imbricated in one another. To define themselves as ethnically separate and different, people who once viewed themselves as barely, if at all, distinct had to act to overcome and undo their historical commonalities. They constructed ethnic identities in a process, as it were, of cultural dis-homogenisation, the deliberate, systematic and effortful production of dissimilarities among themselves.

A particularly common element in these processes of ethnic uncoupling is the systematic forgetting, or suppression, of shared history. Jarman (1999), for example, discusses two important Northern Irish commemorations which take place in Belfast each year, both celebrating events of 1916. One, held by Unionists (the predominantly Protestant supporters of the union of Northern Ireland and Britain), remembers the Battle of the Somme in the First World War and the very many Northern Irish Protestant volunteers killed in it. Unionists regard the Somme as a major historical sacrifice by their people on behalf of Great Britain, a sacrifice for which Britain has ever since owed a great moral debt. On the other hand, the predominantly Catholic, Irish Nationalist community (supporters of a united Ireland) for their part celebrate the Easter Rising, the abortive rebellion of Irish Nationalists in Dublin in the same year as the Somme. The two annual commemorations, Jarman argues, held ostensibly to preserve and remember the past, are also devices for forgetting the past or for eliding those aspects of it which neither of the two communities find it in their interests to recall. Neither side, for instance, publicly remembers the large numbers of Irish Catholic volunteers in the British forces in the First World War. To Unionists the sacrifices of the Somme and of the First World War as a whole are a kind of historical monopoly of their own people. In Irish Nationalist versions of Anglo-Irish history, the memory of Irish Catholics defending the British Empire is equally unwelcome. Even in a strongly divided society such as Northern Ireland, there is inevitably a great deal of historical common ground between the two sides. The formation and maintenance of separate collective identities requires from both of them a principled and complicit forgetting of significant parts of it.

Clearly, people can feel their identities are jeopardised and undermined by too much similarity to certain others, by having too much culture and history in common with those whom they wish to classify as outsiders. Leone (1981) argues that an enduring problem faced by the members of the Mormon Church in maintaining their cultural distinctiveness in the United States is the fact that they are very similar culturally to the mainstream American population – indeed, similar in rather too many ways for their own liking. In the course of its history, he suggests, the Mormon Church has tended to differentiate itself from the wider society by a device of contrariness, a deliberately perverse flouting of whatever the core prevailing social norms happened to be. In the nineteenth century, when the church was founded, American society had a rigid sexual code. The Mormons accordingly flouted it, outraging public opinion by practising polygyny. But by the 1960s, there was growing public support for the Mormo͞ ͞n their struggle to maintain their distinctive family system in the face of official persecution. Indeed, their problem was that mainstream American society had become too sympathetic towards them. Their response was to adopt deliberately provocative racist policies, excluding blacks from their ministry, a move which alienated much American public opinion and lost them much support, as they knew it would. The Mormons seem to represent what Roosens (1989: 97) calls an 'oppositional counter-culture' or, as Douglas (1993) terms it, an enclave or sectarian community: that is, a group defining itself through dissidence from a majority culture. It seems that for small groups of this kind, too much sympathetic identification on the part of outsiders can be highly unwelcome, posing just as much a threat as hostility and persecution as they try to preserve a distinct identity: hence the Mormons' switch-over from provocative marriage practices to provocative racial policies, when their marital practices ceased to be sufficiently effective at marking them off as 'different'.

Simmel and Freud are among those who have pointed out the way that claims to difference can arise – indeed, are particularly likely to arise – among groups that share a common identity at another, more inclusive level. Hence that tendency of neighbouring states, and closely related peoples, to exhibit what Freud called the narcissism of minor differences (Freud 1930: 114; 1945: 101; 1957: 199; 1964: 91; see also Simmel 1955: 42). Their similarities seem perpetually to threaten each group's sense of identity, and so each clings to some small distinguishing marks, investing them with disproportionate significance. Freud's important insight here was to realise that only people with much in common develop these intense needs to differentiate themselves. It is the commonalities between them that drive them to seek differences. This insight is echoed today by those analysts who view globalisation, and perceptions of a growing worldwide homogenisation of culture, as key factors provoking resurgences of ethnonationalism and other particularistic assertions of difference (see, for instance, Featherstone 1990; Friedman 1994; Hughes-Freeland and Crain 1998; Meyer and Geschiere 1999). It is those who imagine they have the most in common – or fear that they have, or fear that they may come to have, the most in common – who are most likely to categorise each other as different, as opposites or inversions of one another. It is they who have the most at stake in differentiating themselves.

I would, though, slightly amend Freud's insight in one respect. The resemblances which give rise to the narcissism of minor differences are, of course, socially constructed perceptions of resemblance and not necessarily actual, objective resemblances. This narcissism is therefore not just a matter of exaggerated perceptions of difference, but must also involve the construction of these threatening perceptions of undifferentiation and over-resemblance which provoke, in reaction, the overstated claims of distinctiveness. To understand how a narcissism of minor differences might arise, one must first understand the discursive production of cultural claustrophobia – the stifling resemblances and excessively close commonalities – which the narcissism, as it were, attempts to deny and negate. These images of over-similarity might need to be actively reinforced, or even deliberately created, before they trigger the sorts of chauvinism Freud had in mind. Hence nationalist ideologies often draw force not just from rhetorics of distinctiveness, but also from those complementary rhetorics of corrosive homogenisation which portray the nation's distinctive culture and identity as under threat from the outside (see Forbes and Kelly 1995; Handler 1988). Whether these are in some sense 'real' threats is another matter.

Contemporary social commentators often argue that the rapidly increasing rate and volume of transnational flows of culture are not, as one might have expected, producing global homogenisation. On the contrary, they seem to be giving rise to growing assertions of local distinctiveness and heterogeneity (Featherstone 1990; Friedman 1994; Sibley 1995: 183–84). As people become in many respects culturally less diverse, they seem to imagine or claim they are becoming more so. Some authors suggest that the two processes are connected causally. Meyer and Geschiere, for example, argue that contemporary 'global flows' of culture provoke reactive attempts at 'cultural closure'.

> There is much empirical evidence that people's awareness of being involved in open-ended global flows seems to trigger a search for fixed orientation points and

action frames, as well as determined efforts to affirm old and construct new boundaries ... It looks as if, in a world characterised by flows, a great deal of energy is devoted to controlling and freezing them: grasping the flux often actually entails a politics of 'fixing' – a politics which is, above all, operative in struggles about the construction of identities. (Meyer and Geschiere 1999: 2, 5)

Meyer and Geschiere seem to imply that there are certain basic human needs for secure identities and stable social categorisations; hence, as increasingly global circulations of culture undermine old frameworks of belonging, so people may seek or cling to closed and exclusive identities as a defensive reaction. Appadurai (1999), similarly, suggests that as identities become increasingly fluid, uncertain, ambiguous and contingent, so people seek increasingly – and sometimes increasingly violently – to assure themselves of closure and fixity.

A basic psychological need for secure identities may of course exist, but I do not think it is necessary to posit such a need in order to understand the linkage between contemporary processes of globalisation and assertions of diversity. Rather, one has only to examine the way that all claims to stable, bounded cultural identities seem inextricably connected with, and to imply, a corresponding negative counter-imagery of dissolution and flux. Ethnicity and nationalism can define themselves especially powerfully in opposition to precisely the kinds of images of homogenising and solvent flows which globalisation processes can so readily be seen to represent. These are the very images which can help to create and sustain their cultural particularism.

Hannerz (1992) suggests that contemporary social anthropology is responding to globalisation by abandoning old assumptions of objectively bounded societies and cultures. Anthropologists no longer presuppose the existence of delimited groups or cultures, but problematise the boundedness of the phenomena they study. One approach they can take is to focus on processes of cultural hybridisation and creolisation. But, as Jenkins (1997: 29–30) points out, these conceptions themselves seem to imply that a world of discrete cultures did once exist. In other words, they belong to the same conceptual universe as the older view of culture, and thus seem to be relics of it (see also Ohnuki-Tierney 2001: 239). But if Hannerz is right, it is ironic that many of the communities and actors we study seem to have now stepped into our former shoes. They appear strongly inclined – even increasingly so – to represent the world as if it were composed, or ought to be composed, of delimited groups of very much this sort, each possessing its own discrete 'culture' (see, for instance, Stolke 1995).

In short, at a time when anthropologists no longer tend so readily to assume the existence of bounded cultures and societies, it seems to be increasingly vital for us to understand why those whom we study seem to have appropriated, and now employ, representations of boundedness of very much this sort, so that the concept of culture once developed by anthropologists is now overtly politicised in public discourse (Wright 1998). Hastrup reminds us that to make politicised claims to an 'inviolable and autonomous culture' can be a vital strategy of resistance, perhaps even of survival, for many communities (1995: 155; see also Nadel-Klein 1991: 514–15). Anthony Cohen argues likewise that small communities can very effectively mobilise their members in collective action by representing themselves as having endangered boundaries – as having essential qualities, for instance, or distinctive ways of life which are under threat from the outside – as they may indeed truly be (A.P. Cohen 1985: 109; 1986). Smith (1986: 217) suggests in a similar way that it is particularly the small nations – which is to say, the majority of nations – that depend most heavily on their cultural distinctiveness for their sense of identity. But it is clear that, even in the largest and most powerful nations or coalitions of nations, political actors may view their cultural identities as under threat from the outside or represent their identities as under threat in order to justify barriers to immigration (see Balibar 1988; Stolke 1995). In short, nations in general increasingly appear to their members as defensive 'enclave' cultures, encompassed, surrounded and threatened by globalised culture and, to some extent, defining themselves oppositionally in relation to it.

The key point here is that cultural forms are never first global and then locally appropriated. Rather, as anthropologists have often shown, such forms become global only through countless particular local appropriations and adaptations. Thus, the same social actors who perceive globalisation as a threat are very often also its agents, and their relationship to it is compounded of resistance and desire, rejection and attraction. Let us take, for example, the Japanese kamikaze pilots of the Second World War, whose letters, diaries and other writings have been examined by Ohnuki-Tierney (2001, 2002). These were certainly ardent nationalists but, far from being in some sense narrowly chauvinist, they were among the most cosmopolitan Japanese of their generation. Most were students at prestigious universities, widely read in European literature and philosophy. Their own patriotism was strongly influenced by their readings of French, German and Russian nationalist writers. They kept diaries in French or German, read Goethe and Baudelaire, many were Marxists and some were Christians. To these fervent champions of the local and particular, occidental culture may have represented their Other, but it was clearly an Other that also embodied a profound part of themselves (Ohnuki-Tierney 2001: 230–34). What Ohnuki-Tierney rightly calls the 'mutually constituent' opposition of the global and the local is an existential conflict within the consciousness of the social actor, and seems to take its most acute form in the subjectivities of cosmopolitans (2001: 237–40).

Conclusion: the Mimetic Misrecognition of Mimesis

In this and the previous chapter, I have sought to question the idea that ethnic and national identities are most usefully understood as based on perceptions of difference. The problem with this view, I have tried to show, is that representations of difference and alterity, though of course central to ethnicity and nationalism, nevertheless always seem to be bound inextricably to perceptions of similarity. In fact, they seem to be elaborated specifically in antithesis to certain kinds of resemblances. The Other, as Sax (1998) argued, always appears to embody aspects of the Self.

It is perhaps not surprising that this should be so. In the context of ethnicity and nationalism, cultural differences are social relationships. They are not mere ethnological dissimilarities, like those that might be found to exist between the French, say, and the Hittites. Rather, as Barth showed long ago, they are distinctions conceived, valorised and communicated by people interacting with one another, as ways of structuring their interactions. In this context, cultural difference is a particular idiom of sociality. Ethnic and national 'differences', in this sense, are much better conceptualised as muted or broken resemblances. I have outlined three broadly distinct configurations which these muted similarities seem often to take, configurations in which the Other is valorised respectively as inferior, superior and equal to the Self.

In one configuration, which I called difference-as-inferiority, the cultural Other is made to represent censored and disclaimed attributes of the Self. On the surface, the Other therefore appears essentially alien. But behind this façade of radical alterity lurks a hidden identity between Self and Other, in which the Other represents what Said called 'a sort of surrogate and even underground self' (1978: 3; see also p. 95). The Other, ostensibly one's opposite, is at a deeper level an expression of one's self-image. In a sense, such processes of projection are the opposite of imitation, a kind of anti-mimesis. To imagine an Other that inverts the Self, that embodies everything the Self disowns, is to simultaneously create and repress an intimate resemblance.

Another configuration, difference-as-superiority, is the pattern of identification with the Other that occurs in the emulation of other ethnic or national identities. Here, a culturally foreign Other is valorised positively rather than negatively, attributed with that superiority Armstrong (1982: 296) calls cultural ascendancy. It offers models, rather than anti-models, for the Self. Instead of a projection that ascribes unwanted attributes of the Self to the Other, this is a process – often covert and surreptitious – of introjection, a mimetic appropriation of desired attributes of the Other.

In the third configuration, difference-as-equality, the Other is conceived as essentially similar culturally to the Self, in some respects far too much so. Here, actors define their ethnic or national identities by marking themselves off contrastively from others with whom they are categorised as sharing common features of identity at some more inclusive level. This situation corresponds to Freud's portrayal of the narcissism of minor differences, in which groups differentiate themselves from those with whom they are also closely identified, doing so by negating or diminishing these commonalities in some way. So, as we saw, Australian nationalists define their national identity by fracturing a felt similarity to the English, their deep ties with class-ridden England providing the foil against which they contrast their own nation as egalitarian. In a stronger disavowal of similarity, ethnic minorities in the United States claim their own separate and distinctive cultures in a language that masks their cultural commonalities.

The feature that these three configurations of Self and Other have in common are perceptions of a similarity – indeed, an oversimilarity – of some kind. In each case, the key characteristic of the Other is that it embodies some resemblance, or some excess of resemblance, to the Self, and these felt resemblances provide a kind of background on which ethnic boundaries and national differences are engraved. Actors may etch these distinctions lightly, setting themselves off from one another by cultural microdifferences ('our' Tolstoys, Prousts, national sports, opera companies etc., versus 'theirs'). At the other extreme, they may posit radical contrasts, inversions and categorical oppositions among themselves: dichotomies of spirituality versus materialism, equality versus hierarchy, reason versus emotion, and so forth. But, in every case, these constructs seem to be sustained over time as attempts to counteract, diminish or repress to some extent an awareness of shared identity. They are intimately linked to perceptions of – perhaps too much – similarity.

Ethnicity and nationalism seem then, at one level, to be ways of altering cognition, even of distorting it, in a very specific direction. They act upon an unwanted consciousness of shared identity and shift it towards a consciousness of unlikeness. Hence, in creating certain kinds of relations of dissimilarity among people, they also create, as we have seen, their own underworlds of disguised resemblances, denied commonalities and submerged identifications with the Other. These distortions are not just a feature of ethnicity and nationalism themselves, but seem to have influenced their study as well. In trying (as one must) to understand them from within, from the perspective of actors and their discourse, one tends to see differences more readily than the processes which produce and support these differences and keep them visible. For actors to imagine themselves different, they have to imagine resemblances – and may have to work to reproduce resemblances – against which they can make differences continue to appear.

5

Property, Personhood and the
Objectification of Culture

Introduction

In a seminal argument, Handler shows how nationalism is connected
intimately to Western conceptions of personhood: specifically, to an ideology
which, following Macpherson (1962), he calls 'possessive individualism'. This
ideology represents persons as bounded, unique and autonomous entities that
define themselves through the things they create and own. A 'nation' is, in
effect, an imagined individual of precisely this sort writ large. The proof that
a people are a nation is conceived to lie, above all, in their visible possession
of a distinctive 'culture' of their own creation, demonstrating their national
identity (Handler 1988: 192). Ethnic and national differences, then, are
purported contrasts between such conceptually objectified cultural
repertoires, and between the social groups which identify with them or are
identified with them by others.

By pointing to the key role of concepts of property and personhood in
shaping the nationalist world-view, Handler's argument raises an important
question. As their ethnographic fieldwork experiences tend to make
anthropologists particularly keenly aware, property is a social relationship –
a relation, not between people and things, but between people in regard to
things (Bloch 1975; Carter 1989: 126–32; Goody 1962: 284–87; M. Strathern
1985: 197–99; Whitehead 1983). Accordingly, constructs of property can vary
significantly from one society to another. The notions of personhood in
possessive individualism, in particular, are clearly culture-bound (see Dumont
1970; M. Strathern 1988). A key problem Handler's analysis therefore raises
is how ethnic and cultural identities are constructed in societies which do not
have this ideology of possessive individualism, but instead employ other
notions of property and personhood.

An answer to this question, I suggest, can contribute a great deal to a
proper understanding of contemporary ethnicity and nationalism themselves.
A comparison with non-Western forms of cultural identity can help us to

highlight the culturally specific features in which the Western forms are grounded. In particular, it may shed light on why these forms seem, as I have tried to show, grounded in relations of distorted and denied resemblance.

LiPuma (1998: 56) points out that recent anthropology has come to stress differences between the Western concept of the individual and the concepts of the person indigenous to Melanesia. According to this view, Melanesian societies tend to posit the person, not as an individual, but as what M. Strathern (1988) calls a 'dividual', or relational person, conceived as embedded inextricably in social relationships with others – indeed, in a sense, as constituted by such relationships. LiPuma cautions wisely against overdrawing such contrasts, or portraying Western and Melanesian representations as somehow incommensurable. Rather, he suggests, a tension between relationality and individuality is probably intrinsic to the constitution and lived experience of persons everywhere. But societies do differ in which of these two aspects they mask and which they stress. The indigenous Melanesian models, he argues, tended to minimise or marginalise the actual existential separateness and individuality of persons and to valorise their relationality. Western notions of the individual, on the other hand, valorise conceptions of autonomy and boundedness and tend ideologically to de-emphasise the equally real and inescapable relationality of personhood. The key task is to identify the kinds of social conditions under which either one of these two ubiquitous dimensions of personhood is likely to be more or less overtly cognised and culturally elaborated. This is an important question for anthropologists seeking to understand contemporary Melanesia, given that:

> concepts such as nationhood, liberal democracy, civil rights, and electoral politics presuppose at least a Western-like image of the individual (ideologically defined as an autonomous, self-animated, and self-enclosed agent). The emergence of the nation-states of Melanesia, oriented toward and encompassed by Western culture and capitalism, entails the evolution of Western-like conceptions of the individual ... All of these motivate the emergence and increasing visibility of the individual facet of personhood because *the individual is the main and mythologized locus of those types of desire particular to modernity.* (LiPuma 1998: 53–54, italics in the original)

As we have seen, Melanesian societies in precolonial times seem to have represented cultural practices as forms of property. But I want to suggest that they applied conceptions of property and personhood different in their principal emphases from those of contemporary Western societies, and therefore gave rise to forms of cultural identity unlike those of modern nationalism and ethnicity in certain key respects. The comparison I will make with these Melanesian systems will suggest that the distinctive feature of modern nationalism and ethnicity is, just as Handler has proposed, the specific conception of culture as a patrimony 'belonging' to the nation or ethnic group as an imagined individual. It will also suggest that a conception of cultural practices as forms of property – according to the culturally and historically variable ways in which property relations are conceived – is a key feature, not just of modern nationalism and ethnicity, but also of other, in some respects quite different, ways of representing cultural identity, predicated on different conceptions of personhood.

In this chapter, I argue that contemporary ethnicity and nationalism seem to differ from the indigenous Melanesian forms of cultural identity in two related ways. First, cultural borrowings – though no less common among nations and ethnic groups than they were among groups in precontact Melanesia – tend to be ideologically de-emphasised, marginalised or under-cognised. Secondly, a more pronounced role is given to the disvaluing and rejection of the culturally alien. To put this contrast the other way round, the Melanesian societies tended not to seek to deny their own mimetic foundations, but treated cultural borrowing and importation as fundamental to the construction of their own collective identities. Accordingly, they did not on the whole seem to elaborate ideas of difference-as-inferiority to the extent that their contemporary counterparts tend to do.

Rather, the positive valuation of the cultural Other – the relation I called earlier difference-as-superiority – was much more openly elaborated and readily acknowledged in Melanesia. In differentiating themselves from one another culturally, Melanesians in general did not seem particularly preoccupied with seeking to exclude or disvalue exogenous cultural forms, or with representing their own particular cultural practices as inherently superior to those of other groups. Their concern was rather with regulating or manipulating the flow of cultural forms through trade, gift-giving and practices resembling licensing and franchise. The indigenous Melanesian understandings of cultural identity, like their understandings of personal identity, emphasised the ontological primacy of linkages and connections – here, the sorts of flows of cultural forms and practices that are an inevitable part of human interactions across group boundaries anywhere.

One very fundamental consequence of this was that these Melanesian identities tended not give rise to ethnic conflicts: that is, conflicts understood specifically as connected with cultural 'differences' or arising from such differences in some way. The societies were certainly not peaceful. It is just that they tended not to imagine warfare and feuding as associated with differences of 'culture'. They had violent conflicts, but not violent ethnic conflicts.

It is particularly when juxtaposed with the forms of cultural identity characteristic of precontact Melanesia, that contemporary ethnicity and nationalism appear as based on relations, not so much of 'difference' as of elided, fractured and muted resemblance. For as I have tried to show, mimetic relationships among nations or ethnic groups are intrinsic to the way these cultural identities are constituted, just as they were among groups in precontact Melanesia. In Melanesia these processes tended to be strongly valorised culturally. Under ethnicity and nationalism, on the other hand, they tend more often to be under-cognised, ideologically denied or represented negatively. A language of ideas in which to express such processes positively is much less developed.

If the mimetic foundations of national or ethnic group identity tend to be elided and denied, it is presumably because such elisions and denials are intrinsic to the modelling of such groups as a particular kind of collective person: these elisions play an important role in producing and sustaining images of collective individuality. Furthermore, when a group is imagined as an 'individual' in this way, possessing both its own internal unity and integrity, and its own discrete and bounded 'culture', its unity and its culture can seem linked together. Social order and cohesion can come to be seen as connected with cultural homogeneity, and a connection appears to form between violent conflict and cultural 'difference'. In other words, the Western theories of social order and conflict I referred to in the introduction to this book may, ultimately, be an expression of certain key cultural assumptions about the nature of personhood and property.

Cultural Fluidity and Change in Precontact Melanesia

Let me begin by outlining the ways in which cultural identity in precolonial Melanesia was connected with indigenous notions of property and personhood. As we saw earlier, these societies tended to reify cultural practices in ways that denied the creation of these practices by human beings, misrepresenting processes of human invention as processes of revelation or acquisition. On the other hand, they often acknowledged cultural interrelatedness and interchange quite openly, or, more accurately, insisted upon them: groups were likely to disguise even those cultural practices which actually were their own endogenous creations as gifts from gods, culture heroes or other outsiders. If these practices did not originate in transactions with outsiders, then such transactions had to be fabricated retrospectively, for only in this way could the practices be rendered valid, authentic and legitimate.

It was therefore perfectly possible for Melanesians in precolonial times to imagine cultural forms themselves as timeless and unalterable, while recognising that the distribution of these forms among groups and actors was manipulable and subject to change. A group's fund of cultural property could be understood to be fluid and negotiable rather than fixed for all time. In this sense, culture was objectified in ways that did not necessarily seek to stop change but could allow, or indeed encourage, constant change in the surface details of culture.

There is a good deal of evidence that the cultural practices – especially the religious practices – of many Melanesian societies were in constant change long before the colonial period. Much of this evidence has been very usefully brought together and examined by Brunton (1989), who suggests that the explanation of this cultural and religious lability lies in the nature of the indigenous political systems; these, he argues, were characterised by a high degree of fragmentation and instability which made durable religious and other traditions difficult to sustain. My own, rather different, interpretation is that this tendency to cultural flux is best viewed, not as a kind of 'cultural instability', as Brunton (1989) calls it – for this might suggest that stable cultural traditions are somehow normal or desirable – but as a concomitant of the high degree of commoditisation of indigenous cultural forms and a perfectly expectable part of the workings of the often region-wide trading and exchange systems (see Harrison 1993a).

The Siuai people of Bougainville provide one example, among many that might be put forward, of this connection between the commoditisation of ritual forms and their susceptibility to change (for other cases, see Harrison 1993a). At the time of Oliver's study, in the late 1930s, the Siuai had a standardised shell currency which they used in a very wide range of transactions, and trade, commerce and exchange were highly developed (Oliver 1955: 339, 341–42).

Virtually every Siuai adult practised a specialised craft or variety of magic, and some individuals possessed several such specialities (Oliver 1955: 306). All magical services were performed for fees and some of these techniques were an important source of wealth, their owners admitting readily that they practised them in order to gain money and influence. For instance, the services of magical practitioners called *mikai* were highly remunerative. A *mikai* possessed a spirit-familiar, whom he could bid to carry out a wide range of tasks, such as divining the causes of illness, retrieving captured souls, discovering and killing thieves, and many others. Aspiring leaders, or Big Men, seemed particularly attracted to this role as a means to wealth and influence. Songi, a prominent Big Man on whose career much of Oliver's ethnography focuses, was a *mikai* and often admitted openly that he practised in order to earn money and advance his political career (Oliver 1955: 91–92, 305, 355, 428, 446).

Apart from certain forms of magic owned by descent groups, all property rights in magic were held by individuals and these rights were bought and sold as valuable commodities. In keeping with the competitive and individualistic tenor of much of Siuai life, the world of Siuai magic seems to have been essentially a market, its driving force being a constant quest for new market niches. A characteristic of this market was its volatility and its high turnover of short-lived magical forms: 'There are fads in magic, just as there are fads in crafts and music. A particular variety of litigation-winning magic may earn money and notoriety for its owner for a year or so, but a few unsuccessful episodes and the appearance of new magical fashions will transfer public interest elsewhere' (Oliver 1955: 305, footnote omitted).

Oliver observed that Siuai religious beliefs and practices were probably changing constantly even before European contact, and he insightfully attributed this fluidity to the absence of an 'institutionalized tribal priesthood exercising a vested interest in maintaining fixed beliefs and practices' (1955: 444; see also pp. 61–62). Certainly, the Siuai were culturally conservative and ethnocentric in some respects. They regarded most of their 'customs' (*onoono*) – their rules of behaviour, techniques of magic, agriculture, and so forth – as having been established by their ancestors and as superior to those of their neighbours. On the other hand, they eagerly acquired cultural traits from their neighbours, especially magical techniques (Oliver 1955: 80; see also p. 92). Their attitudes towards magic and ritual were essentially pragmatic and instrumental. They did not seem deeply committed to any particular forms or dogmas. Their interest in the plethora of magical goods available for their consumption simply concerned whether or not they worked: hence 'the alacrity with which they acquire and test new magical devices' (Oliver 1955: 444) and their readiness to abandon or modify old ones.

Precolonial Melanesian cultures such as this could indeed appear unstable if we take individual sociocultural groups as our units of analysis, and assume that their fundamental problem was to ensure the continuity of their particular local traditions across the generations. From the viewpoint of any given group, one might indeed see constant discontinuity and change. But this apparent instability disappears if we take intergroup relations as our focus. We simply see groups embedded in systems of trade and exchange and maintaining perfectly stable long-term relations with each other by producing and exchanging a variety of goods – including cultural or religious forms.

'Lamarckian' Identities

As a result of such processes, cultural proprietary rights were often shared across group boundaries. In many parts of Melanesia there were male initiatory cults and secret societies in which important ritual sacra and religious knowledge were controlled by senior men. The initiation ceremonies and other rituals, staged to cement truces and alliances, could involve participants from many different cultural groups. In this way, ambitious men might gain admission to the secret cults of several peoples, and thereby acquire the rights to introduce the rituals into their own communities (Barth 1987: 8–9; Forge 1990; Oosterval 1961: 52–53). In contrast to the exclusiveness of cultural affiliation which Western forms of nationalism tend to demand (Handler 1988: 49), groups and individuals in precolonial Melanesia could have rights in, and affiliations to, several cultural identities at once (Linnekin and Poyer 1990a: 9).

The social systems within a given region could in this way become linked in complexly intertwining networks of rights in cultural, and especially ritual, property. Errington and Gewertz (1986) describe Chambri society, for instance, as based explicitly on the importation of culture from neighbouring societies. Chambri, as they put it, is a 'confluence of powers', having drawn together the ritual traditions of a variety of other peoples. What unified a community of this sort and gave its people a sense of their distinctiveness from their neighbours was their perception of possessing, not so much perhaps their own unique culture but, rather their own unique combination of elements of other cultures. Cultural differences and commonalities among people could be conceived in an imagery of transactional networks and lines of transmission rather than of discrete and bounded entities. An important consequence was that foreign cultural practices were often valued very positively, and mimetic processes were recognised as having a fundamental role in the construction of cultural identities. Another consequence was that political enmities were not conceived as homologous with cultural 'differences' between groups. Communities sharing the same language and culture were just as likely to fight and make war as those that viewed themselves as culturally and linguistically different – indeed perhaps more likely to do so (de Lepervanche 1973: 1; Langness 1973: 146–47).

Linnekin and Poyer (1990a), developing the argument of Watson (1990), describe Western theories of cultural identity as a 'Mendelian' model, in which an ethnic group is represented as a bounded, culturally distinct people sharing a common identity through blood, parentage or ancestry. In the precolonial Pacific, Linnekin and Poyer propose, cultural identities were 'Lamarckian', as Watson (1990) puts it; they reflected the current state of people's relationships with their social and political environment. Groups and individuals could change their cultural affiliations relatively easily, or maintain more than one cultural identity at the same time. In short, identity was labile, situational, non-exclusive and achieved rather than ascribed (Linnekin and Poyer 1990b: 9).

Certainly, local communities in precolonial Melanesia often seemed distinguished from one another, not so much by each claiming to have a unique 'culture', but by each having a kind of portfolio of property rights in a unique combination of ritual complexes in which its neighbours simply owned different combinations of shares (see Harrison 1987). In the 1950s, the Ngaing people of the Rae Coast of New Guinea numbered between eight hundred and nine hundred, divided into about twenty local communities. Traditionally, these were politically independent war-making units, though they were also linked by trade, intermarriage and a structure of dispersed matriclans. A community consisted of several patriclans, or patriclan-like groups, each of which had a separate magical and ritual patrimony: a cult house (or a section of one in the case of a cult house shared by several clans), slit-drums, gourd trumpets, drum melodies, secret magical formulas and a variety of other sorts of material and intangible religious property. In each patriclan there were normally one or two prominent men, who achieved their position by success in important activities such as warfare and ceremonial exchange and, especially, by mastering their clan's ritual knowledge (Lawrence 1965: 198–203, 217–18).

According to myth, the important elements of Ngaing material culture were created by deities who revealed to the first human beings the technical and magical knowledge associated with their use or manufacture. Some Ngaing localities credited quite different gods with having created the same item of culture. Ngaing magic involved the symbolic re-enactment of the deities' acts, and the recitation of spells containing the secret names of the deities or of the artefacts they created. Bows and arrows, slit-drums, hand drums, wooden bowls, shell and dog-tooth valuables, bull-roarers and so forth all had their specific deities and associated myths and magical spells. There were deities associated with the control of the weather, with the fertility of taro and other crops, with the institution of pig exchange and the growth of pigs, and with the ceremonies of male initiation. All the deities had their abodes in specific locales within or outside Ngaing territory, and thereby had particular areas within which people owed them allegiance and possessed rights in the mythology and rituals relating to them (Lawrence 1965: 208).

Most of the twenty or so local communities had their own war gods, but affiliations to many other deities cut across political and even linguistic boundaries. Some deities were common to the Ngaing as a whole, and others to particular Ngaing regions, but in both cases many deities were shared with a variety of neighbouring groups. From the point of view of religion, the territory of the Ngaing and their neighbours was cross-cut by many overlapping and intersecting ritual domains. These had little correspondence with group structure, though they seem, in at least some cases, to have corresponded to routes taken by the deities in mythical journeys. Within each of these domains, people took an intensely proprietorial attitude towards their deity and mythology. Any attempts by outsiders to use religious secrets without formally purchasing the rights to them were strongly resisted and treated as theft (Lawrence 1965: 203–6, 215).

There were great local variations in details of ritual and culture among the Ngaing. The Ngaing themselves were just one of many small groups in their area with different languages and systems of kinship and descent. But these peoples were interrelated by trade and all seem to have had structures of ritual organisation similar to those I have described (Lawrence 1964: 9–28; 1965: 222–23). And they all seem to have shared the same conceptions of religious knowledge as property, and of their gods as goods. The structures of affiliation to patron deities, in many cases cross-tribal and linking groups differing in language and social structure, constituted in their totality a regional network of ritual interrelationships. The gods of these societies did not, *pace* Durkheim (1976 [1912]), correspond to groups but to patterns of interconnections between groups.

The male cults of the Abelam people were focused, in a rather similar way, on beings called *nggwalndu*, clan spirits which men represented in painting and statuary and in the elaborate façades of their cult houses. Within this overall common framework of ritual there was considerable diversity among the Abelam in ritual, art styles and forms of ceremonial organisation. These elements themselves constantly changed and diffused, and such borrowings were helped by the fact that Abelam communities had essentially similar clan structures and in many cases shared common names for clan spirits. Men could be initiated into the male cults of villages other than their own, on payment of a fee, and would then be entitled to replicate the rituals and sacra back in their own villages (Forge 1990: 163–64).

The Abelam villages also exported their rituals to the Arapesh and to other peoples on their borders: 'Rights to hold ritual, objects to serve as the focus of secret ceremonies, ritual paraphernalia, spells, and instructions for ceremonies were sold to neighbors for many pigs and shell-ring wealth items. The sales were sometimes outright, but more usually attempts were made to "lease" ritual complexes and claim payment each time they were staged' (Forge 1990: 163). A sale or lease of a ritual complex to a non-Abelam village was arranged by the leaders of the two villages, and involved lengthy negotiations. For the sellers demanded very high fees including pigs, high-grade shell valuables, and large amounts of food while they prepared the requisite masks, carvings, paintings and head-dresses. Once the preparations were complete, the sellers carried the sacra to the purchasers' village in a massive armed display, demonstrating their power by destroying and pillaging property along the route. In some cases they stayed to take part in the ritual and made considerable demands on their hosts' hospitality, but otherwise they simply took their payment and went home (Forge 1990: 164–65).

In precolonial times the sellers usually carried out the work of preparing the sacra in their own village, partly for their own safety and partly to make it clear that ownership of the ritual still remained ultimately with themselves. For they would deliberately omit many of the most vital parts of the ritual, particularly the secret names of the *nggwalndu* and the spells by which they were invoked. Whatever the Arapesh may have thought they were buying, from the Abelam point of view what were being sold were primarily valuable and magically powerful objects, not full title to the rituals necessary for their reproduction and manufacture. Some Abelam acknowledged that the Arapesh might in time grow strong by their acquisitions of Abelam rituals, however partial and incomplete the versions they obtained. But since the purchasers did not know fully how to use the objects they bought, the Abelam regarded the buyers as liable to be harmed rather than benefited by acquiring them (Forge 1990: 163–65).

The Abelam population seems to have been an expanding one, and their villages not only fought each other but were aggressive in their relations with their Arapesh neighbours as well, and had been displacing them northwards for much of their known history (Forge 1966; Tuzin 1976: 72–76). The Arapesh, for their part, in their position of relative military weakness, seem almost to have fetishised the culture of their powerful and dominant neighbour.

It is significant that the Abelam sought to define these transactions only as leases and to keep the ultimate 'copyrights' in their rituals by withholding important religious secrets and by demanding payments each time a ritual was staged. Perhaps Arapesh villages acquiesced in these demands on the understanding that they would receive further disclosures of ritual knowledge; but in the final analysis any demands for wealth would presumably have needed effective threats of force to back them up. At any rate, the Abelam villages seem to have sought to keep their Arapesh trade partners in long-term indebtedness and dependence, their principal aim being the extraction of wealth. The main items of Abelam wealth, essential to their entire exchange system, including bridewealth payments, were shell rings which they were able to obtain only from the Arapesh in return for pigs. Forge argues that the Arapesh never tried to exploit their monopoly; they misperceived themselves as dependent on the Abelam, though the real situation was quite the reverse (1990: 165).

Culture as a Prestige Economy

Let me try to sum up the main respects in which Melanesian ethnic identities seem particularly unlike Western forms of ethnicity. Many of the collectivities of precolonial Melanesia existed by virtue of a pronounced awareness of their embeddedness in regional trading and exchange systems, in which dances, rituals, religious representations and so forth moved along the same channels and networks as bird plumes, shell valuables and other prestige goods. These exchange systems were the foundations on which cultural identities were built. In a sense, groups had no choice but to participate in these systems: their only choice was whether to participate more or less. So the precise ways in which cultural symbols entered into the Melanesian exchange systems were variable. At one extreme, some societies were quite parsimonious with their cultural practices. We saw earlier that the groups studied by Schwartz in the Admiralty Islands imposed in this way relatively tight restraints on the access of outsiders to their cultural practices. The Abelam, similarly, sought to keep key parts of their religious knowledge to themselves when selling or leasing ritual complexes to their Arapesh trade partners. From their point of view it was above all the religious knowledge which they held back – the ritual elements they did not give in the exchanges – that served critically to continue to distinguish them from the Arapesh.

At the other extreme, many other groups seem to have been relatively profligate, regularly offering one another prestations of songs, dances, ceremonies and other expressive practices, in much the same way that groups in some parts of Melanesia exchanged prestations of yams, pigs or pearl-shells. In other societies again, the key actors were ambitious entrepreneurs who bought, practised and sold magical and ritual techniques on a relatively open market, feeding the resulting income into financing their political careers as Big Men. The Siuai people, it will be recalled, readily commoditised many magical and ritual practices, buying and selling them along with many other kinds of goods, both among themselves and with outsiders.

The cultural repertoires of groups such as these could be understood as mutable, provisional and ever open to negotiation, rather than as permanently fixed and static in their content or needing to be conserved and protected from change. Nor were they visualised as necessarily wholly singular and discrete. These groups could define themselves by claiming to possess, not so much their own bounded and distinctive 'cultures' but their own distinctive combinations of resemblances and overlapping cultural interconnections with others.

Cultural forms could also be represented, not so much as belonging to ethnic groups as internally homogeneous totalities, as collective 'individuals', but as distributed unequally among different social categories or segments within such groups. Characteristically, those actors with privileged access to these cultural prestige goods were the same political actors who also controlled the circulation of tangible prestige goods such as shell valuables. High social status, defined in terms of age, gender, descent, personal achievement or some combination of these and similar factors, conferred the most important entitlements to both types of resources.

So, for example, men excluded women and junior males from much of their ritual and religious activities as much as – if not more than – they excluded adult men of other communities. Indeed, many of the cultural forms trafficked in these societies (male initiation rites, in particular) were modes of excluding women or protecting the male body from being harmed by them. Although cult objects and rituals were often said to have originally 'belonged' in mythical times to women, until men 'stole' them (see Gewertz 1988), this ideology served only to emphasise and justify men's present-day control of these cultural resources.

Many of these societies appeared culturally highly extroverted and acquisitive. Often, their rituals and other expressive forms were conceived to have origins distant in space rather than in time and drew their prestige and authenticity more from their foreignness than from their antiquity. The key concern was less with keeping out alien cultural practices, than with transacting such practices so as to establish relations with outsiders or across group boundaries.

We can, of course, find instances of ethnocentrism in precolonial Melanesia and elsewhere in Oceania (see, for instance, Kertzer 1988: 19; Knauft 1985b: 327–28). But, perhaps just as often, we also see evidence of broadly positive valuations of cultural differences. The perception of such difference seems at times to have been accompanied by a strong perception of other cultural identities and practices as having a potential value for oneself and of one's own cultural symbols as potentially a value for others. In short, cultural practices were conceptualised as quasi-objects capable of being used to establish relationships between groups or across their boundaries, and even perhaps in some cases to represent groups as constituted by these relationships with one another.

Because neighbouring peoples often viewed their respective cultural repertoires as interdigitating, overlapping and open to change, rather than as discrete, static and fixed for all time, one might be tempted to regard these indigenous Melanesian forms of cultural identity as analogues of those contemporary 'hybrid' forms thought by some analysts to be increasingly characteristic of Western postmodernity. But I think this would be misleading. As we saw in an earlier chapter, notions of cultural hybridity inescapably imply counter-notions of cultural purity. Melanesians did not create such dichotomies, most basically because they did not conceive of cultures as the kinds of discrete totalities that could possibly be 'pure' and unmixed in the first place.

Most crucially and fundamentally, Melanesian identities were not based, to the same degree as Western ethnicity and nationalism are, on the denial, suppression and forgetting of cultural resemblances. Their forms of cultural identity involved the misrecognition and denial of something else: namely, the human authorship of culture. People conceived themselves as transactors, not creators, of the cultural practices which defined their identities, disclaiming the sort of authorship on the basis of which (if it were acknowledged) ethnic groups culturally and historically 'individualised' in the Western sense could develop. Equivalent elaborations of the role of cultural interchange in the construction of national identities are not absent from the West, but they exist within an overarching conception of the group as essentially 'individual'. In this respect, the two patterns, each with its own forms of ideological distortion, nevertheless help to illuminate each other. This is why I have sought, at several places in this book, a comparative vantage point from which to view modern nationalism and ethnicity, placing these side by side with the systems represented by precolonial Melanesia. For each seems to valorise and culturally elaborate what the other tends to suppress and elide: each can contribute to the understanding of the other by revealing the very processes which the other tends ideologically to mask or hide.

Postcolonial Melanesian Identities

I want now to outline the significant ways in which these identity constructions have changed (and are currently changing) since close European contact with this region of the world began in the late nineteenth century, processes in which indigenous constructs of cultural identity have been replaced, or are currently being replaced, by Western notions of the ethnic group or nation as a collective individual.

I shall suggest that a key difference between the older Melanesian objectifications of culture and the newer ones associated with the colonial and postcolonial period lies in the models of property on which they draw. In precolonial Melanesia, the critical feature of religious representations is that they could enter the trade and exchange systems as a category of luxury or prestige goods, convertible from and into other forms of wealth. If the models underlying these older Melanesian reifications were thus indigenous notions of prestige goods, the underlying models in contemporary Melanesian representations of 'custom' and traditional culture – and in the Western models of nationalism and ethnicity they derive from – seems to be the concepts of a legacy or inheritance. Thus the two patterns share an important common feature at a certain level: both involve representations of culture as property. It is the underlying conceptions of property (at least as applied to cultural symbols) that differ.

Over the past two decades or so, much research has focused on the emergence of new ethnic and national identities in Melanesia and other parts of the postcolonial South Pacific, processes often accompanied by objectifications of 'traditional culture' or 'custom' as a form of collective property. The seminal contribution of Handler (see especially Handler 1988) to the theoretical understanding of ethnicity and nationalism in general, though arising from an examination of cultural politics in the Canadian province of Quebec, has had an important influence on research into the construction of 'tradition' in the contemporary South Pacific (see, for example, Foster 1995a: 20; Foster 1995b: 154, 176–77; Jolly and Thomas 1992b; Keesing and Tonkinson 1982; Linnekin 1990; Linnekin and Poyer 1990a, 1990b; Norton 1993; Thomas 1992). As Foster (1992: 284) among others has noted, colonialism has been viewed in much of this research as the key factor in giving rise to these hypostasisations of culture, especially those involving objectifications of entire 'traditional' ways of life as cultural wholes.

Some authors recognise that comparable processes occurred even in precontact times. Otto (1991: 144), for example, following Mead (1975) and Schwartz (1975), argues that the peoples of the Admiralty Islands were highly conscious of their cultural differences long before colonialism. Jolly, similarly, writing specifically of Vanuatu, argues that Melanesian societies were keenly self-aware culturally even before the colonial period, as was amply demonstrated by the widespread borrowing and trafficking of cultural elements:

> songs imported from elsewhere were often sung in a foreign language rather than being translated, dance styles were named for their place of origin long after they were purchased, sculptural styles for ceremonial figures were known as emanating from a certain place and might be exchanged or bought ... In precolonial polities such differences were not ranged as entire folkloric ensembles, nor were material items or ritual forms taken to be icons of cultural wholes, but there was still self-consciousness of one's language, of one's way of life as not being the one, the only way to live. (1992: 59)

Some writers on the politics of tradition in the Pacific suggest very plausibly that cultural self-consciousness of some sort may be universal: in other words, that people nowhere simply 'live' their cultural practices, but always reflect upon, evaluate, discuss, modify and dispute them, though this self-awareness may become particularly heightened, or take specifically politicised forms, in colonial contexts (see for instance, Jolly 1992: 58–59; Jolly and Thomas 1992a: 241; Keesing 1993: 592; Linnekin 1990: 170; 1992: 253).

Both in precontact Melanesia and in contemporary Western forms of ethnicity and nationalism, we have populations with cultures possessing a strongly developed 'self-reflexive' component, as Schwartz called it, consisting of representations (and, of course, misrepresentations) of their internal cultural differences and commonalities. In both cases it is, above all, élites, or those representing their interests, who are the main agents in transmitting cultural ideas and practices through physical and social space. It is therefore also among such social actors that this consciousness of cultural diversity and of the relativity of cultural practices is most pronounced and it is they who are the principal agents in the processes of cultural objectification. In short, in both Melanesia and the West, self-conscious cultural identities are in large part élite constructs. They represent cultural difference and identity as conceived by the dominant, or on their behalf, and therefore have to be seen as an aspect of power, and as serving power.

I cannot hope to summarise here the burgeoning literature on the politics of culture in contemporary Melanesia (see, for example, Foster 1995a). I shall simply note that many parts of Melanesia have seen the emergence of an explicitly conceptualised sphere of 'tradition' or customary behaviour, often called in pidgin *kastom* and frequently defined by contrast to other spheres of contemporary life such as *bisnis* (commerce), *gavman* (government) or *lotu* (church) (Foster 1992; Otto 1992). *Kastom* consists of codified rules and behaviours understood to preserve important aspects of a given people's ancestral way of life; and it has sometimes served as a political symbol around which ethnic groups have mobilised against each other or against the colonial powers (Keesing and Tonkinson 1982). Increasingly, it is employed in this politicised way in the inter-ethnic conflicts now emerging in some of the new South Pacific states.

What I wish to do here is to identify certain concepts of property or of possessions which seem implicit in contemporary Melanesian representations such as *kastom*. We saw that cultural practices tended to be objectified in precolonial Melanesia as transactable prestige goods or valuables. The emerging ethnicities and nationalisms of postcolonial Melanesia, in contrast, tend to reify a group's cultural symbols as a heritage or legacy from the past. That is to say, central to these modern constructs of national and ethnic identity are conceptions of inheritance. Throughout Melanesian history, the construction of cultural identity has thus involved processes of objectification; what has changed, or is changing, are the models of property that underlie these reifications. Such objectifications are not in themselves a new phenomenon in Melanesian societies or a product of colonialism. Rather, the forms they take have altered, or are altering, in ways concomitant with changing conceptualisations of the nature of property, or rather of those forms of property that have key political significance. Crucially, they are changing in accord with the changing nature of Melanesian political élites. Both in modern Melanesia and in the past it seems to be the particular definitions of property deployed by power-holders that play the key role in determining the way in which cultural identity and difference are constructed.

LiPuma (1998), Foster (1995c) and others have examined the growing salience which modernity is giving, above all, to the figure of the individual in a wide range of contexts in contemporary Melanesia. LiPuma, in particular, makes the crucial observation that Melanesians certainly did not lack conceptions of the individual in the past, but rather that expressions of individuality tended to be morally and ideologically disvalued in certain respects. Melanesians knew and recognised the 'individual' perfectly well. But, to them, the paradigm of such a figure was the sorcerer, the very archetype of the purely selfish, antisocial person:

> [U]ntil the progress of Westernization sorcery was the indigenous name for instances and acts of individuality. So a person who was inordinately successful in relation to others (in hunting, pig-raising, etc.) was suspected of sorcery ... I would suggest that one reason that the advance of modernity is being accompanied by an upsurge in the practice of sorcery is that they share the same underlying epistemology. (LiPuma 1998: 69–70; reference omitted)

The advance of modernity is entailing, not so much the introduction of new concepts of the person, but rather the revaluation of already existing ones: in particular, an increasingly positive, rather than negative, valorisation of individuality, self-interest and lack of obligation to others.

Notions of individuality were thus not absent from precolonial Melanesian societies, but they were expressed in special contexts. Principal among these was the realm of sorcery beliefs, as LiPuma (1998) shows, and also warfare. Manambu men, for instance, undertaking warfare and head-hunting raids, underwent rituals to transform themselves temporarily into beings no longer quite human, recognising no social ties, driven to kill, capable even of killing their own families (Harrison 1993b). Cultural images of autonomous individuality were therefore not lacking, but they were understood to represent a dimension of personhood that could only realise itself fully through the violation of social ties with others. Hence it manifested itself quintessentially in forms such as the sorcerer and ritual homicide, figures deemed at best morally ambivalent and at worst pathological. Sociality, in short, was quite simply assumed (see Iteanu 1983; M. Strathern 1980: 196; 1988). It was taken for granted as the background from which persons as 'individuals' lacking a sense of accountability to others could sometimes emerge, or be made to emerge. But it always provided the grounds of the existence of even these transgressive figures, who could come into being only in their attempts to extricate themselves from it.

The same cultural logic could be applied to collectivities: a group too could in certain contexts represent itself, or be represented, as an 'individual' in this sense – namely, when it appeared wilfully to isolate itself by withholding its cultural practices from outsiders, or in some other way refusing to transact or engage with others. When groups guarded their cultural practices closely in this way, imposing many restrictions on their reproduction by outsiders, they were treating their cultures more as if these were their private property than an exchange resource.

Linnekin and Poyer (1990a), among others, have shown how cultural and ethnic identities of a Western sort – in which such images of culture as private property are valorised positively rather than negatively – are now emerging in Melanesia and elsewhere in the South Pacific (see also Foster 1995c; LiPuma 1995). Larcom (1982) gives an account of these processes specifically among the Mewun of Vanuatu. Until the 1980s, the Mewun specialised in producing dances and many other expressive forms (which they referred to generically in pidgin as *kastom*), and formally presenting these as gifts to other groups in special rituals. Larcom shows how in the 1980s, after Vanuatu gained independence, the Mewun and other neighbouring ethnic groups began, under the influence of the national government, to redefine the concept of *kastom*, in keeping with Western concepts of ethnic nationalism, as referring to unchanging, sacrosanct bodies of traditions belonging exclusively to individual social groups. In Western nationalism – perhaps according to the 'Mendelian' logic attributed to it by Watson, Linnekin and Poyer – cultural property rights, once generated, are normally only heritable, like an entailed estate.

I referred earlier to Handler's view that a central feature of nationalism is the representation of culture as a kind of reified collective possession according to the logic of possessive individualism. This is a logic in which property is understood to arise from the act of creation or authorship, and cultures appear as human products belonging rightfully to their creators and thereafter to their heirs, with ownership conceived as transmitted by ancestry or blood (see Handler 1988: 6, 17, 46–47, 50–51, 153, 192; see also M. Strathern 1988: 322–23).

The varieties of modern ethnic nationalism being adopted by states such as Vanuatu, or at least by their political élites, seem to follow closely the pattern identified by Handler, in which cultural groups are represented – which is, of course, to say misrepresented – as collective individuals of this general sort, discrete entities to which people have fixed and exclusive affiliations (see also LiPuma 1997). But there is also an underlying continuity, a phenomenon which has remained constant over a considerable period of Melanesian history: namely, the imagination of cultural practices as possessions, and the reification of culture as a form of property. Always, an important direct influence on the ways in which cultural identity has been constructed in Melanesian societies has been the manner in which property has been conceptualised. If we accept Handler's insight that nationalism models cultural property after the concepts of private property characteristic of capitalism, in accordance with the logic of 'possessive individualism', the forms of cultural ownership characteristic of an earlier time in Melanesian history seem to have been grounded in the concepts of property entailed in the prestige economies, and in the trading and gift-exchange systems, characteristic of this ethnographic region. In short, a key factor which seems broadly to distinguish precolonial and postcolonial cultural identities in Melanesia is their underlying mode of objectifying culture. Once, cultural practices tended to be reified as transactable prestige goods; now, they tend increasingly to be reified as an individuating inheritance or legacy from the past.

These changes in emphasis occurring in the conceptions of property and personhood in contemporary Melanesia must be understood in the context of the changing nature of Melanesian political economies and élites. As we saw, political leadership in precolonial Melanesian societies tended to be grounded in prestige economies in which cultural practices – in particular, ritual practices – could be treated as forms of wealth, with proprietary rights or claims over them being transmitted in acts of exchange. The emerging middle-class political élites, on the other hand, play their key role in the construction of modern national identities through their involvement in formal education, the media, the arts, the armed forces and party politics. Their underlying model of ethnicity and nationalism draws on ideas of a 'culture' as a kind of collective birthright, inheritance or legacy, to be carefully preserved and handed down intact from each generation to the next. But their constructions of cultural identity remain unchanged and continuous with the precolonial past in one important respect: namely, in the representation of cultural practices and symbols as possessions. Interestingly, these élites often continue to refer to the same cultural practices as symbols of identity, but in radically recontextualised ways. For example, 'traditional' music or dance performances – many of them, originally, cultural ephemera created as part of perhaps quite transitory alliances between small kin groups during the precolonial or early colonial period – are now kept alive as expressions of ethnic, or even national, heritage (see Lawrence and Niles 2001). Contemporary nationalists in Melanesia can thus claim – in a sense, quite rightly – that little has changed, that the present remains essentially continuous with past tradition. Of course, such claims obscure the way that the powers to construct cultural identities are shifting, or have shifted, into the hands of new kinds of élites, whose conceptions of the nature of property and of the person have much less in common with those of the past.

6

Cultural Piracy
and Cultural Pollution

Introduction

In the previous chapter, I have tried to outline two complementary ways in which cultural identity can be conceived by social actors. In one, 'cultures' are understood as discrete entities attached to social groups as exclusive legacies, thereby differentiating these groups from one another. In another, culture is a transactional resource intended for circulation between social groups, and groups are thereby connected to one another principally by networks of cultural commonalities and resemblances. Perhaps people everywhere give some recognition to both of these two alternative dimensions of cultural identity. And undoubtedly both of them have some correspondences with reality. But societies do seem to vary in which of these two patterns they valorise or emphasise ideologically. Contemporary Western, or Western-derived, forms of ethnicity and nationalism give ontological primacy to the individuality of groups, though they certainly also acknowledge that groups can at times choose to enter into relations of cultural give and take with one another. The precolonial Melanesian forms gave primacy to the relationality of groups, though acknowledging that any group could partially withhold itself from communication with others at times, thereby making itself to that extent appear 'individualised'.

Notions of culture as an individuating legacy, a private inheritance from the past, were thus not absent from precolonial Melanesia, but they seem to be given a particular primacy in contemporary Western, or Western-derived, conceptions of ethnicity and nationalism. I want now to examine folk models of this type in more detail, focusing in particular on the close connections they appear to have with rhetorics in which the culturally alien is disvalued and 'difference' is likely be represented negatively as inferiority.

I shall argue that models of identity of this type, based on ideas of culture as a legacy or birthright, tend to be haunted by one of two recurring visions (or, as we shall see, by both together). In both of these recurring images, 'cultures' appear as entities capable of being endangered, undermined or destroyed from the outside. In one, a group appears as under threat from the intrusion or imposition of foreign cultural forms. In the other, it appears threatened by the foreign consumption or misappropriation of its own local cultural forms. A group's cultural distinctiveness and individuality, in short, are imagined as things that it can lose, and lose in two ways: either by being forced to adopt the lifestyle and cultural practices of others, or by having its own lifestyle and practices copied or purloined by others. The first image employs a rhetoric of cultural pollution, and the second a rhetoric of cultural appropriation, piracy or theft.

My perspective implies that the fundamental anxieties to which conceptions of culture as an inheritance give rise are concerned, not with difference and otherness but, quite the opposite, with imaginings of homogeneity and lack of distinctiveness. In an earlier chapter, I called these sorts of anxieties 'cultural claustrophobia'. Images of cultural appropriation and pollution are two alternative ways in which social actors may envisage this claustrophobic homogenisation as capable of occurring. There are perhaps other kinds of discursive imagery of cultural homogenisation and claustrophobia, but these two varieties do seem to me to be widespread, basic and closely connected expressions of an underlying conception of culture as a particular form of property. Let me illustrate each of them in turn, and try to shed some light on the circumstances which give rise to them.

Pollution and the Other

In her classic study of ideas of ritual purity and defilement, Douglas (1966) argues that social boundaries tend to be represented symbolically as bodily boundaries (see also Jacobson-Widding 1983b). Groups that maintain strong barriers between themselves and outsiders are, she suggests, likely to have a corresponding preoccupation with protecting the margins of their members' bodies from contamination. For example, they may associate outsiders conceptually with disease and defilement. The rhetoric of right-wing European nationalisms seems to exemplify Douglas's thesis, with immigrants and foreigners often being compared, implicitly or explicitly, to germs, invasive organisms or parasites attacking the body of the nation (R. Cohen 1994). But this imagery is by no means restricted to modern nationalisms. The Mohave Indians of California linked outsiders with disease in a very similar way:

> [Xenophobia] is a major moral theme that conditions Mohave relations with all other ethnic groups – including their former allies, the Quechans. Intimate physical contact with non-Mohave that involved combat, sexual intercourse, food-sharing, or handling of material possessions was perceived by the Mohave to cause their most basic psycho-physiological disorder, which they termed either 'enemy' or 'foreign disease' ... Foreign disease is mythologically foreordained as the prototype of all disorders. (Gorman 1981: 56; see also pp. 64, 68)

After the United States authorities suppressed warfare, the Mohave developed the belief that they could contract 'foreign disease' merely by dreaming of interacting with outsiders (Gorman 1981: 60). Some societies make a symbolic association between foreigners and noxious substances or represent foreign cultural practices as physically harmful in some way. In nineteenth-century China, for example, the long-standing official hostility to Christianity was greatly intensified by the growth of missionary activity and, from 1860, 'the empire was deluged with a growing torrent of violently anti-Christian pamphlets and tracts' (Paul Cohen 1963: 45). This literature accused Christians of drinking menstrual blood or employing it in their rituals, of gouging out the eyes of dying Chinese converts to make silver by an alchemical process and of many other sorts of perversions and outrages against the bodies of Chinese people (Paul Cohen 1963: 31, 50–51, 54, 90, 291).

As a more contemporary example of the same sort of thinking, many French intellectuals decried the development of the Euro-Disney entertainment complex (opened in 1992 outside Paris) as – in the words of one of them – a 'cultural Chernobyl', referring to the Soviet nuclear reactor disaster in 1986 that contaminated large areas of Russia, Ukraine, Europe and Scandinavia (Forbes 1995: 255). It was as though they visualised this American-style theme park as spewing the cultural equivalent of effluent or toxic waste across the French cultural landscape. In short, in a wide range of times and places, the representation of cultural practices as 'foreign' has involved equating them, metaphorically or literally, with substances deemed noxious and contaminating· with menstrual blood, radioactive fallout, bacteria, and so forth. They have been imaged as polluting, attacking or infecting the indigenous cultures or the actual bodies of local people, or both.

The key analysis of the deeply implicated role of notions of purity and pollution in the construction of ethnonationalist identity is undoubtedly Handler's (1988) study of cultural politics in the province of Quebec in Canada. Handler argues persuasively that the representation of culture as a kind of reified possession is one of the central features of nationalism. The most fundamental imperative of a nation or ethnic group is to define for itself a 'culture', a body of 'authentic' custom, immemorial and sacrosanct. This codification and cataloguing of a national culture is an attempt – albeit futile and self-defeating – to fix and freeze it, to stop cultural change (Handler 1988: 51, 67, 77). In this way, nationalists reify, or 'objectify', their 'culture' as their nation's property, as a patrimony capable of being encroached upon, appropriated, adulterated, defended, conserved, displayed, amassed, lost, and so forth.

Handler suggests that nationalism objectifies culture in such a way as to make groups appear to themselves as self-sufficient 'essences' independent of each other (1988: 194). Some kinds of nationalism view such groups as having to be kept separate and pure; some involve strongly devaluing the cultural Other, or perceiving oneself as devalued by the Other (see Hall 1993).

Thus, the Quebec nationalists he studied envisage their nation as forever menaced with being overwhelmed politically, economically and culturally by larger and more powerful entities such as English-speaking Canada and the United States. To the nationalists, these collectively comprise Quebec's defiling cultural Other, threatening perpetually to adulterate and extinguish its national identity as embodied in the French language, rural folk traditions, and so forth. Fundamental to Quebec nationalism and, Handler suggests, to all nationalisms, are these sorts of images of the nation as an entity needing to be safeguarded and bounded against an outside world envisaged as a source of contamination, extinction and death (1988: 47–51). They are a part of the way nationalism 'objectifies' culture: representing it as a sort of possession, thing or entity vulnerable, among other dangers, to being corrupted, undermined or disintegrated by hostile external forces.

Ohnuki-Tierney (1995) observes likewise that '*purity* of self is at ethnicity's and nationalism's symbolic core' (p. 234; italic in the original). She examines certain comparable ideas of purity and impurity entailed in the construction of Japanese national identity. For much of Japanese history, food – and in particular, rice – has served important roles in Japanese representations of identity in relation to other peoples. Especially significant is the symbolic contrast drawn between imported, 'foreign' rice, viewed as inferior, impure and contaminating, and Japanese, native-grown rice, whose perceived 'purity' is both a metaphor and a metonym for the pu...., of the Japanese national self.

This, then, seems to be a common way in which the theme of cultural pollution can be developed symbolically: other groups and the cultural practices attributed to them are represented as inferior in bodily, physiological idioms of defilement and contamination. In seeking to understand these conceptions of purity and defilement, one needs to distinguish two separate aspects which they can present. On the one hand, outsiders can be represented as contaminating in themselves, in their very bodies; on the other hand, their cultural practices, or symbols of their identity, can also be represented as contaminating. Of course, both foreign people and symbols of foreignness can together be seen as defiling. The Nazis, for instance, made systematic attempts to purify German of all foreign words, representing these loanwords as a kind of infection of the national language, in the same way that they represented Jews and others as an infection in the body of the German nation. Just as the nation had to be purged of its unwanted people, so the language too had to be rigorously cleansed of these foreign words – the 'Jews of language' as Adorno described them (Morley and Robins 1990).

But foreign culture can be seen as polluting without its bearers necessarily being seen as so. French nationalist attitudes to Anglo-American culture seem to be of this type. The French Academy was founded in 1634, with one of its principal aims described as follows:

> nettoyer la langue des ordures qu'elle avait contractées, ou dans la bouche du peuple, ou dans la foule de Paris ... ou par les mauvais usages des courtisans ignorants (to cleanse the language of the filth it had acquired, either in the mouths

of the people, or among the Paris crowd ... or from the improper usage of ignorant courtiers). (Ball et al. 1995: 265)

Ever since, a strong concern with the defence of the French language, and language purity, has characterised the Francophone world – in metropolitan France, Africa, Canada and elsewhere. The French government passed laws in 1975, and again in 1994, banning the use of foreign terms in commerce, business, advertising and work contracts (Ball et al. 1995: 264). The official variety of French:

> being the product of three centuries of constant refinement, is felt by many to need preserving from 'contamination'. This may come from within, taking the form of 'sloppy usage', 'bad grammar', or 'misuse of words' ... Alternatively contamination may have an external origin, the main threat at the present time being the proliferation of English terminology. The French language, moreover, can be perceived as embodying French/francophone cultural identity and values (there is, for example, a long-established mythology that French is clearer, more logical, and better suited to abstract thought than other languages). Consequently there lurks in the background the conviction that any threat to the language is also a cultural threat in a more general sense. It can hardly be a coincidence that René Etiemble's celebrated attack on the influence of English on French, *Parlez-vous franglais?* was published in 1964, when Gaullist anti-Americanism was at its height. So preservation of the language can be seen as fundamental to the preservation of national or ethnic identity – be it the identity of the French nation against encroaching Anglo-Saxon values, that of the Québecois against the anglophone Canadians, the Walloons of southern Belgium against their Dutch-speaking compatriots in Flanders, or the centralized power of the élite in many 'francophone' African states against tribal fragmentation. As a result, *la défense de la langue française* is a serious issue in francophone society. (Ball et al. 1995: 266)

These concerns are focused particularly on the perceived subversion of the French language by English, seen as a symptom of a much broader and more general threat to the French way of life, even to French national honour, posed by Anglo-American culture, and American culture in particular (Trotter 1993: 276). Such conceptions locate the source of pollution, not in American people as such, but in their cultural products or exports. Many French may be deeply concerned with the penetration and subversion of their culture by American popular culture; but, clearly, they have no equivalent concerns with the possible penetration of their national boundaries by an influx of American people.

The Piracy of Identity

In this respect, French nationalism differs in an interesting and instructive way from the nationalism of the Basque region of Spain. Arana, the nineteenth-century founding father of Basque nationalism, 'dedicated many years of his life attempting to cleanse its lexicon of Spanish "borrowings" and interferences' (Conversi 1997: 64). But, in addition, he strongly opposed the immigration of Spaniards, whom he called *maketos*. As part of this, he and his Basque nationalist movement laid very great stress on preserving the Basque language as an exclusive possession of the Basque people – whom he defined in racial terms – and sought to prevent Spanish immigrants into the Basque country from learning it. The nationalism of Arana was rigidly exclusive, attributing an innate immorality to Spaniards, their mere presence among the Basques 'corrupting the Vizcayan [Basque] soul' (Heiberg 1980: 333). Spanish immigration was portrayed as a threat both to the Basque people's exclusive possession of their language, and to their racial purity:

> The Vizcayans are as much bound to speak their national language, as not to speak it to the *maketos* or Spaniards. It is not to speak this or the other language, but rather the difference between languages which is the great means of preserving ourselves from the contagion of Spaniards and avoiding the mixing of the two races. *If our invaders were to learn Euskera, we would have to abandon it*, carefully archiving its grammar and dictionary, and dedicate ourselves to speaking Russian, Norwegian or any other language, as long as we are subject to their domination. For the Catalans it would be a great glory if the Spanish government appointed Catalan as the official language of all Spain; on the contrary, if it were to do the same with Euskera, it would be for us the final blow of unavoidable death dealt from the most refined diplomacy. (Conversi 1997: 173; italics in the original)

Arana wrote that a single Spaniard who knows Euskera – the Basque language – is more dangerous to the Basque nation than a hundred Spaniards who do not:

> Here we suffer greatly when we see the name 'Pérez' at the bottom of a poem in Euskera, when we hear our language spoken by a *riojano* teamster or a Santander salesman, or by a Gypsy ... [F]or us it would be ruin if the maketos resident in our territory spoke Euskera. Why? Because the purity of race is, like language, one of the bases of the Vizcayan banner ... *So long as there is a good grammar and a good dictionary, language can be restored even though no one speaks it. Race, once lost, cannot be resuscitated* ...
>
> *Many are the Euskerianos who do not know Euskera. This is bad. Many are the maketos who know it. This is even worse.*
>
> Great damage can be done to the Fatherland by one hundred *maketos* who do not know Euskera. Even worse is the damage that can be done by only one *maketo* who knows it ...
>
> In the heart of the Fatherland, every *Euskeriano* who does not know Euskera is a thorn; every *Euskeriano* who knows it and is not a patriot is two thorns; every Spaniard who speaks Euskera is three thorns. (Conversi 1997: 175–77; italics in the original)

An old Basque legend equates foreigners with the Devil, implying that outsiders, like Satan, only want to learn Euskera to do evil to Basques. So long as outsiders do not know the language, the legend suggests, the Basque people will be safe from harm:

Traditionally, before the spread of nationalism, there had been a pride among many Basques in the unintelligibility of their language. The contention that no foreigner had ever been able to master it worked as a strong psychological barrier against amalgamation and 'evil infiltrations'. According to an ancient legend, the devil once visited the Basque country to learn the language and make disciples. He tried for weeks, but was defeated and returned to hell after having learned no more of the language than *bai* (yes) and *ez* (no) … Thus not only was Euskera God-given and crucial to the definition of Basque identity, but popular ethnicity considered language to be an 'ethnic barrier' against foreign infiltrations. Hence Arana's refusal to allow the immigrants to learn the language was not his own idea but derived from centuries-old attitudes. (Conversi 1997: 60; references omitted; see also pp. 85–86)

In common with many other modern nationalisms, those of France and the Basque region have a strongly linguistic flavour, with language and the felt need to preserve linguistic distinctiveness playing a central role. And both French and Basque nationalists see their languages, and their cultural identities more broadly, as under threat from the outside and as needing constant protection. But the two nationalisms seem to exemplify two contrasting ways in which a community can represent its cultural identity as at risk. It may, on the one hand, be concerned primarily, like French nationalism, to protect the 'purity' and integrity of its language from adulteration by foreign linguistic forms. Alternatively, it may, like Basque nationalism, be preoccupied more with protecting its language against use or reproduction by outsiders. If the principal concern of some nationalisms is with keeping foreign culture out, with preventing or limiting its diffusion inwards, the main concern of others seems to be with keeping their own indigenous culture in, with limiting or controlling its diffusion outwards.

These are both ways of constructing the collective Self by means of a conceptual opposition to a potentially or actually threatening Other. But this menacing Other may, it seems, be envisaged in two opposite forms: either as culturally intrusive, expansionist and contaminating, an invasive influence which has to be repelled, or as a covetous, acquisitive, extractive Other from whom one's culture has to be sequestered away. In short, some groups seem to enclose themselves in boundaries against the pollution of their culture and others in boundaries against the piracy of their culture.

As another example of perceptions of cultural piracy, let us consider the complaints among certain Aboriginal artists in Australia that their work is widely reproduced by entrepreneurs without their permission on merchandise such as T-shirts (Altman 1989: 304). These artists, who were at the time of Altman's study trying to have their works protected by copyright, were thus seeking the same sanction by which artists, inventors and business corporations worldwide prevent others from profiting from their creations and inventions: namely, the law of intellectual property. An older and more direct device capable of protecting some kinds of valuable commercial and other privileges from being copied is secrecy. Initiatory cults and secret societies, for instance, surround their most important symbols with taboos and restrictions, treating them as mysteries revealed only to adepts. Indeed, many Australian Aboriginal religions are themselves precisely of this kind, with myths, rituals, songs and graphic designs often being treated as clan secrets restricted to initiated men (Keen 1994; Morphy 1991).

Ethnicity is sometimes the basis of craft guilds, castes, or other occupationally specialised groups, and the protection of the group's identity is closely linked to the protection of a livelihood or an economic monopoly. Roosens (1989) made a study of the ethnogenesis of the 'Hurons' of the province of Quebec in Canada, a group claiming ancestry from the Native American people of that name. These are craft specialists who regard their right to manufacture 'Indian handicrafts' as a key element of their cultural identity, an activity over which they claim 'a sort of moral monopoly' (Roosens 1989: 98):

> If one examines the objects produced and analyzes them in terms of art history, one may conclude that no object for sale in a local store has anything to do with the products of the Hurons of the pre-Columbian period and even little to do with the culture of the Hurons of the nineteenth century. The canoes are no longer made of bark and are no longer repaired with resin; the leather jackets with fringes have nothing to do with the former clothing of the Hurons, nor do the headdresses with feathers down the back. Most of the moccasins are at least partially machine-made and not from the same kind of leather as previously; miniature objects, like the small tomahawks and most of the beadwork, are fodder for tourists who want to buy cowboy-film stereotypes for their children or relatives. Nevertheless, any French Canadian who would produce such objects would be branded a forger. (Roosens 1989: 98)

But cultural symbols of a much more abstract sort than songs, myths, graphic designs or native handicrafts can also be treated as exclusive cultural possessions, as valuable assets needing to be protected from piracy. For example, some ethnic groups identify themselves with particular styles of discourse and may react with hostility if other groups appear to be imitating these forms of expression. Let me give an example which comes from a society in which an indigenous minority perceive members of a dominant majority to be trying to misappropriate a discourse of 'ancestral' land rights.

In a study of sheep farming communities in New Zealand, Dominy (1990, 1995) shows that these white farming families, many of which have farmed the same estates for generations, have developed notions of emotional and spiritual relatedness to the land, analogous in many ways to those of the Maori. Dominy's ethnographically sensitive portrayal of these farmers' world-view has been criticised by Levine (1990) on the grounds that it provides – whether intentionally or not – an ideological justification of the farming communities' claims to land and is therefore highly damaging to Maori interests. Levine points out that many Maori do not only resent what they see as attempts by white New Zealanders to assimilate them and eradicate their culture. They also resent the more subtle and insidious 'reverse assimilation', as Levine (1990: 6) calls it, in which whites (as Maori see it) unjustly appropriate Maori values and plagiarise the language of indigeneity and connectedness to the land, to which the Maori feel that they alone are entitled.

The attachments which the sheep farmers feel to their land may be, to them, an authentic outgrowth of their collective experience over the generations, and as deep and genuine as those of the Maori. But, to Maori critics and their supporters, any claims of this sort amount to a kind of forgery or usurpation, a wrongful assertion of indigeneity and of moral equality with the Maori. In this dispute, and in other cases I shall describe later, we see social actors assuming that ethnic identity symbols – which may range from designs printed on T-shirts to abstract discourses of indigeneity – 'belong' to social actors or groups very much as though they were a form of property (see Handler 1988). These proprietary rights may be asserted, for instance, through aesthetic judgements, as in the claim often made by black Americans that '[o]nly African-Americans can appreciate African-American music' (Frith 1996: 108). An identity symbol employed by those to whom it 'belongs' is accepted as in some sense 'authentic'; but deployment by others may be decried as an 'imitation', or indeed as a 'theft', of another group's qualities and attributes. One way in which the identities of individuals or groups can be attacked is thus to disparage their symbolic practices as counterfeits, stolen from their rightful owners.

For instance, accusations of cultural borrowing were a common theme in anti-Christian writings in China for several centuries. This literature attacked Christianity using rhetorics of both cultural pollution and cultural piracy. The seventeenth-century writer and official Yang, for instance, accused Christianity of having plagiarised its doctrines of heaven and hell from Buddhism. Another influential work of the following century argued that the Christian countries had originally been Buddhist and Moslem but stole the doctrines of these faiths and incorporated them into their own religion (Paul Cohen 1963: 26, 30): 'By characterising Christianity as a religion which, far from adding anything new to the "traditional" religions of China, was actually taken from them, Christianity was placed in a position in China which was at best superfluous' (1963: 31). By the eighteenth century, the claim that Christianity had copied its key tenets from Buddhism was taken for granted by almost all non-Christian Chinese who wrote on Christianity (Paul Cohen 1963: 32–33). The nineteenth-century geographer-official Hsu, in his account of the history of the countries of Europe, described Christianity in these terms as having no separate identity as a religion, on the grounds that it 'is an offshoot of Buddhism, that some of its most important doctrines were established by Moses long before Jesus, and that the only difference between Christianity and Islam is that the followers of the latter did not eat pork' (Paul Cohen 1963: 41).

Of course, 'resemblances' between the religious or other practices of different groups may sometimes be purely coincidental. More accurately, it is very much a matter of perception whether practices even resemble each other in the first place, and 'piracy' is clearly sometimes entirely in the eye of the beholder. Let us consider the sixteenth-century Dominican priest Diego Durán, one of the most sympathetic and knowledgeable Spanish writers of his time on Aztec culture and history (see Todorow 1984: 209–10). Durán was struck by what he saw as parallels between Aztec religion and Christianity: the Aztecs had a festival which reminded him of Christmas; certain of their cosmological ideas seemed strangely reminiscent of the doctrine of the Trinity. Durán felt highly ambivalent about these similarities, unsure whether to feel gratified by them or repelled and threatened. On the one hand, he thought that they might be evidence that the Aztecs had received Christian teaching in the distant past (perhaps St Thomas had visited them), in which case the resemblances were positive and deserved to be valued. But another, deeply sinister, possibility also occurred to him: namely, that: 'the devil had persuaded and instructed them [the Indians], stealing from and imitating the Divine Cult so that *he* be honored as a god ... the devil our cursed adversary forced the Indians to imitate the ceremonies of the Christian Catholic religion in his own service and cult, being thus adored and served' (quoted in Todorow 1984: 210). Durán in the end resolved the doubts that plagued him by concluding that the Aztecs must be one of the lost tribes of Israel. But my point is that the resemblances between Aztec religion and Christianity which perplexed him were just as much his own creations as was the theory of satanic plagiarism by which he sought to explain them.

Claims of cultural piracy are thus accusations which social actors may level at others when they perceive certain similarities between themselves and these others to be in some way threatening. Of course, it may be quite obvious to the observer that no copying could really have taken place; or it may be impossible to determine who, if anyone, has actually copied from whom. The main question for the observer concerns perceptions: why social actors, in certain circumstances, may come to view perceived resemblances between themselves and others negatively, as a challenge to their identity or their interests, and act to safeguard themselves from such threats.

As instances of what Weiner called inalienable possessions, these symbolic practices are felt subjectively not to be external to the self, but to be defining constituents of it; often, they cannot be appropriated by others without a deep sense of injury and violation of one's integrity. These assumptions are evident, for instance, in the dispute between Greece and the former Yugoslav republic of Macedonia over the ownership of the name of Macedonia and other symbols associated with the ancient kingdom of that name. One such symbol is the figure of Alexander the Great, and another the emblem of the sixteen-pointed sun, or Star Vergina, which appears – provocatively, from the Greek point of view – on the Republic's flag.

From the Greek nationalist perspective, then, the use of the name 'Macedonian' by the 'Slavs of Skopje' constitutes a 'felony', an 'act of plagiarism' against the Greek people. By calling themselves 'Macedonians' the Slavs are 'stealing' a Greek name;

they are 'embezzling' Greek cultural heritage; they are 'falsifying' Greek history. As Evangelos Kofos, a historian employed by the Greek Foreign Ministry, told a foreign reporter 'It is as if a robber came into my house and stole my most precious jewels – my history, my culture, my identity.' (Danforth 1993: 4)

We can find similar conceptions of culture as property among West Indians in Britain. Abner Cohen (1993) shows how this ethnic identity emerged into self-awareness in the 1970s with the annual Notting Hill Carnival in London as its pre-eminent symbol. He describes the struggles of the West Indian community to establish and maintain this identity in the face of repeated attempts by the authorities to suppress the carnival and, later, to take control of it and so co-opt it. West Indians couched their resistance in terms of the inalienability of their culture, with assertions such as: 'Carnival is inside our blood. It is ours and cannot be taken from us' (Abner Cohen 1993: 32). Nothing could express the inalienability of identity symbols more clearly than the notion that one's history and identity are a treasured possession, like jewellery, or that one's ethnic practices are bound into the substances of one's body.

Cultural Identity and the Body: the Imagery of Transgressive Flows

Such symbols can generate powerful allegiances and feelings of primordial belonging, making these allegiances appear inescapable. I want to suggest now that much of their emotive power may derive from the way that the folk understandings of identity which I have just tried to outline are connected with certain ontogenetically primitive understandings of the body.

I have distinguished two related kinds of discursive imagery which seem often involved in the construction of cultural identity. One is an imagery of pollution, in which a group represents its culture as threatened by invasion and replacement by some other or others. The second comprises images of piracy or appropriation: here, a group represents its cultural practices as threatened by being purloined or incorporated by others. That is, its members perceive the reproduction, or unwarranted reproduction, of their cultural practices by outsiders as harming their interests in some way. Certain aspects of their identities, it seems, appear to them as a sort of scarce resource, needing to be protected from usurpation by non-members.

Both discourses thus evoke images of transgressive movements of cultural symbols across imagined boundaries. But they differ in the direction – inward into the Self or outward from the Self – of these conceived transgressive flows. A proper understanding of a group's self-constructions must therefore involve understanding the ways in which it may seek to draw particular types of boundaries around some putative 'cultural repertoire' which it claims to possess – boundaries of purity (defending its cultural repertoire from pollution), of ownership (defending it from appropriation), and perhaps of other kinds – thus representing itself as differentiated from its sociocultural environment. But, in either case, the fundamental anxieties here seem to concern possibilities of loss of cultural integrity and the dissolution of identity. I suggest that much of the emotive power and persuasiveness of such discourses derives from other, deeper, imageries of bodily dissolution and the loss of physical integrity.

As we saw, the work of Douglas (1966) on notions of ritual purity and pollution revealed the close interrelationships between categorical, social and bodily boundaries. The first two appear to be rooted, phenomenologically, in bodily experience (see also Leach 1964). Hence the power of images of bodily defilement in symbolising the transgression of boundaries of any kind. Boundaries are defined, above all, by being represented as endangered, challenged or transgressed: either by things (such as the anomalous animal taxa in the Hebraic dietary laws) that transgress categorical boundaries by their very existence, or else by human actions, such as witchcraft or incest, that transgress moral boundaries. In both cases, notions of impurity and ritual pollution are intrinsic to the construction of ordered categories.

But I would add a reminder that a key feature of social categorisations is that their use tends to be egocentric. They are primarily schemes for ordering relations between the Self and some Other or Others, categorising them as closer or further apart in social space. The relations they define are normally ones in which the actor himself or herself is actually located. Thus the boundary between two social categories is usually asymmetrical: from the situated perspective of the social actor, it has two qualitatively different faces, one looking from the outside in and the other from the inside out. There are therefore two qualitatively distinct and complementary ways in which actors can imagine such a boundary being threatened or transgressed: from its far side, and from its near side. Actors may, on the one hand, visualise the Self being invaded by things belonging to the outside – by foreign objects, by the not-Self. This is the realm of pollution symbolism: of ideas of invasion by dirt, waste, disease, decay, foreign matter, of intuitive notions of hygiene and contagion (see, for instance, Rosin and Nemeroff 1990). In many cultures, such conceptions are manifested in beliefs that witches and sorcerers can magically shoot or implant objects into their victims.

But the boundaries of the body can also be transgressed if the things of the Self pass outward to be alienated and lost. Here is a different symbolism of bodily harm: not of pollution, but of extraction or depletion of the body's vital contents. This too is a rich theme in myth and folklore worldwide. It is, for instance, the realm of beliefs in witches and sorcerers who consume their victims' life substance by extracting their vital organs, stealing their body fluids, sucking their souls from their bodies, and so forth (see, for instance, Canessa 2000).

In some cultures, it is as though the body's boundaries were conceived as a sort of membrane through which things can pass safely and readily in one direction but not in the other. The body is understood to be at risk primarily, or only, from one direction. Lindenbaum (1984), for example, has identified two contrasting kinds of gender systems in New Guinea cultures. Both of them construct a rigid boundary between maleness and femaleness, but they do so in opposite ways. One of them elaborates male fears of female pollution, portraying menstruation and childbirth as dangerously defiling to men. The other focuses on the dangers of the loss of semen in heterosexual intercourse, representing women as avid consumers of the life-giving powers that semen is imagined to contain. In both systems, women are seen as posing dangers to men's bodies – causing them to sicken, weaken, age prematurely and so forth. In one, women do so by contaminating men and, in the other, by consuming and depleting them (see also Kelly 1976).

In many cultures, these two types of imagined harm are closely blended. The figure of the Hollywood vampire embodies both kinds of danger simultaneously, consuming his victims' life-blood and infecting them with his own vampirism. But, in all these cases, what seem to be at stake are ontogenetically primitive understandings of the unity and integrity of the body and its boundaries – boundaries conceived as having an outward side protecting the body from contamination, and an inward side protecting it from dissolution or depletion.

Here, then, I suggest, lies part of the source of that deeply emotional, primordial, quality of the attachments to which ethnicity and cultural nationalism can give rise. These are forms of identity and belonging which resonate, in the way they are constructed, with what are perhaps deep-rooted and widespread intuitive understandings of the body. I referred earlier to those writers in nineteenth-century China who attacked Christianity on the grounds that it was both a religious deviance and a mere plagiarism of Buddhism: in other words, that it was both different and not different from Chinese religious orthodoxy. This double condemnation seemed echoed in the similarly double body imagery in which they portrayed Christians as polluters of Chinese bodies (by their ritual use of menstrual blood and so forth), and as organ-robbers who extracted Chinese eyes to make silver. Of course, it is unlikely that representations of the body and representations of cultural identity are usually homologous with each other in any simple way. The point is rather that ethnic practices characteristically are bodily practices. Ethnic identity tends to be, in a very immediate sense, inseparable from the treatment of the body, intimately and deeply inscribed on it.

> [S]ome groups without distinctive physical features to mark them apart from other groups have deliberately created them. Thus circumcision, scarifying, tattooing, filing teeth, piercing or otherwise changing the shape of nose, ears, tongue, lips, all become badges by which to identify those who belong and those who do not, sometimes with highly complicated effect.
>
> Less permanent but hardly less distinctive are the changes made for this same purpose in the body's extensions, beginning with the hair; for example, the scalplock of some North American Indians, the monk's tonsure, the sideburns of

the Hasidic Jew, the uncut hair and beard of the Sikh ... Then there are the distinctive marks that can be made on the body's surfaces, caste marks in India, painted patterns on the skin, as in parts of Africa and Oceania. Beyond these come clothes, dress used to distinguish bodies that would all look alike – more or less – undressed, all the 'native costumes' which occur from nation to nation, group to group, sometimes from village to nearby village, giving to each one the identifying distinctiveness it needs to feel. (Isaacs 1975: 42–43; footnote omitted)

The modes of dress, adornment and bodily comportment of women, especially, are often important ethnic, religious and cultural boundary markers. As a result, these are often subject to a high degree of control and are particular likely to become contested territory, in situations of ethnic conflict (see, for instance, Graybill and Arthur 1999: 12; Kandiyoti 1996; La Rue 1994).

My point is that the kinds of transgressive movements of cultural practices across boundaries which often preoccupy ethnic and nationalist discourses lend themselves very readily to being envisaged as transgressions of the boundaries of their members' bodies. Goffman pointed out long ago that institutions such as asylums and prisons impose standardized modes of dress on their inmates as deliberate violations of their normal sense of self. On entering the institution, inmates have their personal possessions removed and are issued with uniforms. Their 'identity kit', as Goffman calls it, is thus taken from them, and they are made to experience a 'mortification of self' in which 'the boundary that the individual places between his being and the environment is invaded and the *embodiments* of self profaned' (Goffman 1968: 271; italics in original; see also Dittmar 1992: 109).

Simmel points us to the other, complementary way in which this boundary can be invaded and the embodiments of self profaned: namely, by having one's 'identity kit' imitated or appropriated by others. Hence that inherent transitoriness of which Simmel wrote in his essay on fashion, in which, as he saw it, fashions are always created by the upper classes and abandoned as soon as the lower classes start to copy them (Simmel 1971: 200, 296, 302). Again, élites experience these mimetic usurpations as trespasses at the somatic level, as unwanted bodily commonalities appearing between themselves and others.

What tends to distinguish ethnicity from other forms of social identity is the especially close connection, if not isomorphism, between the boundaries of such groups and the somatic boundaries of their members. Cultural boundaries are, to a particularly pronounced degree, embodied boundaries, inscribed in the bodies of people themselves and in their largely routine and taken-for-granted everyday practices. Because ethnic identities are lived in and through the bodily routines of everyday life, they comprise 'total' identities, ones that subsume the whole being of social actors, pervade their social existence and can be lifelong. Moreover, the identification of these actors with their nation or ethnic group tends to have a markedly kinaesthetic character, as if the collectivities to which they belong were their own embodied Selves writ large (see, for instance, van der Veer 1994a: 85ff). When the boundary between the self and the collectivity grows blurred in this way,

'I experience any attack on the symbols, emblems, or values … that define my ethnicity as an attack on myself' (Roosens 1989: 12). One's relationships with these symbols and with one's own body have become inextricably merged.

7

Cultural Boundaries, Cultural Ownership

Every property is an extension of personality; property is that which obeys our wills, that in which our egos express, and externally realize, themselves. This expression occurs, earliest and most completely, in regard to our body, which thus is our first and most unconditional possession. (Simmel 1950: 344)

Introduction

The discourses of cultural piracy and pollution, I suggest, are best viewed as twin aspects of a single model which seems often to underlie contemporary claims concerning cultural identity. This implicit folk theory of cultural identity might be briefly summed up in the following way. First, cultural practices and symbols are in certain respects things (they are 'objectified', as Handler (1988: 14–16) puts it), and can in principle be transmitted, circulated, accumulated and so forth, much like objects. As we shall see, many cultural symbols *are* objects or, more precisely, practices relating to them: objects such as sacred sites, antiquities, museum objects and, indeed, national territories and ethnic homelands themselves.

Secondly, discrete and enduring cultural identities are understood to come into existence through the imposition of an order, in which unrestricted transfers of these objects or objectified patterns of action are brought under control and discontinuities are introduced into the unregulated flow of cultural forms and practices. This folk model thus seems implicitly to posit a kind of potential condition of uncurbed cultural diffusion, through whose control and negation collective identities crystallise, each attached to a stable, fixed inventory of cultural 'traits'.

An inexorable implication of this folk model is that every such inventory of cultural practices appears susceptible to loss, dispersal and extinction. A group's cultural identity is therefore always to some degree provisional, insecure, conceived as something it can 'lose' (see Handler 1988: 47–50). This loss of distinctive identity can be conceived to occur through the replacement of one's local culture by alien ones (flows of foreign culture inward) or through the appropriation of one's culture by foreign ones (flows of local culture outward), or through combinations of both of these processes. The implication is that a group must safeguard its cultural identity by controlling the flow of cultural forms into and out of its repertoire of symbolic practices, because if it does not protect its cultural boundaries in this way it will be absorbed by its environment and dissolve back into the surrounding identity space.

These images of pollution and appropriation are aspects of a single underlying conception of culture as a particular form of property: namely, the patrimony or inheritance. Certainly, they are often collapsed into each other in everyday folk discourse. Hence, for example, Irish nationalists in Northern Ireland may describe themselves as having been 'robbed of our language' (De Rosa 1998: 109), speaking of cultural assimilation (the suppression of the Irish language and the imposition of English) as the 'theft' of an important part of their heritage. In other words, nationalists may use the language of property and theft to describe any kind of perceived harm to their cultural identity. Both cultural appropriation and cultural pollution alike are attacks upon their property, disinheriting them of what is rightfully theirs.

In this model, then, every culturally distinct collectivity depends for its existence on defending an exclusive association with a region of a wider identity space inhabited also by others. The symbolic practices understood to differentiate these groups, and the rules of purity and proprietorship relating to these practices, are the boundary markers and coordinates in this space. Each group must prevent others from appropriating its practices or prevent them from imposing their own practices, or do both. Each remains a distinct entity for so long as it can keep the others from trespassing in these ways into its proprietary domain.

In the symbolism of cultural identity, the difference between Self and Other takes the form of a contrast imputed to exist, a frontier drawn in the imagination, between one's own group's cultural identity symbols and those of some other group or groups. What I shall call cultural boundaries are the imagined lines demarcating these bodies of symbolic practices. Thus, the discourses of ethnicity and nationalism, for example, not only reify the cultural repertoires of groups, but separate these repertoires by boundaries similarly reified and objectified too. Such boundaries are linked closely to a view of cultural identity as something inherently vulnerable, needing to be protected and conserved. They are a key element in the ideologies of fixed identity and in the models of clear-cut cultural difference which nationalist and ethnic actors often employ in social action.

But this folk model of identity does not make such groups inherently xenophobic. As we shall see, groups can have soft boundaries and can even be culturally highly acquisitive, expansionist, or both. And it goes without saying that the strength of such a boundary, and indeed its very existence, is often contested within the group itself (I discuss some examples of this in a later chapter). My point is that, as Schwartz reminds us, 'in order for people to "have ethnicity" they must have at least two (and usually more) ethnic groups' (1975: 107–8). In other words, ethnic identity is inherently relational and contrastive. Anderson implicitly makes the same point in relation to nationhood. The 'imagined community' which in his view constitutes a nation is always a limited (that is, an exclusive) one: 'No nation imagines itself coterminous with mankind. The most messianic nationalists do not dream of a day when all the members of the human race will join their nation' (Anderston 1983: 7). No nationalists, even the most ardent, want to convert the whole world. Again, to paraphrase Schwartz, a nation can only exist if there is at least one other one. What poses a threat to an individual nation or ethnic group is not the existence of others who are 'different'. On the contrary, as Anderson shows for nationalism and Schwartz for ethnicity, it needs such others. Each depends on others for its very reality and has no existence apart from theirs. The most fundamental threat to its being is the possibility of slippage into undifferentiation, of falling back into homogeneity, of lapsing into similarity with outsiders.

Thus, certainly, the folk rhetorics of identity which I have tried to outline can allow groups to represent themselves as more or less outward-looking, more or less amenable to various sorts of mutually enriching cultural give and take – but on condition that their cultural boundaries are not erased altogether and all distinction lost between inside and outside. For, according these discourses of identity, the distinction between the cultural Self and Other depends irreducibly on stopping at least some transmission of culture between them: on regulating the movement of foreign culture inward or of local culture outward, or both, so preserving this critical and yet imagined boundary against erosion.

Cultural Boundaries, Hard and Soft

The problem I address in this chapter is why these boundaries seem to be drawn more or less strongly or acutely in some circumstances than in others. Some communities – or, more accurately, social actors in some contexts – seem to create relatively stark and rigid distinctions between their own group's practices and those of outsiders. Others seem to tolerate more permeable boundaries, and may even value change or indeterminacy in the perceived distribution of cultural characteristics among groups.

In seeking an answer to this question, one needs first to distinguish conceptually between cultural boundaries and social boundaries. By social boundaries I mean divisions drawn between social groups or categories, demarcating human collectivities (see Barth 1969). It goes without saying that many groups show a marked concern to divide their social worlds in this way into two distinct kinds of people: insiders and outsiders:

> This mythical unity, this imagined community which divides the world between 'us' and 'them', is maintained and ideologically reproduced by a whole system of

what Armstrong (1982) calls symbolic 'border guards'. These border guards can identify people as members or non-members of a specific collectivity. They are closely linked to specific cultural codes of style of dress and behaviour as well as to more elaborate bodies of customs, literary and artistic modes of production, and, of course, language ... They are cultural resources which are used in the struggle for hegemony which takes place, at any specific moment, not only between collectivities but also within them. Different, sometimes conflicting, cultural border guards can be used simultaneously by different members of the collectivity. (Anthias and Yuval-Davis 1992: 33)

The first point to note is that it is not just cultural boundaries that can be weak or strong. Social boundaries can, of course, vary in the same way also (Banton 1983; Smith 1986: 47). Groups may be more or less permeable to outsiders, more or less difficult to join – or to leave. In this regard, social and cultural boundaries seem closely correlated:

An incipient nationality is formed when the perceptions of the boundaries of community are transformed: when soft boundaries are transformed into hard ones. Every cultural practice ... is a potential boundary marking a community. These boundaries may be either soft or hard. One or more of the cultural practices of a group, such as rituals, language, dialect, music, kinship rules, or culinary habits, may be considered soft boundaries if they identify a group but do not prevent the group from sharing and even adopting, self-consciously or not, the practices of another. (Duara 1996: 168)

And of course, as Duara reminds us, these boundaries may be hard in relation to some categories of outsiders, soft in relation to others (1996: 169).

One can point to innumerable cases in which communities are quite indifferent to the adoption or reproduction of their practices by outsiders (or certain categories of outsiders) and even welcome this sort of borrowing. To some, transactions across their cultural boundaries are an opportunity rather than a threat. In certain situations, even having one's cultural practices 'appropriated' can be welcomed. Afonso points out that exiled Tibetans – unlike some Native American groups I shall discuss later – approve of New Age interest in their shamanistic traditions, viewing it as useful to their political goals: 'Whereas Native Americans are critical of such usurpations, the Tibetans in exile use the appropriations as utilitarian symbolic capital to expand western audiences and to extend sympathy for the Tibetan cause across the spectrum' (1998: 122).

A very important observation often made on ethnicity and nationalism is that group boundaries – social and cultural alike – are drawn most starkly by those who perceive their identities as in some way threatened and insecure and are defined specifically towards outsiders perceived as posing this threat: 'Ethnicism is fundamentally defensive. It is a response to outside threats and divisions within. It seeks a return to the *status quo ante*, to an idealized image of a primitive past. It emerges when the group's sense of ethnicity is attenuated and impaired, or when it is challenged by shattering external events' (Smith 1986: 55). Forsythe makes an argument of this sort in relation to national identity in contemporary Germany. Germans, she suggests, show a greater propensity than other European nationalities to view foreigners in their midst as a 'problem'. Turkish migrants and their cultural practices – such as the wearing of headscarves by women – tend to be seen as 'pollution'. The reason for this heightened concern with the 'foreigner problem' among Germans, Forsythe argues, is that many Germans perceive their identity as weaker and more threatened than the other national identities in Europe (1989; see also Kandiyoti 1996: 316).

Conversi, in his discussion of minority nationalisms in Spain, draws a striking contrast between two sorts of nationalisms: one exemplified by the Basques, the other by Catalans. Catalan nationalism rests on a rich and flourishing high culture, giving it a secure cultural identity and a confident, 'inclusive' or 'integrationist' attitude to outsiders. Basque nationalism, on the other hand, is of a rather more xenophobic, exclusionary or 'exclusive' variety, principally – so Conversi suggests – because Basque cultural identity is weaker, its distinctiveness from the rest of Spain much less pronounced:

> Where [shared culture and values] flourish, not only do they become a central part of the nationalists' claims, but they also add cohesion to their struggles; i.e. the availability of pre-existing cultural 'markers', which help to differentiate the group from its neighbours, facilitates the organisation of united political action. The common elements chosen as core values can work both as mobilising symbols and as points of reference for a wide political p.....orm and large constituencies. Conversely, the absence of shared cultural distinctiveness is likely to encourage political fragmentation within nationalists movements. In this case, the movement is bound to rely on an 'antagonistic identity'. Such an identity is one constructed essentially through the opposition of the ingroup to one or more outgroups. All identities are in some way based on opposition, but an antagonistic identity focuses more on the need to define one's own group by negative comparison to others, and by exclusion. This border-definition process is carried out by a radical re-evaluation of the positive traits of the ingroup and a parallel devaluation of those of the outgroups. Borders are stressed rather than content, i.e. the group's culture. (Conversi 1997: 5; see also pp. 162, 185, 220, 262)

Conversi's argument implies that it is nationalist movements with the weakest cultural identities and the least developed positive cultural content that have the strongest cultural boundaries. In other words, these boundaries are compensatory: they are defensive reactions to too little actual difference. Preoccupations with cultural pollution and piracy can conceal a deep unease that one may not be sufficiently distinct from the outsiders after all.

Again, what seems most to threaten a group's identity is not difference but the possibility of sameness and loss of distinction. But it is the loss or blurring of distinction between themselves and lower-ranked groups in particular that social actors are likely to fear most. In this respect, there is an especially close connection between cultural boundary discourses and the relation which I called difference-as-inferiority. Groups draw their cultural boundaries most firmly against those others they class as exemplifying a kind of lesser cultural status. They are most concerned with protecting themselves from assimilation and from appropriation by lower-ranking others. Indeed, cultural piracy and pollution discourses are deeply involved in the categorisation of others as culturally inferior. To represent others as seeking either to appropriate one's symbolic practices or to replace them invasively with their own practices is, in a sense, to define them as embodiments of difference-as-inferiority.

Horowitz (1985) argues that ethnic groups whose boundaries and identities are weakening – because they are faced either with what he calls 'differentiation' (splitting) or 'assimilation' (incorporation by another) – may react with cultural revival movements. In such movements – Linton (1943) called them 'nativistic' – minorities attempt to resist assimilation by reviving or forcefully asserting selected aspects of their culture. Ostensibly concerned with recovering or perpetuating tradition, these movements are often in fact processes of ethnogenesis. In other words, nascent ethnic groups, their identities not yet securely founded, are struggling to establish themselves against opposition. Cultural boundaries are strongly stressed in contexts such as these:

> Bakonjo [a people of Western Uganda] borrowed Batoro rites and language, Kurds in Iraqi cities underwent Arabization, Basques became Castilianized, and the line between Sikhs and Hindus was uncertain.
>
> The cultural revivals that emerged in response reflected an awareness of the danger of a fading group identity. They tended to emphasize the history of separateness and even hostility between the groups. Memories of insults were recalled. Languages were 'purified' of words that derived from the language of the neighbouring group. Religious practices were cleansed in the same way, in the name of returning to some former states of orthodoxy that may or may not have existed. Group identity was thus infused with a new or revived cultural content that served to demarcate the lines between groups more clearly, thereby reducing the ease with which individuals could cross group boundaries. (Horowitz 1985: 72)

Of course, in such situations groups often employ discourses both of pollution and of piracy together (and perhaps others too), and do so in an equally forceful way. The problem for the observer is usually therefore to understand the ways in which such rhetorics are in practice combined in concrete situations. Let me outline two cases of ethnogenesis, illustrating the ways in which these discourses are employed jointly in the formation of ethnic identities. My first comes from Abner Cohen's (1993) rich and fascinating analysis of the history of the Notting Hill Carnival and of the key role this festival played in the emergence of West Indian identity in Britain.

For the first five years or so of its existence (1966–70) this carnival was a relatively small, working-class event attended by a few thousand people. Although several ethnic communities were involved in it (there were Irish, Turkish-Cypriot and Czechoslovak bands, for example), the overall symbolism of the carnival was predominantly British or English, the themes of the masquerades including English monarchs, the novels of Dickens and scenes from Victorian London. Politically, the carnival expressed opposition to landlords and local authorities over issues such as housing shortages and extortionate rents (Abner Cohen 1993: 10–20).

During the first half of the 1970s, a collective West Indian ethnic identity developed in London, arising out of shared experiences of unemployment, police harassment and poor housing conditions, and this emergent community adopted the carnival as its focal symbol. Within a few years, the carnival had became exclusively West Indian in its leadership and in musical and cultural form, a process accomplished, first, through the deliberate removal of all artistic and cultural content not deemed to be West Indian (Abner Cohen 1993: 1–2, 21–32). Cohen writes of one of the main organisers of the carnival at this time:

> He jealously developed and guarded the West Indian character of the celebration and discouraged the incursion of 'foreign' cultural forms into its structure ... [F]rom the start, during the first few years of the carnival when it was multicultural in its arts and music and multi-ethnic in attendance, and was referred to as a fair, he strived to turn it into an exclusively West Indian celebration, to 'purify' it of the contamination of native British cultural forms ... [T]here was at the time a sustained, conscious effort to establish cultural and social boundaries, to achieve a distinctiveness that would mark the identity and exclusiveness that would be necessary for the articulation of a corporate West Indian organisation. (1993: 113–14)

To many of its West Indian organisers, the carnival was a quintessentially West Indian cultural event which had, in effect, been misappropriated by outsiders and adulterated by white British culture. As they saw it, establishing a distinctive West Indian collective identity involved removing these admixtures from this key symbol of their heritage and so recovering it as their rightful property: 'The West Indians had tended to reify the concept of carnival, that is to treat it as if it were a material object, and to regard it as being exclusively their own' (Abner Cohen 1993: 76).

Their appropriation (but to them, repossession) of the carnival as a symbol of identity eventually came to be legitimised by a revision of its history. From the start, a white community worker had been acknowledged by everyone as the carnival's originator and as its leader for its first few years. But, in the mid-1980s, some of the West Indian leaders 'discovered' that the carnival had actually been founded by a West Indian woman in the late 1950s (Abner Cohen 1993: 5–6, 62–78).

While the West Indian community took the Trinidad Carnival (itself originally an expression of black emancipation, protest and resistance) as their model, this community did not predominantly originate from Trinidad but from a variety of islands, many of which did not have a tradition of carnival (Abner Cohen 1993: 5, 21–32). The great interest and significance of Cohen's study are therefore that it is one of relatively few detailed analyses of the historical genesis of an ethnic identity and its cultural symbolism. This identity symbolism was constructed, I would argue, by selecting an existing cultural form (essentially, a working-class street festival) and subjecting it to two processes of exclusion: one concerned with pollution (removing all but 'West Indian' cultural and artistic content from it) and the other with ownership (extricating the festival itself from its predominantly white working-class cultural context). Both processes crucially involved, of course, the removal of outsiders from decision-making and leadership roles.

In short, it was not that an already-formed West Indian community took over the carnival as its cultural heritage. Rather, this West Indian identity seems to have generated or produced itself, as it were, in the very process of appropriation itself. It did so, moreover, primarily in relation to one cultural Other: namely, British white majority culture. But some cultural identities are defined, or generate themselves, in contrast to more than one cultural alter, and may come into existence presenting different kinds of boundaries to each of them. Greek national identity is a case in point. Greek nationalism arose in the eighteenth and nineteenth centuries in relation to two primarily significant alters: the Ottoman empire and Western Europe (see Friedman 1994: 118–23; Herzfeld 1987, 1995; C. Stewart 1994). This was a double process, in which the Greek élite, as Friedman observes, 'was working its way into the West and extricating itself from the Ottoman empire' (1994: 132). The Greek nationalists viewed their language and culture as having been adulterated over the centuries by Turkish influences, which had to be thoroughly rooted out if Greeks were to reassert their true national identity. At the same time, these nationalists were greatly concerned with the custodianship of the classical past, and with what they viewed as the theft of much of the Greek classical heritage by Western European nations, particularly Britain and Germany. Stewart (1994), for instance, discusses the deep concerns of nineteenth-century Greek nationalists to establish modern Greeks as heirs of the classical Hellenes, in opposition to the claims of some other European nationalities – especially certain German nationalist scholars at the time – to be the rightful inheritors of Hellenic civilisation. Similarly, Herzfeld shows how contemporary Greek nationalists see the expropriation by the West of classical antiquities as part of a more abstract expropriation of 'all rights to the understanding of the Classical past, or to define its very nature' (1987: 20). Conversely, the efforts of nationalists to reclaim these relics are implicitly assertions that classical Greece forms a special part of 'their' history and identity (Herzfeld 1987: 20, 53, 57–58). While these concerns tended to focus on the proprietorship of material culture such as antiquities and museum objects, the deeper issue at stake for Greek nationalists was, and remains, the much more abstract, moral right to be recognised as the true successors of the classical Hellenes and their civilisation (Herzfeld 1987, 1995).

Like West Indian identity in Britain, the formation of Greek national identity seems to have involved two simultaneous processes of exclusion. But in the Greek case each process was directed at a different cultural Other. One process, directed towards the Ottoman East, ‥s intended to reclaim Greek culture from pollution; the other, directed towards the European West, was concerned with reclaiming Greek culture from appropriation. These two processes were intimately connected: to the nationalists, the Greek nation had to 'purify' itself of Turkish adulterations to re-establish itself as authentically Greek and thus as the rightful inheritor of the classical Hellenic legacy.

I earlier described cultural boundaries as rhetorical devices. But clearly, they are often more than just this; ethnic groups do at times try actually to engineer such barriers and to exercise very real control over cultural flows (see, for instance, Tomlinson 1991: 17–18). Of course, as Eriksen reminds us, ethnic or nationalist 'revitalisation' movements, aimed at returning to 'tradition' and restoring an imagined former cultural purity, always in fact involve unacknowledged innovations (1993: 86). Thus, for instance, the Greek linguistic purists of the nineteenth century introduced French and German syntactic structures into the supposedly 'pure' national language they were creating (Hertzfeld 1995: 229). Naturally, Greek nationalists did not portray their language, culture and national identity as novel constructions, but as the revival or reconstruction of something that had existed all along. To them, the Greek nation was, and always had been, historically continuous with classical Greece (though, as Friedman (1994: 118) points out, the very image of classical civilisation to which they referred was in fact a historically quite recent invention of the Western European Renaissance). The problem, as they saw it, was that their nation had lain submerged for centuries under Turkish influences and had been dispossessed of much of its patrimony by Western Europe. What was therefore needed for this identity to re-emerge was to reverse the cultural flows which had compromised it in the first place: to purify Greek culture of its Turkish accretions and to reassemble the classical heritage in Greek hands.

These cases suggest that many cases of ethnogenesis can be understood as processes in which a group, as it were, extracts itself from a state of undifferentiation, or relative undifferentiation, within its sociocultural environment. This self-extraction involves, above all, social actors gaining, for the group they are seeking to define, acknowledgement as a possessor of a distinctive inventory of cultural forms and practices. Two main sorts of discursive strategies are employed here. One is preoccupied with the removal of imagined alien admixtures from the group's symbolic repertoire. The other is concerned with gaining a monopoly of the use or control of the repertoire and with excluding outsiders from it. A culturally distinct group is formed – that is, is disembedded from its surrounding identity space – through the successful discursive imposition of boundaries and separations around an inventory of symbolic practices: distinctions of ownership versus appropriation, of purity versus pollution, or some combination of both.

Hence a recurring problem for ethnic and nationalist actors – and one that becomes especially acute in situations of conflict – is that Self and Other may appear not to be satisfactorily distinct from each other. Ways often have to be devised to make them more different – or, rather, to appear to be so. Ethnic differences seem, then, to be the products of a specific type of purposive activity aimed at generating apparent dissimilarities out of relations of similarity – even, perhaps, as we shall see, aimed at creating resemblances in the first place in order to subvert them. Culturally distinct groups tend to emerge through processes in which social actors work to reject, diminish or undo certain of their conceived commonalities, making themselves seem to one another less alike. To preserve their distinctive identities thereafter, they may have to make a constant effort to constrain the recognition or expression of their likenesses.

8

Power and the
Negotiation of Identity

Introduction: Two Patterns of Internal Conflict

An important question concerns the ways in which these representations of
cultural appropriation and cultural pollution serve the interests of power, in
particular the interests of élites. These are the social actors who
characteristically play the leading roles in nationalist movements and in the
construction of national identities (Antonnen 2000; Bauman 1992; Conversi
1997: 257; Jacobson-Widding 1983a: 24; Nederveen Pieterse 1996: 31; Sharp
1996: 93; Smith 1986: 178; Verderey 1990: 94). The theme of this chapter is
therefore competition for power within groups, focusing on the ways in
which this conflict is often closely connected with the negotiation and
definition of cultural identity. We shall see that two particularly widespread
and recurrent patterns of internal competition of this sort seem to arise
among people linked by a sense of shared culture. One pattern is linked with
ideas of cultural pollution and the other with notions of cultural
appropriation or piracy – but both, here, occurring within the group itself
rather than across its boundaries. In the context of ethnicity and nationalism,
both patterns originate in a particular conception of the group as a property-
owning individual, and of culture as a collective legacy or inheritance.

Appropriations from Within

In his study of the symbolic and ritual dimensions of modern politics,
Kertzer observes how postwar Italian political parties sought competitively
to be identified with the historical legacy of the wartime Italian resistance
(1988: 70–71). In a rather similar way, the Brazilian military regime of the
1970s sought to bolster its prestige and patriotic legitimacy by appropriating
slogans and songs connected with the national soccer team (Kertzer 1988: 74).
Of course, it has been common throughout history and across cultures for

political authority to carry with it special expressive functions and privileges, and for the holders of power to possess – or to seek – a kind of monopoly of their societies' sacred symbols. An early study of indigenous African political systems contains a classic discussion of the 'mystical values' associated with political office in Africa: the notion that a chief has a special religious relationship with his land, that he is responsible in ritual for its prosperity, sets his power within a framework of moral values (Fortes and Evans-Pritchard 1940: 16–22). Alternatively, in Marxist terms, these sorts of beliefs are regarded as ideological mystifications of power (Bloch 1986; Keesing 1982). But, if political office-holders may use ritual symbolism to legitimise their power, the question this raises is what legitimises their control of these symbolic resources in the first place. From one perspective, the ritual powers and prerogatives of a king or chief are really no different in kind from his sumptuary privileges, his entitlements to wear special regalia or to receive tribute. What need examining are how such exclusive proprietary rights in religious symbolism are themselves established and how they are protected if they are challenged or infringed.

In the community of Kalauna, in Papua New Guinea, each clan has a distinct heritage of 'customs' (Young 1971: 60–69): its own myth cycles, cosmological knowledge, magic, ceremonies or ceremonial functions, ritual paraphernalia and so forth. In Melanesian societies, these sorts of ceremonial and cosmological specialisations typically support ascribed inequalities of rank, albeit only of an incipient kind (Harrison 1990; Morauta 1973).

For example, each local community in the Trobriand Islands owns its own systems of magic. These always include gardening magic, connected closely with the community's territorial rights, and sometimes other types of magic as well. Malinowski observed a tendency for high-ranking subclans to expand into the villages of other descent groups and take over their land rights and magic. The typical strategy is for a woman of high rank to marry into a lower-ranking village, and for her sons and descendants to establish there a new branch of her subclan. In time, the hosts gradually surrender to these honoured incomers the titles to their land and to all their magical powers, and myth is eventually adjusted to legitimise the new status quo (Malinowski 1935: 362–69; 1948: 117–26).

The status of the highest-ranking subclan, the Tabalu, is based on their ownership of the most powerful and feared form of magic, the magic of rain and drought (Powell 1967: 168; see also Malinowski 1922: 66–67; 1935: 83, 328, 362). Malinowski provides strong evidence that the Tabalu subclan settled in their 'capital', the village of Omarakana, in precisely the way I have mentioned, and that the magic of rain and sun had originally been the property of this village's autochthonous subclan. A process of this sort seems to be reflected in myth. The indigenous subclan in Omarakana has a very typical Trobriand origin myth, according to which one of its ancestresses, on her emergence from underground, gave birth to rain and to various animals associated with the magic. But the myth goes on to state that she or her successors later ceded the magic to the Tabalu (Malinowski 1935: 342–43, 347, 367). So myth, as Malinowski points out, is revised to account for the vicissitudes of history. In other words, it seems that the incomers not only acquire their hosts' property in land and magic but take over and adapt the origin myths of their hosts as well. Malinowski speaks of Trobriand subclans as 'owning' their myths, in the sense of being credited with ultimate authority on them (1922: 329), and more recently Weiner has described Trobriand origin myths as 'among the most coveted and valuable forms of knowledge' (1977: 40), and it does seem that, in the processes which Malinowski describes, the control of myth is itself one of the key resources that is surrendered to the immigrant subclan. A series of adjustments are made in the control of land, of magic and of myth, and the transformation of the incomers from outsiders into insiders is simply the restructuring of this total set of material and intellectual property relations.

Malinowski suggests that it is due to the immigrants' higher rank that they are able to appropriate their hosts' hereditary privileges. But, if the high rank of the Tabalu is based in the first place on their possession of the magic of rain and drought, it would surely follow that they in fact acquired their present rank only by gaining ownership of that magic. The processes which Malinowski describes are not, as he seems to have thought, the consequences of pre-existing differences in rank. They are actually processes of competition or negotiation for rank itself, and the differentials in the ownership of magic which are their outcomes are emergent and provisional distinctions of rank.

The characteristics of these sorts of power-conferring possessions as property – however property may be locally defined – emerge particularly clearly when their ownership is in dispute. There have been centralised political systems in which it was perfectly possible to take control of a state by capturing its ritual paraphernalia or ceremonial emblems of government. In ancient China, for instance, a state could be conquered by capturing its art treasures and ritual vessels. For these art collections, very much like the tutelary gods of the Roman cities, represented, and in a sense physically embodied, the autonomy and statehood of each polity (Chang 1983; Yang 1996: 102). Among the eastern Anuak, a Sudanese people, kingship was based, in a rather similar way, on the possession of certain sacred emblems. There was constant rivalry for possession of these heirlooms, which:

> could not be taken from the holder without a fight to the death. This was not a single combat, but a pitched battle between the supporters of the emblem-holder and those of his rival ... To hold the emblems, the most sacred objects that existed in this part of the country, was a matter of prestige for the village where they were kept as well as for the individual holder, and gradually ... more and more villages came to be linked by their rivalry for this prize. (Mair 1962: 65; see also Evans-Pritchard 1940)

In contemporary societies too, political conflict often involves struggles of a similar kind over the control of important collective symbols, whether material or intangible. C. Stewart (1998) describes the differing conceptions of Greek national identity at stake in the disputes between the State and Church in Thessaloniki over the control and ownership of the Rotonda, a major classical monument. Hetherington (1998) shows that the contested control of sacred sites and spaces such as Stonehenge has played an important role in contemporary identity politics in Britain (see also Chippendale 1990).

A similar point is illustrated in Jakubowska's (1990) analysis of the power struggles in Poland during the 1980s between the communist government and the 'Solidarity' opposition movement. At the centre of these processes was a struggle over what Jakubowska calls the moral monopoly (1990: 11) to use the symbols of Polish nationalism: the national colours red and white, the anthem and nationalist religious iconography such as the image of the Black Madonna of Czestochowa (see also Mach 1994). Jakubowska shows that the government's attempts to appropriate these key emblems of Polish identity, and so cloak itself in legitimacy, failed in the end precisely because the majority of the people saw these attempts as illegitimate, as attempts to misappropriate a symbolism that was not the rightful property of the government. Again, if ritual symbolism serves to legitimise political authority, the question this begs is how the political authority's control of this symbolism itself comes to be accepted as legitimate. The case of recent Polish politics, at least, would seem to suggest that deploying the symbols of national identity cannot itself create legitimacy but can only test it, because legitimacy includes – perhaps, in fact, it ultimately is – the very right to employ this symbolism in the first place. There must already be a publicly accepted entitlement to use these symbols before they can be utilised to any political effect.

In short, such would-be monopolisations may very well fail or, indeed, backfire upon those who attempt them. In contemporary party politics, the commonest objects of such attempted usurpations are probably God and the national flag. Before the United States presidential elections of 1992, the Republican candidate, George Bush Senior, appeared to suggest that his party had a closer relationship with God than did the Democratic Party. The result was a stern rebuke from American Church leaders, who warned Bush that God is not a Republican and does not belong to any particular political party.

> God is neutral in this year's presidential election, and the Republican Party's attempt to conscript him into the conservative cause is blasphemous, American church leaders have combined to declare.
>
> God may not even necessarily be an American, the Baptists warned, appealing to all parties to 'refrain from any further attacks based on religion'.
>
> The National Council of Churches, the Baptist Joint Committee on Public Affairs and a third group of ecumenical church leaders have all written to President Bush and the Republican Party to complain that 'the partisan use of God's name tends to breed intolerance and to divide'.
>
> President Bush last week condemned the Democratic Party's platform for leaving out 'three simple letters, G-O-D'. And his party convention earlier this month was marked by the new influence of the Christian Coalition and speeches which warned that the country was facing 'a religious war for the soul of America'.

'We need to be very clear that God belongs to no one side, for we believe that we all belong to God,', 23 church leaders, including President Bush's own religious leader, Bishop Edmond Browning of the Episcopal Church, said in their letter to the White House. (Walker 1992)

This, then, illustrates one way in which an important collective symbol can become a focus of conflict among sections of the same group: namely, when one party attempts to use it for its own advantage in a way which appears to others to be improperly monopolising what is the common property of the whole. In another variation of this pattern, there are situations in which two or more opposed political factions compete for the monopoly of some collective symbols, in a manner reminiscent of the institutionalised rivalry among the eastern Anuak over the emblems of the kingship. Observers of British party politics, for instance, have often noted how the Conservative Party appeared in this way to monopolise cer.....i key icons of British identity during their long period in government from 1979 to 1997. It seemed to many political commentators in the 1980s that the national flag, in particular, had become almost a totemic emblem of the Conservative Party, whose monopoly was given its most powerful and triumphalist reaffirmations at the Party's annual conferences. This monopoly seemed to remain unchallenged until 1995, when the Labour Party set out to appeal to British nationalism at its own conference. A well-known political journalist reflected at the time:

The minutes before the leader of the Conservative Party makes the leader's conference speech are quite a spectacle. Land of Hope and Glory resounds around the conference hall; everywhere Union Jacks are waved unashamedly. There'll be somebody with John Bull whiskers and a Union Jack bowler. As the speech progresses, so the patriotic fervour mounts.

The message is hardly subliminal. The Conservative Party is the party of the nation, the patriot's party. Nor is it just a political fiction. Most members of the Conservative Party think of themselves in these terms. Conservatism, England (but not Scotland and Wales) and the Union are as one.

The British left views the whole affair with cynicism and ridicule – after all, conspicuous patriotism is the last refuge of the scoundrel. But in doing so it has sold the pass. The Conservative Party has appropriated the flag, and in so doing has gained a massive political advantage.

The great Conservative hegemony rests on a number of key icons; owning the flag is one of the most subtle and effective. The message is: Conservatives are the custodians of England, the non-political guardians of the English order. Government and state belong to them.

The truly audacious part of [Labour Party leader] Tony Blair's speech yesterday was that he set out deliberately to begin to capture this ground ...

It is not just enough to establish the case that the Labour Party has changed – it needs to gather around it the legitimacy of the flag and the idea that it speaks for the majority. It is the one nation Labour Party – and if he could get away with it you feel he'd like to see a few Union Jacks waved in the conference hall. Most Labour Party members would probably gag at the prospect, but [for] the Union Jack to join the red rose [a Labour Party emblem] would send an unmistakable message that Labour not only aims to win an election – but to contest territory the Conservatives have made their own ... and to contest it using language and symbols that have so far been the preserve of the Conservatives. (Hutton 1995)

A year and a half later, in May 1997, Labour won a landslide election victory. In many respects, British general elections seem to be won by whichever party is able convincingly to identify itself with certain key emblems of British identity, such as the flag. It is particularly significant that political observers, as one can see, use the language of property and ownership to describe the way in which British political parties contest in this way their associations with key icons of national identity. It is as though these icons were understood to play a role very much like that of the sacred emblems of the eastern Anuak kingship or the ancient Chinese ritual vessels of state.

Pollution from Within

There is, then, a recurring pattern of factional conflict within the nation or ethnic group, in which factions compete to monopolise certain key symbolic attributes of the group or struggle to wrest them from one another. At one level united by a common cultural identity, by a shared allegiance to the same emblems of belonging, the protagonists are divided at another level by rivalry over the control of these symbols.

I want to contrast this with a second common pattern of internal conflict. Here, the goal of one or more of the factions is to replace certain of these symbols and supplant them with others. Let me begin with an example. In 1964 the President of Haiti, François Duvalier, changed the Haitian flag, an event described by Nicholls (1979: 234) as one of the most extraordinary episodes of Duvalier's rule. Duvalier had been trying to impose the new flag since he came to office in 1957, but it took him a further seven years to become powerful enough to do so.

The roots of this dispute go back more than a century and half to 1804, when Dessalines, leader of the struggle against France, proclaimed independence and took the title of Emperor. He adopted an Imperial flag of two vertical bands, one black and one red, with the black placed nearest the mast. He was assassinated in 1806 and Haiti split into two states. One was led by a black general who became King Henry I in 1811, and this monarchy retained the Imperial flag. The other, a republic, adopted a flag of blue and red horizontal stripes.

After the death of King Henry in 1820 and the reunification of Haiti, the republican flag was adopted as the national flag. But it had become associated with mulatto dominance of the political system. The Imperial flag of Dessalines, on the other hand, was associated with blacks and with their political aspirations, and they sought to have it reinstated. So began a long-term struggle over the national flag, a dispute which flared up intermittently for the next century and a half as part of the jockeying for power between the two political factions.

To Duvalier and other black leaders, the flag of Dessalines, founder of independent Haiti, was the sole authentic and legitimate national flag. The story grew up that Dessalines had created it by taking a captured French tricolour and tearing off the white band, an act obviously symbolic of driving out the white French oppressors. He had then changed the blue band to black, to stand for the black people of the nation. The position of the black band next to the mast symbolised the closeness of the blacks to the land and their right to dominate. When Duvalier finally succeeded in restoring the Imperial flag in 1964, it was meant to demonstrate both his own personal dominance and the coming to power of the new élite which he represented (see Nicholls 1979: 33, 78, 213, 234–35).

In a very similar way, after a revolution, the new regime usually seeks, as Weiner (1992: 8) points out, to obliterate all the symbols of the old, for fear that these might serve as a focus for counter-revolution. It was in this spirit that the Bolsheviks renamed St Petersburg 'Leningrad', the French revolutionaries created a new calendar, with new names for the months of the year, and the English Protestants in the Reformation took the Catholic furnishings out of the churches and refitted the interiors in the Puritan style. In effect, the new holders of power are putting their mark or stamp on the institutions of their polity to make these institutions their own. The outlawing of the Mass and the other measures taken to suppress Catholicism during the English Reformation illustrate the same point. All citizens were required by law not only to abjure Catholicism, but to take an oath of allegiance to the king as head of the Church and so acknowledge his exclusive rights to their religious and political loyalties (Hughes 1957: 154–88).

What is usually at stake in situations such as these are competing visions of the group's identity, differing ideological viewpoints, alternative conceptions of the group's history and culture. Among the competing factions and interest groups which a nation or ethnic group encompasses, some inevitably harbour quite divergent views of its identity (Lebovics 1994; Tomlinson 1991: 18). Smith, for instance, discusses the conflict between 'Byzantine' and 'Hellenic' versions of Greek nationalism (1986: 203). Fox, examining the rise of Hindu nationalism in India, shows how the creation of this political ideology involved: 'a struggle through and over cultural beliefs about Indian nationalism. Through this struggle, Hindu nationalism works toward dominance or hegemony over national consciousness. My general proposition is that what may end up as *the* national culture starts out as one contending nationalist ideology among several. No nationalism is natural; they are all constructed through confrontation' (Fox 1990: 63).

Paine, similarly, describes the ways that competing sections of contemporary Israeli society seek to promote their own particular versions of Israeli nationality and culture, their own definitions of 'Jewishness'. In Israel:

'there are groups who enact their lives as though they are living in different Israels from one another. Each group, each "Israel", is an attempt to constitute Jewish identity in Israel. Antagonistic versions of that identity become bastions of ideology' (Paine 1989: 123; see also pp. 127–28). A situation such as this is, in effect, one of competing orthodoxies: different factions within the nation are trying to impose their own representations of the group's identity and to marginalise or exclude others.

Mixed Disputes

There are, then, two particularly commonly recurring varieties of conflict in the cultural politics of the nation and ethnic group. What they have in common is that they are both based on a shared preconception of a group's 'culture' as a kind of collective legacy or patrimony. One is a pattern of conflict over the control or custodianship of this cultural heritage, or of key symbols of it, and involves attempts by one or more factions to usurp or monopolise these symbols in some way. The second is a pattern of conflict over what exactly the group's heritage is: it involves disputes over this cultural legacy's definition. The underlying issue in both of these varieties of factional conflict, an important resource for which the players are implicitly competing in both cases, is clearly people's political allegiances. For a basic assumption they seem to share is that attachments to these enduring symbols express political loyalties. Whoever rightfully owns the key symbols of a group's historical and cultural identity thereby also owns its members' allegiances. Hence the principal actors in these conflicts tend to come from among élites and power-holders.

Of course, both sorts of conflict very commonly occur together. An important arena for this kind of mixed competition has to do with the allocation of prestigious roles in ritual. Communities often define themselves by distinctive and, sometimes, socially highly exclusive rituals (Abner Cohen 1974; A.P. Cohen 1985; Leach 1954). A community staging one of its important ceremonies may, at one level, be expressing its sense of identity and unity. But often this is only outwardly so, and the performance may in fact be preceded by intense power struggles among its performers and organisers. These behind-the-scenes or sometimes open disputes are public tests of the political support each contestant can muster, not only in regard to ritual claims, but in regard to other claims as well, such as to political office or the control of economic resources. A ritual may be intended by the group staging it as a display of solidarity – particularly, perhaps, in relation to outsiders. But it is also a display – perhaps implicit, or perhaps overt and triumphant – of the current state of often changing and contested power relations within the group itself.

Viewed sociologically, these struggles are an integral part of the preparations for the ritual. In a sense, the struggles are an integral preliminary phase of the ritual itself, with a successful performance of the ritual as simply their temporary and provisional resolution. As a means of demarcating group boundaries symbolically, this preparatory phase of internal conflict is as effective and important as any assertions of unity which the ritual may later make.

What I mean is that it is always an insider's right – and often a jealously guarded one – to take part in such disputes. What defines membership in a group is therefore not the entitlement merely to take part in its rituals. Perhaps more importantly, the right to fight and compete for the important roles in these events is itself often a closely guarded prerogative as well, and may be a special privilege reserved for an élite. For example, let us take Abner Cohen's (1980, 1993) study of the Notting Hill Carnival, and its key role in the emergence of West Indian ethnic identity in Britain. In the late 1970s, internal conflicts among its organisers resulted in the formation of two rival organising committees with opposed views of its purpose. One group saw the carnival as non-political, an essentially artistic or cultural festival; another, more openly radical faction wanted its message to be one of protest against racism. This struggle for the right to control and direct it was a contest between competing interest groups within the same ethnic community to determine its meaning, and thus in a sense to shape the definition of West Indian identity in Britain.

Ever since Robertson Smith (1889: 16–17), rituals have often been observed to have a paradoxical character: they seem, as practices, to alter relatively little over history, while the meaning attributed to them is changeable (Pareto 1935: 607; Radcliffe-Brown 1952: 155–57). This constancy of form and variability of interpretation, as Boas (1955 [1928]: 128) called it, has been examined by Bloch (1986) in his study of the history of the Merina circumcision ritual in Madagascar. At one stage, the ritual was carried out by the elders of localised descent groups; with the formation of a powerful state, the symbolically central episode of it became a royal ritual presided over by the king, with descent groups forbidden under penalty of death to perform it. After the conquest of this state by France, it became once more a descent group ritual, but this time functioning as a symbol of resistance to colonialism. But, throughout this long history of political upheaval, during which it served the purposes of a succession of quite different political regimes, movements and ideologies, its basic form remained remarkably unchanged and constant. Like the ritual vessels of the ancient Chinese state, many rituals seem over history to have circulated unchanged and carefully preserved through the hands of many different owners.

The stability of ritual forms and the manipulability of their meanings have also been illustrated by Gajek (1990) in her study of Christmas under the Third Reich. In the late 1930s the Party began a systematic attempt to transform Christmas for propaganda purposes into a Germanic, specifically National Socialist festival and to dissociate it from Christianity and the Church. In contrast to the Merina kings with the circumcision ritual, no attempt was made to turn it into a ceremony of state; the family's rights to celebrate it were left unchanged, and an attempt was made simply to appropriate the 'copyright' with the assistance of bogus 'Germanic' folklore produced by the Ministry of Propaganda. The new version was recognisably the same ritual, with the same basic elements: the family gathering, the decorated tree, the exchange of presents and so forth. But by introducing small modifications to its symbolism, the intention was radically to change its ideological content from a message of peace to one of militaristic nationalism and the duty of self-sacrifice in war. My point is that this attempt to alter the ritual ideologically, to remake its meaning while conserving its form, was clearly an attempt to transfer its institutional associations from the Church to the National Socialist Party: in other words, to redefine the structure of property rights in which the ritual was located.

Kertzer describes how the Party tried also to take over and remake Easter, the traditional marriage ceremony and other rites of passage, as well as appropriating the socialist ritual of May Day. In a rather similar way, the Soviet state, having tried unsuccessfully to suppress traditional Christian rituals, later resorted to appropriating them and trying to remove their Christian content (Kertzer 1988: 45–46, 166–67).

The aim of suppressing or refashioning the rituals of some group in this way is, of course, to integrate or absorb the group by supplanting its symbols of identity with one's own. So, for instance, the Soviet state tried repeatedly to abolish its peoples' religions: not only Christianity, but also Buddhism, Islam, the tribal 'shamanistic' traditions and the rest. The purpose was not merely to destroy. It included the positive aim of replacing the old, disapproved rituals with new, 'secular', officially sanctioned socialist rites designed to express loyalty to the state (Binns 1980; Cheater 1986: 271–78; Lane 1981, 1984).

The Protestant Reformation is a particularly clear case of a struggle of this sort over the interpretation and control of ritual. Many writers on the Reformation have noted its essentially conservative nature (see, for instance, Chadwick 1964: 65). The Reformers saw themselves not as creating a new Church, but as simply returning to scripture and ridding the Church of historical accretions and distortions (McGrath 1988: 3–4). They made certain changes to ritual; but it is significant that the only changes they introduced were to those aspects of ritual that they saw as giving an unjustified status and power to the priesthood. These included the Latin liturgy and the practice of communion in one kind, in which the priest in the Eucharist reserves the chalice for himself and gives only bread to the laity. Above all, the Reformers objected to the conception of the Eucharist as a sacrificial offering performed by the priest, to the notion of the priest, as Weber put it, as 'a magician who performed the miracle of transubstantiation' (1930: 117). The very earliest experimental alterations to this ritual were made in 1521, when Luther's associate Carlstadt said Mass in lay dress and, speaking in German, gave communion in both kinds (Chadwick 1964: 58; Green 1964: 126, 144). If the Reformers were Lévi-Straussian *bricoleurs*, it was clearly not the existing pattern of symbolism they sought to modify, but the structure of property rights regarding it. Their aim was to reorder these property relations radically, while making the fewest possible alterations to the symbolism itself.

The changes they made to ritual were, of course, part of wider reforms in doctrine and Church organisation. Clerical marriage opened up the priesthood to all adult males and followed necessarily from the Reformers' doctrine of the priesthood of the laity – the doctrine that all believers, not only ordained priests, have a priestly vocation. Translations of the Bible into the vernacular attacked the authority of the clergy and the Pope to interpret scripture, by making scripture directly accessible to anyone who was literate. The doctrines of predestination and justification by faith completely subverted the mediatorial powers of the clergy, as did the Reformers' rejection of the notion of purgatory and the system of penances and indulgences based on it. The aim of the Reformers was perhaps summed up succinctly in Luther's assertion that 'what is the common property of all, no individual may arrogate to himself' (quoted in Green 1964: 132). The aim was not in fact to abolish the functions and privileges of the priesthood and papacy, but to redistribute them in such as way as to incorporate them into every individual or, more accurately, into every man: this, I think, is the meaning of Luther's claim that 'we are all priests and there is no difference between us' (quoted in Green 1964: 132; see also McGrath 1988: 141). Ostensibly, the Reformation was a dispute over the means to salvation. But at another level it was a struggle between interest groups sharing the same system of religious symbolism, but having divergent theories of the structure of its proprietorship, which, in turn, implied divergent conceptions of the person. What the Reformers sought was to maintain the existing religion, but to reallocate property rights in it in a radical new way – not only between individuals but, as it were, within the individual as well.

The degree to which the Reformers' version of the Eucharist altered the medieval original or conserved it seems to have reflected the balance between the Reformers' twin goals of establishing an identity distinct from the medieval church, and establishing a legitimacy based on continuity with the past. We know that each side regarded the other's variant of the ritual as illegitimate and sought to eradicate it and impose its own. The participants regarded these as utterly different and opposed sets of ritual practices and doctrines whose irreconcilability could only end with one emerging hegemonic. They seem, in other words, to have viewed their conflict as one of competing orthodoxies, each aiming to eliminate the other.

But objectively, the differences between the medieval and Reformers' versions of the Eucharist were small. In fact, a case could be made for considering them as the 'same' ritual, and the conflict as a struggle for the custodianship or proprietary control of this shared cultural object (see Harrison 1992). But the Eucharist, perhaps like most rituals, is best regarded as actually a class or family of symbolic objects sharing both resemblances and differences. Regarding the differences – that is, those aspects of the medieval ritual they sought to alter – the Reformers aimed at eliminating the rival variants. But in relation to the commonalities – those aspects of the ritual the Reformers conserved – their strategy was proprietary. That is, their aim was to be acknowledged the only true custodians of Christianity's key sacramental ritual.

At one level, then, competing factions which attribute competing 'meanings' to a ritual are making assertions about its ownership or control, about access to privileged roles in the event and to the authority these roles confer. In other words, they are putting forward conflicting theories of the proprietorship of the ritual. At the same time, they are often also, in doing so, making conflicting assertions about the core values and beliefs that define the ethnic group or nation that practises the ritual, and are offering alternative visions of the group's historical identity.

Conclusion: the Politics of Heritage

Clearly, it is common for a nation or ethnic group to harbour several competing representations of its history, culture and traditions. And there seems to be no necessity for any overall agreement within the group over which of these various versions is definitive. Moreover, factions may compete with one another for some kind of privileged association with core symbols of the group's historical or cultural identity (or with symbols they assert to be central in this way). Here too, there need be no overall consensus. Indeed, it seems that these are typically both important focuses of cultural politics among élites jockeying for power, prestige and legitimacy.

A group thereby has internal cultural boundaries, just as it has external ones. And both are constructed in very much the same way: that is, through the use of discourses of cultural pollution and appropriation. The more closely we look at any group that claims to possess a common 'culture', the more it reveals itself to be composed of factions and subfactions contesting its internal cultural boundaries in much the same way as occurs with contested boundaries between groups. An internal faction or interest group may appear to its rivals to be making unwarranted attempts to monopolise part of the group's cultural heritage. Or it may appear to be seeking to redefine the group's identity in ways that other factions oppose. In other words, in their sectional struggles, competing actors can represent cultural piracy and pollution as occurring from within.

These competing factions can continue to view themselves as belonging to one such group and not to two or more only for so long as a consensus exists among them that one, and only one, definitive version of their historical identity does exist in principle. An ethnic group or ethnonation thus seems to be a collectivity whose members accept, minimally, that they constitute a single collective individual, possessing no more than one bounded cultural and historical heritage. But they may not necessarily agree on which particular heritage they share in this way or on which factions or fractions (if any) may have specially close associations with it. If this fundamental premise is abandoned, the group is no longer one group – at least in the eyes of some of its members – but has become two or more.

9

Identity as a Scarce Resource

Self-definition does not occur in a vacuum, but in a world already defined. As such it invariably fragments the larger identity space of which its subjects were previously a part. (Friedman 1992: 837)

Cultural Boundaries and Social Boundaries: Élites and Social Exclusion

My argument raises the problem of identifying the situations in which social groups and actors employ particular kinds of cultural boundary discourses. It is important to discover why, for instance, communities may be preoccupied with perceptions of cultural pollution in some circumstances or in relation to certain kinds of cultural Others, and why they sometimes mobilise themselves collectively through discourses of cultural appropriation instead (or employ both sorts of discursive imagery together, or perhaps even some other kinds).

To begin to answer these questions, I return to the distinction I drew in Chapter 7 between cultural and social boundaries. Cultural boundary rhetorics provide ideological grounds on which social boundaries and distinctions are drawn. That is, cultural boundaries are discursive devices with which actors try, successfully or otherwise, to convince others of the truth of their perceptions and definitions of certain social divisions. Rhetorics of cultural pollution portray insiders as those who faithfully honour and uphold the group's traditions, customs and doctrines, while outsiders are those who follow other ways, deemed inferior and defiling. Rhetorics of cultural appropriation, on the other hand, define insiders as those uniquely privileged to reproduce the group's traditions, customs and beliefs; outsiders are defined as such by being excluded from these prized entitlements. In one case, the demarcation between in-group and out-group is drawn in the idiom of cultural purity, and in the other it is drawn in the idiom of cultural ownership.

Durkheim (1976 [1912]) pointed out long ago that symbols of collectivities tend to be attributed with certain qualities of sacredness by their members.

And of course the key distinguishing symbolic attributes of many ethnic groups have an explicitly religious character or, indeed, actually are religious confessions. But it seems that people can construe the sacred in this context in two rather different ways, depending on the kinds of cultural boundaries they imagine. On the one hand, the members of an ethnoreligious community may view themselves as obliged, above all, ιο exclude outsiders from their faith, perhaps even keeping secret much of their system of religious observances and beliefs. The Druze people of Lebanon exemplify this pattern. Originating in the eleventh century, they are an ethnic community based on endogamy, secrecy and exclusion, practising an hereditary religion (Hitti 1928; Smith 1986: 111–12, 123).

The principal concern of some other ethnoreligious groups, on the other hand, is to keep their faith pure, their religious practices and doctrines uncontaminated by foreign influences. The Old Order Amish communities of North America illustrate this pattern. For them, a key religious duty is to reject all that is worldly, modern and thus alien (Hostetler 1968). Here, it is ideas of the purity, rather than the exclusivity, of practice and belief that play the key role in the construction of ethnoreligious identity.

The difference between these two understandings of the sacred reveals itself most clearly in attitudes to evangelisation. It seems perfectly natural to purity-focused ethnoreligious communities to seek out converts or even to feel that they have a sacred duty to spread their faith. From this viewpoint, a religion may be understood by its devotees to be enhanced by being more widely shared. But to groups which build their identities on processes of exclusion, the mysteries of one's faith are a precious resource not to be given away to the unworthy. Evangelising would be a betrayal or senseless desecration of them. To disseminate one's religion freely is only to diminish and devalue it (see Harrison 1995b). Thus the two rhetorics of identity lead to two rather different ways of conceptualising the sacred.

But both kinds of preoccupation with the integrity of the cultural boundaries of one's group seem to reflect a preoccupation with the integrity of its social boundaries – with limiting or regulating the movement of insiders outwards, or of outsiders inwards, or both. Some groups seem to be concerned principally with the defection or loss of personnel. This is the type of collectivity that Douglas (1993) calls a sectarian or 'enclave' culture: one whose members define themselves by dissidence or opposition to a surrounding cultural majority (see also Castile and Kushner 1981). Douglas suggests that the characteristic preoccupation of such a community is 'leakage of members' (1993: 51). Presumably, such leakage need not necessarily involve actual outmigrations or physical departures. It is rather a matter of the transformation of identity, a re-definition of social affiliation. Such a group seeks above all to resist the assimilation of its members into the majority society outside. Its principal concerns in relation to its cultural identity, I would suggest, will stress pollution. French nationalism is of this type, with its marked sense of the dangers of pollution by American or Anglo-American culture. The fears among American conservatives in the 1950s of the suborning of their nation by 'Communism' were of the same type, as are the anxieties of the Old Order Amish regarding the corruption of their youth by American modernity. It is the perceived inward spread of foreign or alien ideas and practices that poses the key threat.

Of course, movements of cultural practices and meanings accompany movements and interactions of populations; a group trying to keep out foreign cultural practices or ideas may try to keep out foreign people as well, and vice versa. Hence, for example, the attempts by the isolationist rulers of seventeenth-century Japan to rid their country of Western influences. The measures they took included banning foreign books, giving up the use of firearms in warfare, outlawing Christianity after 1616, and closing the country to missionaries and other foreigners in 1636 (Brown 1955: 42–47; Perrin 1979). They viewed Christianity as a focus of political dissent in their country, a subversive threat to stability and to their own power (Brown 1955: 42–47).

Culturally enclaved groups, then, may indeed seek to exclude outsiders. But they will portray them as unassimilable, as bearers of an alien lifestyle which they cannot or will not abandon and which threatens to spread to their own members. The point is that to groups such as these, it is the intrusion of foreign culture that represents the ultimate threat, whether or not it is accompanied by any incursions of foreign personnel.

Let us now imagine the second, contrasting type of group. Here, what is feared most is not the loss of members, but the incursion of outsiders. The primary concern of such a group is with preventing non-members from crossing, not necessarily its territorial boundaries (if indeed the group has such boundaries), but, crucially, its social boundaries. This is the pattern exemplified by the Druze, and by the Basque nationalists discussed earlier. A group of this sort seeks above all to prevent outsiders from assimilating into it (by marriage, by adoption of the group's lifestyle, language or religion or by some other means of affiliation). This is probably the most basic situation in which groups take steps to restrict or monopolise their symbolic practices: namely, when their members wish to keep unwelcome outsiders from claiming membership (or, indeed, to drive out members no longer wanted).

Of course, many kinds of collectivities besides ethnic groups and nations employ emblems of identity and badges of membership. In an earlier chapter, I discussed the use of logos, names and emblems by business corporations to regulate who may and may not trade under their identities. Many sorts of social groups have formal or ...formal rules about the use of their identity symbols and may protect them as assiduously as Harrods does its trademark. Rights to bear or use these emblems may be conferred when new members join the group, perhaps in a rite of passage. The entitlements may then be revoked with similar formality if they leave.

Ballard, for instance, describes the way that motor cycle clubs in Northern Ireland mark themselves off from one another with distinctive styles of dress and other insignia. The use of a club's insignia or 'colours' is the exclusive right of its members; members who leave must cease using them, a rule which can cause a little inconvenience for members who have had these emblems tattooed on them: 'Members who leave amicably have their club tattoos endorsed with their dates of membership. Those leaving as the result of a dispute generally have a certain length of time in which to have any tattoos reflecting club membership covered or removed' (Ballard 1998: 123).

With social groups such as these, the role of badges of identity is to distinguish counterfeit and genuine members, rather than counterfeit and genuine products. To have the power to regulate or restrict the reproduction of one's group's symbolic practices is to be able to define who is and is not a member, who does and does not really belong to one's group, who may or may not rightfully claim to share its identity. Outsiders may have various motives for wishing to adopt a group's practices and thus claim membership. A *nouveau riche* may feel that his new-found aristocratic lifestyle expresses his authentic inner self; the bank robber may view the clerical dog-collar he sports as just a convenient disguise; the counterfeiter selling cheap goods in imitation of famous brand names is concerned merely with quick profit. But, whatever the motive, the aim is essentially the same: to alter, permanently or temporarily, the presentation of one's identity, discarding or suppressing one identity and assuming the signs of another, replicating it as persuasively as possible.

These are actions against which many groups perceive a need to protect themselves if they see those whom they wish to exclude trying to misrepresent themselves as insiders. A fundamental vulnerability of emblems of identity is that they can be imitated or adopted by people with no right to them. Hence many groups have informal ways of protecting their identity or its symbols from piracy. Gambetta, discussing the use of these kinds of signs among organisations such as the Mafia, argues that one common device is to make the emblems in some way costly to acquire and difficult to forge (1991: 70). His theory explains, among other things, why induction into privileged groups so often involves undergoing some kind of painful mutilation. It may be relatively easy for someone to sport a regimental tie to which he is not entitled. But to pass as a *yakuza* in Japan is more costly. Severed fingers and whole-body tattoos are badges of identity likely to discourage all but the most determined impostors.

Obviously, the more exclusive an ethnic group or category is or the more privileged it is in some way, the more concerned its members are likely to be with restricting the use of their symbolic practices, because the more likely these identity symbols are to attract unwelcome imitation. A group of this kind will probably be strongly preoccupied with drawing distinctions between insiders and outsiders, current members and ex-members, or between genuine members and pretenders who falsely assume its trappings, and with trying to ensure that these trappings remain its exclusive property.

It hardly needs pointing out that ethnically defined élites characteristically have strong vested interests in preventing their distinctive habits from being copied and their identity thereby reproduced by lower-placed groups and individuals intent on status-climbing. A well-known example is the processes of caste-climbing and Sanskritisation in India, in which – if we follow those who interpret caste as comprised of ethnic groups or corporate communities – lower-placed groups move up the caste system by taking on the lifestyle and rituals of a higher caste, often in the face of intense opposition from other groups (Bailey 1970: 95–100; Kertzer 1988: 112–13; Srinivas 1952: 24–31).

It is unnecessary to review in any detail here the diverse practices which élites employ to index their status, and the equally diverse ways in which they try to protect their practices from reproduction by outsiders (see Parkin 1979). Élites may keep a monopoly of education, focused perhaps on exclusive access to a scriptural or classical language (Bourdieu and Passeron 1977; Gellner 1983: 2–18). They may adopt exclusive leisure patterns priced beyond the means of the lower placed, or reserve for themselves the use of special foods, clothing and so forth by means of direct sumptuary laws (Miller 1987: 135–36; Veblen 1934).

They may simply react with naked violence to attempts to copy their practices. Kuper (1973), for example, examines the political significance of clothing in southern Africa during the colonial period. Whites had ambivalent attitudes towards African dress. Missions, particularly, disapproved strongly of 'native clothing' and sought to make their converts adopt a version of European attire. But, on the other hand, many whites were resentful of Africans who presumed to wear 'fashionable' clothing. Indeed, Kuper mentions a case in South Africa in 1942 of a black beaten to death by whites simply for being too well-dressed 'for a Kafir'. Again, we see that 'appropriation' exists very much in the eye of the beholder. While some whites viewed the adoption of European dress by blacks as a trespass on their privileges, some blacks viewed such dress (or certain forms of it) as having been imposed on them by whites as an act of domination. Special 'Africans only' uniforms were developed for some occupations: for instance, a shirt, pair of shorts and an apron for domestic servants, a uniform which many blacks, of course, found highly demeaning. So far as one can tell, the aim seems to have been to impose on Africans a dress code which was similar to whites, but not too similar; similar enough to express the political assimilation of blacks, but not so similar as to suggest equality (see also Evenson and Trayte 1999: 96–97).

A group seeking to prevent outsiders from assimilating is likely, in defining its cultural boundaries, to emphasise the threat of piracy. Its social boundaries, on the other hand, will tend to stress dangers of pollution, classifying outsiders as defiling. As one can see, then, the relationship between cultural and social boundaries is a close one. Each involves discourses of pollution and of piracy, a concern with regulating inward and outward flows either of cultural symbols or of personnel. But they seem related by a kind of inversion in a certain sense. For, the more concerned a group is with keeping its members in, the more it is likely to be preoccupied with keeping foreign culture out. And, conversely, the more it is concerned with keeping non-members out, the more preoccupied it tends to be with keeping its own indigenous culture in.

Of course, a group may very well employ both kinds of discursive imagery simultaneously. Indeed, a particularly common way of seeking to justify the exclusion of immigrant or minority groups is to represent them both as bearers of a foreign culture and as usurpers of national identity, not truly entitled to participate in the host nation's culture. Krohn-Hansen shows how the majority in Santo Domingo represent blacks in this way, both as fraudulent Dominicans and as sources of pollution at the same time:

> Dominican history manifests a process where the state and many citizens classified some mixtures, or embodiments of 'penetration from the outside', as so dangerous sources of pollution and moral degeneration that they once and for all deprived them of rights to claim true 'Dominicanness' ... 'Blacks on Dominican territory' represented an affront for the Dominican state. We have seen that the Dominican Republic has a history of cheating (at least a part of) its black citizens of their real Dominicanness. The state symbolically and violently turned black Dominicans in 'false Dominicans' or 'fictive Dominicans' (by calling them 'Haitians', by accusing them of unlawfully carrying Dominican identity cards, and by expelling them). (Krohn-Hansen 2001: 186)

Clearly, such conceptions can place immigrant or minority communities in a powerful double bind. If they try to maintain distinctive lifestyles of their own, they can be categorised as culturally alien. On the other hand, if they seek to assimilate they can be categorised as impostors, pretenders to a national identity to which they have no right

Resistance and Subversion

One common situation, then, in which the members of a group may employ discourses of cultural piracy is when they perceive themselves to be confronted with a certain kind of appropriation: namely, when outsiders try – or are perceived as trying – to assimilate into their group or to pass themselves off as members of it. This is often, but by no means exclusively, a problem faced by privileged or dominant groups. Their members may find themselves, or imagine themselves, beleaguered by unwelcome outsiders aspiring, so to speak, to the wholesale reproduction of their identity, to the adoption of their lifestyle and the internalisation of their own norms, values and beliefs.

But there are a number of other situations in which notions of cultural piracy come into play in the construction of collective identity. Let us now imagine a second variety of appropriation. This also typically involves subordinates copying practices associated with privilege and power, but in this case their aim is to distance or dissociate themselves from the holders of power, to accentuate the social barriers between themselves and those who dominate them, rather than to remove or cross such barriers. We might envisage this as comprising acts of subversion, defiance and resistance, in which the marginalised seek to adopt the practices of the powerful in such a way as to challenge or undermine their dominance.

Studies of such processes tend to employ the term 'appropriation' as a key analytical notion, suggesting an active process in which social actors borrow cultural symbols from others in such a way as to give these symbols an alternative, and perhaps contrary, meaning, adapting them to their own purposes and to their own perceived advantage. This is especially the case when subordinate groups adopt symbols and practices from dominant groups. Appropriation, in this sense, is cultural diffusion seen (as it must be) in the context of power relationships.

Hebdige (1979) examines processes of very much this sort in his study of postwar British youth subcultures. He argues that all of these subcultures defined themselves largely through processes of *bricolage* in which they 'appropriated' signs from mainstream culture and altered – indeed, subverted – their meaning by using them in deliberately provocative and deviant ways (Hebdige 1979: 102–6; see also Hall and Jefferson 1976).

Comaroff (1985) draws partly on Hebdige's work in her study of the Christian syncretic groups known as the Churches of Zion among the Tshidi in southern Africa. She argues that the Zionist churches appropriated 'core signs from Protestant orthodoxy and the secular culture which bore it' (Comaroff 1985: 197), adopting into their ritual repertoire elements of European colonial culture, such as modes of dress and uniform, as a way of both imitating and challenging the colonial power. Some Zionist churches, for instance, draw on Anglican ecclesiastical dress for their ritual attire: costumes for men include cloaks and staffs, while the women wear bishop's mitres, coloured bright green. In this way, Zionist dress 'appropriates select signs of colonial dominance, turning historical symbols of oppression into dynamic forces of transcendence' (Comaroff 1985: 225).

Several other recent studies of religious syncretism adopt this sort of perspective, in which subaltern or minority groups are seen to draw on the symbols of religious or political authority and to distort them in such a way as to create identities that oppose or challenge this authority. Meyer, for instance, in a study of African Protestantism, speaks of the way that 'indigenous interpretations of Christianity are not *given* by the mission, but *made* by converts themselves in a process of appropriation (often against the meanings missionaries intended to evoke)' (1994: 61). Similarly, Kempf interprets a syncretic cult among the Yawing in New Guinea as constructed through a 'subversive' copying of elements of the colonial culture and religion. For instance, the cult has appropriated the image of the Crucifixion, but refashioned it into an symbol of the male initiation ceremony in which the cult's youths are circumcised; Christ on the cross represents a Yawing novice suffering an initiatory ordeal (Kempf 1994: 120, 122).

At their most extreme, processes of this sort take the form of satirical or parodic appropriations of some other (usually dominant) group's symbols, actions likely to be perceived by the dominant group as a travesty or desecration of its symbols of authority and prestige. Hogbin describes how the men of Wogeo, in New Guinea, can do little except complain among themselves as their womenfolk perform a defiant and mocking pantomime of the men's own secret initiation rites, a subject on which the women are supposed to be quite ignorant (1970: 131, 135). Some groups react punitively or violently to perceived abuses of their identity symbols: witness the criminal penalties in some countries for 'disrespect' to the national flag (see Firth 1973). There are close analogues here with the way powerful business corporations react to mocking or disrespectful uses of their trademarks, claiming that such acts 'diminish' their marks' commercial value.

The Appropriation and Assimilation of Minorities

The examples I have just given can be summed up very broadly as attempts by the relatively powerless to appropriate the symbolic appurtenances of the powerful. Now I would like to turn to the opposite extreme, to situations in which the power relations are reversed, and the privileged or superordinate seek to appropriate the ethnic practices of the subordinate. These are situations in which majority groups borrow from minority cultures, or are perceived as doing so by these minority groups.

A recent development in anthropology and some related disciplines is the appearance of a growing literature on what has come to be known as 'cultural appropriation'. This term refers to a broad range of processes having to do with contested cultural borrowings and imitations, with attempts to appropriate and monopolise ethnic identities and their symbols, and with struggles across ethnic boundaries for the control of heritage and cultural property (M.F.T. Brown 1998; Coombe 1998; Root 1996; Ziff and Rao 1997). It covers all the variety of ways in which the cultural knowledge, traditions and identities of minority peoples can appear to be exploited by outsiders. Here, I can do no more than draw briefly on some the major studies in this emergent field (M.F.T. Brown 1998; Coombe 1998; Root 1996; Ziff and Rao 1997).

One way in which the cultural or subcultural identities of ethnic minority groups can be appropriated and suffer what I earlier called mimetic injury is through processes of commoditisation and the operation of markets in cultural products (see, for example, Root 1996; Ziff and Rao 1997). Hebdige argues that youth subcultures are 'incorporated', as he calls it, by mainstream society through the commoditisation of subcultural signs such as dress and music (1979: 92–96). These are turned into mass-produced commercial objects and so 'become codified, made comprehensible, rendered at once public property and profitable merchandise' (Hebdige 1979: 96; see also O'Donnell 1981: 371). They are assimilated by the mainstream fashion industry or popular music industry by the same processes of commoditisation that incorporate

Aboriginal art into mainstream Australian culture in the form of goods such as T-shirts bearing 'Aboriginal' designs.

Much of the literature on cultural appropriation is concerned with this kind of commercial exploitation of minority cultures. Discussion has tended to focus principally on the commoditisation of the graphic arts, music and pharmacological knowledge of indigenous cultures (Posey 1990; Ziff and Rao 1997). In North America, a number of recent studies discuss the growing tendency of Native American communities to defend what they view as their cultural heritage from use or abuse for commercial purposes by outsiders (M.F.T. Brown 1998; Coombe 1998: 199–204; 236–41; Root 1996: 87–97). Increasingly, indigenous peoples and their supporters seek to protect such commercially valuable aspects of their cultural heritage with intellectual property law. A related development is the growing resistance which some communities seem to be starting to show to the unauthorised use of their cultural imagery in corporate advertising and publicity and the use of Native American proper names as commercial trademarks. Two recent examples are the action brought by the Lakota against a beer distributor over the use of the name Crazy Horse as a trademark (Coombe 1998: 199–204; Newton 1997) and the damages sought by a Pueblo community for the unlicensed use of their sun symbol as an emblem by the state of New Mexico (M.F.T. Brown 1998: 197; see also Castile 1996).

Minority groups may often perceive themselves as having to resist attempts not only by commercial interests, but also by other agencies – the state or a powerful majority, for instance – to co-opt their identity symbols. According to Brown, some of the harshest criticisms of cultural appropriation have come from Native Americans objecting to what they perceive as the misappropriation – indeed, travesty and theft – of their traditional religious ceremonies and beliefs by white middle class practitioners of 'New Age' spirituality: '[N]ative religious leaders express horror at the monstrous cloning of their visions of the sacred. For them, the New Age is a kind of doppelganger, an evil imitation close enough to the real thing to upset the delicate balance of spiritual power maintained by Indian ritual specialists' (M.F.T. Brown 1998: 201; see also Root 1996: 87–106).

These leaders do not welcome attempts by outsiders to identify with them. They view ethnic chic as caricaturing and devaluing their culture and an unwarranted encroachment on it. Clearly, it is by no means only powerful élites who attract unwelcome imitation, and seek social closure and exclusion. As we saw with the Mormons in an earlier chapter, minority groups can view sympathetic and well-meaning members of the majority identifying with them as posing a threat to their cultural distinctiveness. An issue particularly close to anthropologists, of course, is the vulnerability of their own discipline to being represented as a modality of just this sort of sympathetic cultural appropriation. Some of the communities they study seek to assert proprietary rights over the results of scholarly research: to seek to control or restrict access to field notes, photographs and other ethnographic records, to repatriate museum artefacts, and so forth. The South Pacific nation of Vanuatu, after independence, banned all foreign researchers in the humanities for a number of years, on the grounds that Vanuatu culture is national property and may therefore only be studied by its own citizens (Bolton 1999: 4).

A debate in the field of literature, with close parallels to the debates on ethnographic writing within anthropology, concerns the appropriation of authorial 'voice': the issue of whether it is acceptable for white novelists, for instance, to adopt ethnic minority personae in their writing and thus appear to speak for minority groups to which they do not belong (Coombe 1997; Hart 1997). Again, attempts by members of wealthy and privileged majorities to identify with the ethnic Other are not always welcomed.

Some minorities view themselves as already having had important symbols of their identity appropriated by the majority or by the state. Handler (1988), for instance, examines perceptions of this sort in his study of the cultural politics of Quebec nationalism. To the nationalists, an essential part of establishing Quebec as an independent nation was the reclamation of Quebec's cultural property from the control, as they saw it, of the Canadian state. The nationalists perceived the Canadian federal government as having purloined Quebec's *patrimoine*, or cultural patrimony, as having illegitimately represented it as part of an encompassing 'Canadian' heritage and as having often underlined these misappropriations by housing objects which the nationalists considered part of Quebec's heritage in federal museums outside the province of Quebec. To Quebec nationalists, these actions were part of the federal government's wrongful denial of Quebec's nationhood. As we saw, Basque nationalism under Arana viewed the Basque language as vulnerable to being suborned and appropriated by the Spanish state in very much this way.

Again, it is important to remember that the kinds of boundary transgressions which these sorts of discourses portray are not purely imaginary. Groups really do copy cultural symbols and practices from each other, sometimes – as we have seen – in politically charged ways that can quite properly be described as appropriative. Just as obviously, they sometimes actually do try to suppress the cultural practices of others. They may try to impose their own practices, as happens when one group forcibly converts or assimilates another. Majorities may impose special markers of stigmatised or outcaste identity on minorities, as when European Jews in the Middle Ages were forced to wear special distinguishing dress and badges (Smith 1986: 117). A curious variation of this occurred in the apartheid system in South Africa, which tried to create an exclusively African-language education system for Blacks on the pretext of giving them equality:

> [A]n integral part of this policy was not to suppress the African languages ... but to *encourage* them, and to deny Africans access to Afrikaans and, especially, English. This was part of a policy to retribalize all Africans into separate (and isolated) ethnic groups, a policy which can be interpreted as being part of a 'divide-

and-rule' strategy. The Bantu Education Department has as its stated aim the education of all Africans in their mother tongue. Because this was to be education *in their mother tongue alone*, many of the Africans did not regard this as a valuable democratic right, but rather as an attempt to isolate them from each other, from the ruling elite, from possibilities of advancement, and from international literature and other contacts. (Trudgill 1974: 144–45; italics in the original)

In other words, Apartheid aimed to suppress the cultural and political aspirations of Blacks by forcing on them what it claimed were their own cultural forms. My point is that notions of cultural piracy and pollution are not simply fantasy constructs. They are grounded in reality and correspond to processes of cultural politics which actually occur.

Innumerable examples also spring to mind of ethnic groups seeking aggressively to promulgate their own religious, linguistic or other practices, imposing them even by force on unwilling outsiders. Smith seems to have had groups of this sort in mind when he sought to explain why some peoples have been able to maintain a distinctive cultural identity for many centuries without a state, a homeland or even, in some cases, a common language. He suggests that the reasons may lie in the way some ethnic groups possess an ideology of ethnic election, a strong collective sense of being a chosen people.

[L]ong-term ethnic survival depends, in the first place, on the active cultivation by specialists and others of a heightened sense of collective distinctiveness and mission. The members of an ethnic community must be made to feel, not only that they form a single 'super-family', but that their historic community is unique, that they possess what Max Weber called 'irreplaceable culture values', that their heritage must be preserved against inner corruption and external control, and that the community has a sacred duty to extend its cultural values to outsiders. Persians, Armenians, Poles, Russians, Chinese, Koreans, Japanese, Americans, Irish, English and French, to name but a few, have all cultivated this sense of uniqueness and mission by nurturing ethnic values and traditions, through myths of distant origins and symbols and memories of a golden age of former glory. (Smith 1996: 189)

A group of this sort may envisage its boundaries as essentially a moving frontier, continually expanding and incorporating ever more outsiders. Groups encountering such aggressively expansionist, assimilationist, even culturally imperialist, forms of collective identity are perhaps likely to react by enclosing themselves in cultural boundaries which stress pollution.

One can also think of many examples of groups which have appeared highly avaricious culturally, attributing foreign ways with considerable prestige value and adopting them eagerly (see, for instance, Seeger 1987; Tomlinson 1991: 92–94). As we saw in an earlier chapter, both the Romans of the Republic and the indigenous peoples of the American north-west coast appropriated the religious rituals of those whom they defeated in warfare, viewing violent contact with these cultural Others as an opportunity to acquire prestigious trophies from them. Those whom they encounter are perhaps most likely to stress ideas of piracy in defining the cultural boundaries by which they seek to keep themselves distinct from such powerfully acquisitive groups.

Governments, as well, do quite overtly sometimes try to appropriate minority cultures within their borders as deliberate state policy in very much the way imagined by the Basque nationalist Arana. This has often been the fate of carnival in nations with minorities that have this tradition, as the authorities struggle to put these often unruly and rebellious events under some semblance of official control (Sheriff 1999; J. Stewart 1986).

A process of a similar kind happened in Turkey as a result of the government's failure during the 1990s to suppress Kurdish nationalism. Yoruk (1997: 124, 132) describes how support for autonomy was so overwhelming among the Kurdish minority by 1995 that the government was forced to change tactics. Deciding that it could not realistically hope to suppress Kurdish identity, it attempted instead to appropriate key symbols of it: it declared that the Kurdish colours (red, yellow and green) – the wearing of which was at the time illegal – were henceforth more than merely permitted but were actually the traditional Turkish colours. Similarly, the government announced that the Kurdish new year festival, Newroz, was actually a traditional Turkish custom, to be henceforth celebrated officially under the name Nevruz as a national Turkish holiday. The first celebration of the new, official, government-controlled Nevruz took place in 1996, accompanied by military parades, while the state security forces took exceptional measures to prevent any celebration of Newroz. In effect, the goal of the Turkish state was no longer to eliminate Kurdish ethnicity, but to redefine it as part of the greater Turkish whole, and to claim for itself the role of perpetuating it in this appropriated form.

Generalising from this case, one might suggest that this type of appropriation occurs when one group tries to assimilate or subordinate another, but is unable to suppress or eradicate the other's identity; the resort is to appropriate the symbolic practices of the other, and so redefine its own identity in such a way as to incorporate these practices. The Turkish majority, or the state representing it, sought to assimilate the Kurds, not by altering the Kurds' identity, but by altering and redefining Turkishness in such a way as to incorporate Kurdish identity and its symbols: unable to make the minority resemble itself, it had to make itself resemble the minority.

Taken together, the examples I have mentioned point to an increasing resistance by many indigenous communities to perceived appropriations of their cultures by outsiders, perceptions which to some degree involve the reification of cultural 'heritage' as a form of property. Coombe is perhaps right to see this tendency as part of a more general postmodern process of enclosure, as she calls it, of the intellectual commons: the progressive erosion of a public domain of culture by the increasing privatisation and commoditisation of all kinds of cultural imagery and information (1998: 53).

M.F.T. Brown (1998) very usefully examines radical proposals made by some indigenous activists and their supporters to expand the legal recognition and protection of cultural property rights by means of new extensions or analogues of the law of copyright. Conceivably, such legislation might give ethnic communities proprietary rights, for example, in their religious knowledge or ceremonies. As Brown points out, one of the problems with such proposals is their assumption that every particular ceremony, myth or religious symbol 'belongs' unambiguously to such-and-such a culture, and that people too are always ethnically categorisable in exactly the same unequivocal way. To my mind, an important part of the significance of these proposals is their role in the rhetoric of contemporary identity politics: they are, at least in part, assertions of rigid cultural boundaries, and thus of unambiguous – if not reified and essentialised – ethnic identities (see Harrison 1999b).

In asserting these identities, indigenous minority cultures are perhaps likely to employ discourses of cultural appropriation to the extent that their governments no longer pursue overtly assimilationist policies towards them. Indeed, minority groups in many nations clearly perceive cultural appropriation as just as great a threat as cultural assimilation, if not a greater one, to their cultural continuity and distinctiveness. I have already given one example: namely, the case of the New Zealand sheep farming communities and their perceived misappropriations of Maori self-representations of indigeneity. A similar case, described by Whittaker (1994), concerns Ayers Rock, the famous landmark and tourist attraction in Australia and the best-known Aboriginal sacred site.

In 1985, the Australian government transferred the Rock to Aboriginal ownership, amidst intense and protracted controversy in the Australian media. During this period the Rock had became an important focus of campaigns for Aboriginal land rights generally, and indeed an equally important focus of White opposition to such rights. Aboriginal land claims seek legitimacy partly by appeals to the 'sacredness' of the landscape in traditional Aboriginal religion. Some white Australians were, and are, highly sceptical of such claims (see Maddock 1998: 2). But, as Whittaker shows, a particularly interesting aspect of this dispute is the way in which some sections of the white Australian population began to change tactics: rather than try to deny Aboriginal claims, they began in effect to imitate elements of Aboriginal religious discourse themselves, generating their own representations of the Rock's 'sacredness' to Whites. Their manoeuvre, as Whittaker puts it, was: 'to construct sacredness for "all-Australians," or more specifically, for white Australians. This reified spirituality making the Rock a mecca, a site of pilgrimage, a locus of initiation, a totemic icon, and a place to replenish the spirit and commune with the universe and ultimate, lays a claim beyond the reach of dispute' (1994: 328). In other words, these whites sought to emulate the language of Aboriginal land claims because they knew that supporters of Aboriginal land rights could not challenge such a language without undermining their own claims. Opponents of Aboriginal land rights could thus acknowledge that the Rock is sacred to Aborigines and accept such claims to sacredness as incontestable, merely claiming that the Rock is not specially or exclusively sacred to Aborigines; it is sacred in much the same way to white Australians as well, and thus has a very similar spiritual significance for the whole nation.

This strategy represents an interesting shift in the grounds on which Aboriginal land rights have been opposed historically. In the past, the state's refusal of land rights to Aborigines was justified on the grounds of the supposed primitiveness of their religion and cultural attitudes to land. Australian settlers pointed to Aboriginal conceptions of the timeless and unchanging 'Dreamtime' – as they conceived it – contrasting it unfavourably to their own beliefs in progress (see Wolfe 1991). Now, rather than appear hostile to Aboriginal religious beliefs, opponents of land rights are perhaps just as likely to profess, quite the opposite, an ostensible support for them, claiming that whites too share the same kinds of deep spiritual ties to the land.

One factor, then, influencing the kinds of cultural boundary discourses groups employ in defining and defending their identities seems to be the nature of their external political environment. To the extent that they (perhaps quite accurately) perceive the policy of the majority as hostile and assimilationist, minority groups seeking to preserve a distinctive identity for themselves are likely to emphasise notions of cultural purity and pollution. But the more pluralist are the policies of the state, and the more positively and sympathetically minority cultures appear to be portrayed in public discourse, so the more likely such groups are to turn to ideas of cultural ownership and appropriation in their attempts to maintain their distinctiveness.

10

The Politics of Alikeness

Each tongue hoards the resources of consciousness, the world-picture of the clan. Using a simile still deeply entrenched in the language-awareness of Chinese, a language builds a wall around the 'middle kingdom' of the group's identity. It is secret towards the outsider and inventive of its own world ... There have been so many thousands of human tongues, there still are, because there have been, particularly in the archaic stages of social history, so many distinct groups intent on keeping from one another the inherited, singular springs of their identity ... [I]n this sense also there is in every action of translation – and specially where it succeeds – a touch of treason. Hoarded dreams, patents of life are being taken across the frontier. (Steiner 1975: 232–33; see also p. 284)

Introduction

In the previous chapter, I distinguished three varieties of cultural appropriation. In one, a privileged and dominant group confronts attempts by subalterns to assimilate into it or to pass themselves off as members of it. In a second pattern, the appropriation of such groups' symbols of privilege and power by subalterns is parodic and subversive.

In a third pattern, a dominant group, or a state representing such a group, tries to incorporate a minority by claiming to participate in important aspects of its identity and to share its symbolic practices. Thus, the white Australians who seek to appropriate Ayers Rock as a sacred site portray themselves as representing all Australians, black and white. In the same way, the Canadian Federal government represents itself as the custodian of Quebec cultural property in the name of all Canadians (deemed to encompass the people of Quebec); the Turkish state takes over the Kurdish colours and new year celebrations in the name of the Turkish nation, a category which it defines as including the Kurds.

In this chapter, I examine the most radical and hostile form of appropriation of cultural identities. In this, the fourth and final variety of cultural appropriation I want to describe, two or more groups compete for the exclusive control or possession of some important cultural icon or icons.

Often, one group is a powerful majority and the other a minority; in this case, the aim of the majority group is not to incorporate the minority but to dispossess, exclude and marginalise it.

Conflictual Resemblances

Some years ago, a curious dispute arose concerning the ownership of the figure of Father Christmas:

> Festive cheer was in short supply at the 32nd annual Santa Claus World Conference in Copenhagen yesterday as delegates debated whether to 'excommunicate' Finland's Santa Claus amid a row over Father Christmas's true home ... Wearing red robes and white beards – but minus their reindeer – the 132 Santas from 15 countries were considering sanctions against the Finns ... Tensions have been simmering since 1992 when Finland questioned whether Greenland was Father Christmas's true home, suggesting instead that he lived in Finnish Lapland.
>
> The claim elicited a one-year ban from the world Santa conference, but the Finns remain unrepentant. 'We represent the only true Santa. He is alive and well in Finland', said one of Santa's little helpers yesterday ... But Ib Rasmussen, Denmark's head Santa and the conference organiser, was unimpressed. 'This is the last straw. We invited the Finnish Santa to come and explain himself but now we're going to strip him of his white beard and red robe and excommunicate him once and for all.' (McIvor 1995)

A problem people seem to face in small, close-knit social worlds is that they can sometimes appear to themselves to resemble each other a little too much. They may be conscious of sharing many deeply held values, goals and beliefs. But they may not – or some of them may not – always wish to share them. They do not recognise themselves as truly sharing these characteristics, as always jointly possessing them willingly. There is a special kind of conflict that occurs between people who have very much in common and feel they should not.

Of course, it is important to identify the conditions under which people are likely to consider in this way that they resemble each other inappropriately, and have too much in common. In the case of the dispute over the home of Santa Claus, the reason is not hard to find. The 132 Santas may have shared a devotion to the figure of Father Christmas, but they were divided into fifteen nationalities. Their quarrel was very similar to the rivalries between those ancient Greek cities which, all having the same high regard for Homer, all wanted the prestige of being his birthplace. Strongly united in some respects (including a common literary tradition), the cities were deeply divided in others.

Gluckman (1977) viewed situations in which people opposed to one another in one way are allied in another as a key feature of social life. To him, such cross-cutting social relationships limit conflict and promote cohesion in the long term and so play a vital functional role. I do not share Gluckman's functionalist perspective on cross-cutting ties and divided allegiances, as will become clear. But I agree with him that these sorts of ambivalent relationships are ubiquitous, and I shall argue that they represent an important context in which resemblances can become conflictual.

Let me give an example drawn from ethnic politics in the United States. Certain black American academics argue that Western civilisation had African, not Greek, roots and that its true origins have been deliberately hidden by white historians over the centuries for racist motives. These 'Afrocentric' scholars argue that Greek philosophy purloined African thought, that ancient Greece was a mere satellite of African civilisation and that Socrates and many other important figures of the ancient world were in fact Africans, not Europeans. In short, the cultural heritage of ancient Greece is an African heritage, a 'stolen legacy' (James 1954) purloined by whites, and blacks must regain their rightful ownership of it. In response, a number of monographs by white scholars have appeared, defending the orthodox view of ancient history (for both sides of this debate, see Berlinerblau 1999; Bernal 1987, 1991; James 1954; Lefkowitz 1996). Again, Gluckman's perspective can illuminate the sociology of this controversy. On the one hand, the two sides share as academics the same social class and occupation and certain values – including, clearly, esteem for the classical past. On the other, they are divided by ethnicity. Ambiguously united and divided in this way, their shared attributes have become a focus of conflict between them. Members of opposed ethnic groups, or of certain of their respective class fractions, can sometimes wish they had rather less in common and may try to create conflict and division out of the things that unite them. Claims that much of white culture and history has been 'stolen' from Africans have a long history among American blacks. It is in this light that one needs to understand the claim by the Black Christian Nationalist movement in the United States that Christ and the ancient Israelites were black (Firth 1973: 406–11). Similarly, when certain black intellectuals claim that Beethoven and some other famous cultural icons thought previously to have been white were black (Coles 1991), seeking implicitly to appropriate these prestigious cultural icons into their own ethnic group, such claims clearly show that those who make them share the wider society's estimation of the symbolic value of these figures.

Opposed ethnic groups may be linked not only by cross-cutting ties such as those of social class, but also by a great deal of shared history and culture, and may have much of the content of their ethnic identities in common. In Northern Ireland, observers have often noted that there seem to be few cultural differences between Protestants and Roman Catholics apart from the difference in religion (Harris 1972: ix; Jenkins 1997: 118). For example, they share some important cultural and historical icons. In recent years, a Loyalist (pro-British Protestant) paramilitary force called the Ulster Defence Association (UDA) has begun to adopt a number of symbols previously considered the property of Irish Republicanism. Chief among these is the legendary Irish hero Cuchulain who, according to an eighth-century cycle of

Ulster tales, single-handedly defended Ulster from foreign armies. The figure of Cuchulain became an important emblem of Irish nationalism, and his statue stands in the General Post Office in Dublin commemorating the Easter Rising of 1916, which had its headquarters there.

Yet his image has now begun to feature on UDA wall murals in Belfast as an emblem of Ulster Loyalist identity. The attempts to appropriate this figure are part of a larger claim by the UDA that Ulster Protestants are descended from the autochthonous inhabitants of Ireland. According to this version of history, Cuchulain belonged to this race, which was driven out of Ireland by an invasion of the Gaels, the ancestors of the modern Irish, who subsequently 'stole' the Irish language and Ireland's Celtic cultural heritage from their original owners. Ulster Protestants are, it is implied, more Irish than the Irish themselves. Their settlement of Ulster in the seventeenth century was an act of home-coming, not of colonisation; it was the return of Ireland's original inhabitants to reclaim their rightful inheritance (see Buckley 1989: 183, 197; Kiberd 1989: 278, 287–89, 320–21; McAuley and McCormack 1990; Nic Craith 2002: 84, 88, 93–113).

St Patrick, the patron saint of Ireland, is, of course, an important icon of Irish identity, both in Ireland itself and among Irish communities overseas. In Northern Ireland, the figure of St Patrick has tended to be associated with the Roman Catholic, Irish Nationalist community, rather than with the Unionist (pro-British Protestant) population. But in recent years, some prominent Northern Irish Unionists have argued that St Patrick was actually a Protestant, at least in spirit, a forerunner of the Reformation, who embodied the Protestant character and brought Protestant values to Ireland – albeit nine hundred years before the Reformation itself. In this sense, he 'belongs' specifically or principally to the Protestant people of Ireland. This attempt to claim St Patrick is part of a wider process involving attempts to take over a number of Irish legendary and historical figures, a process of identity politics in which some within the Protestant community appear to be trying to 'indigenise' Protestant identity in Ireland (Buckley 1989; Harrison 1995a: 258–59; McAuley and McCormack 1990; Nic Craith 2002: 53):

> Not only did he drive the snakes out of Ireland, but Saint Patrick was Ireland's first 'Prod'.
>
> That's the controversial view of Ian Paisley Jnr, writing today in an Irish-American newspaper.
>
> 'The Christianity which Patrick preached in Ireland was not the Roman Catholicism which he is all too often associated with today,' wrote Mr. Paisley.
>
> 'The early Celtic church was independent and proto-Protestant (a prototype of Protestantism), a matter which has largely been written out of history by sheer ignorance ... When Irish Americans celebrate St Patrick's day, they are celebrating a man who brought Protestantism to this island and effectively developed the idea of religious partition that is separating truth from superstition.'
>
> But the Catholic church disagrees. Jim Cantwell, Press officer for the church, said today it was wrong to regard St Patrick as a symbol of division rather than unity.

'I remember Cardinal Daly and Archbishop Eames [heads respectively of the Roman Catholic and Anglican churches in Ireland] being asked in a light-hearted way who Patrick belonged to. The Cardinal said that the important thing is not who claims St Patrick, it's do we live like him, do we follow his example.

'This is particularly so in a country where we do have divisions.'

Mr. Cantwell pointed out that St Patrick pre-dated Protestants and Catholics as we now know them.

'He would not have recognised himself in these terms. The world was very different. There was no division in Christianity.'

Retired Church of Ireland minister Canon Edgar Turner also stressed today that St Patrick was alive before the church split.

'I would not use the word Protestant for Patrick as he was not protesting against anything. There was no need for him to protest at that stage' ...

He added: 'What we can say, there's no indication of him accepting papal authority or doctrines such as the later doctrines of Mary.'

Ulster Unionist MP John Taylor, who raised the origins of St Patrick in the House of Commons last week, also takes the view that the patron saint should not be labelled a Protestant.

'He was an early day Christian who was in Armagh 1550 years ago this year. He was neither a Roman Catholic or a Protestant', he said.

'He was a Briton, born outside Carlisle. He wasn't even Irish.' (Simpson 1994; parenthesis added)

Icons of ethnic or national identity may at times in some sense express cohesion, just as St Patrick (to many church leaders in Northern Ireland) is a figure wholly transcending sectarianism. But, clearly, the same figure can also be exploited divisively, to promote sectional identities and antagonisms. Groups, it seems, can invoke the same cultural symbols to unite them and to divide them, because the 'sharing' of any historical icon is inherently provisional, contestable at any time by one or more of the factions claiming to share it. A shared symbol is transformed from a focus of common identity into a focus of division when one or more of the sectional groups identified with it appears to be trying to monopolise it in some way or claim it exclusively for itself. This is a conflict in which at least one of these interest groups – perhaps all of them – are struggling to differentiate themselves within the constraints of a closely shared and restricted universe of historical symbols.

These manipulated identities and traditions are therefore rarely 'invented' or 'fabricated' (Hanson 1991; Hobsbawm and Ranger 1983), in the sense of being simply manufactured out of nothing. Rather, as Smith observes, invention is highly constrained by the past, though some groups have 'fuller' pasts on which to draw than others:

[I]n most cases, the mythologies elaborated by nationalists have not been fabrications, but recombinations of traditional, perhaps unanalysed, motifs and myths taken from epics, chronicles, documents of the period, and material artefacts. As inventions are very often such novel recombinations of existing elements and motifs, we may, in this restricted sense, call the nationalist mythologies 'inventions'. Such novel recombinations are pre-eminently the work of intellectuals in search of their 'roots'. (Smith 1986: 178; see also pp. 206–7, 211).

Identities are constructed and negotiated in large part through the recycling, reuse and recontextualising of cultural elements with quite genuinely deep roots in the past (see Armstrong 1982: 205; Eley and Suny 1996: 23; Turton 1997). These can include, I might add, motifs borrowed from the similarly constructed traditions of other groups. For instance, Gefou-Madianou (1999) shows how this sort of borrowing has occurred between mainstream Greek society and the Messogitic minority community of Attica over the past century, with each appropriating symbolic elements from the other in the course of defining and redefining its own identity.

Appadurai (1981) argues persuasively that the past is in many ways inherently quite refractory to political manipulation, and that social actors seeking to adapt history to their own interests have limited freedom of manoeuvre (see also Smith 1986: 176). I want to suggest that a problem ethnic groups in conflict can face is the difficulty of distinguishing themselves from others culturally, because in many cases they share much the same basic stocks of historical materials from which to construct identities, and their means of differentiating themselves from others may therefore be quite constrained. In particular, it may be difficult for a group to define itself without appearing to trespass on the identity of some other. It may appear (intentionally or otherwise) to be seeking to exclude or displace another group from its relationship to key symbols of its identity, threatening to displace it from its position in historical identity space.

Strategies of Overproduction

In principle, a group faced with unwanted resemblances of this kind could just alter the ways in which it represents its identity, abandon some of its symbolic practices and shift to new ones. The sociolinguist Fischer argued that processes of this kind are an important mechanism of language change. Élites, he suggests, tend to develop special language varieties to distinguish themselves from their social inferiors, who in turn tend to imitate these high-status idioms, provoking the élites to create yet further differences. Language change is thus a 'protracted pursuit of an elite by an envious mass, and consequent "flight" of the elite' (Fischer 1958: 52). Some ethnic groups do seem to show, in certain aspects of their identity symbolism, a constant turnover or built-in obsolescence of this sort. Hannerz, for example, argues that continuous innovation occurs in black American music in response to the unremitting imitation of their music by outsiders. As each musical style is appropriated by mainstream culture, so American blacks develop new forms (Hannerz 1992: 112–13).

In some societies processes of rapid turnover or strategies of cultural overproduction are common ways of sustaining difference. Let me take as an example the classic instance of what Mead (1938) described as a Melanesian 'importing culture': the Mountain Arapesh. The Mountain Arapesh villages were linked to those of the Beach Arapesh in networks of hereditary trade partnerships between individual men. These networks formed three principal trade routes called the roads of the dugong, of the viper and of the setting sun. Along these routes the Mountain Arapesh supplied tobacco, bird plumes, pots and net bags, in return for stone axes, bows, arrows, baskets and shell valuables. Besides these material goods, the Mountain Arapesh also regularly purchased masked dance complexes from their coastal partners, who had themselves bought them earlier from maritime peoples who came to them annually on trading voyages. The dance complexes were very highly prized by the Mountain Arapesh, among whom there was an insatiable demand for what they saw as the superior quality of the cultural forms of the coastal peoples; beach villages were referred to as the 'mothers' of the 'daughter' mountain villages to which they supplied these dance complexes. Each dance brought with it new styles of body decoration, songs and techniques of magic and divination. The purchase included physical objects, such as masks and ornaments, but it was not simply the objects alone that were purchased but the rights to copy them. The Mountain Arapesh bought the dances as whole villages in return for large quantities of pigs, tobacco, bird plumes and shell valuables. A purchase of a dance complex was initiated by a leader in the purchasing village who organised the collection of the necessary wealth. It involved making a series of solicitant gifts that often extended over several years.

A newly acquired dance would go out of fashion in a village when a still newer dance came on offer; the old dance was then sold off to another community further inland along the trade route. Thus the dances travelled gradually from one locality to the next into the interior. If the sellers were dissatisfied with the purchasers' offerings, they would usually remove a few elements from the complex rather than sell it entire; and, because inland villages were poorer than their seaward partners, a dance complex tended progressively to simplify and devalue with each transfer. In some cases, the complexes were incorporated into the esoteric rituals of male initiation; alternatively, their purchasers might decide instead to 'show them to the women' and treat the dances as wholly secular (Mead 1935: 8–10; 1938: 333–35).

The cultural differences between the coast and the hinterland seem to have had real economic value to the coastal and maritime peoples, for they generated a net inflow of wealth. While their inland partners were, in effect, trying to collapse these cultural distinctions, the coastal peoples for their part presumably sought to preserve them and so continue to capitalise on their value (see Mead 1938: 335). It was not the content of their culture that the Beach Arapesh were trying to hold constant, just the differentials between their culture and that of the hinterland. The results were, on the one hand, the constant production or supply of novel dance complexes by the maritime and coastal peoples and, on the other, the perpetual striving by the hinterland peoples to emulate the perceived elegance and sophistication of the coastal cultures. In its endless attempts to appropriate these cultures, Mountain Arapesh culture was running to stand still. The Beach Arapesh were running to keep one step ahead. In both cultures there was thus a constant turnover of symbolic forms. To call this situation one of cultural instability is perhaps true, but it misses the point. The Beach Arapesh, at least, presumably had no intention that either their culture or that of their trade partners should remain stable: indeed, quite the reverse.

If the Mountain Arapesh appeared to wear their culture lightly and were able to shed old rituals and adopt new ones readily, it was because these cultural forms were not conceptualised as 'traditions', as possessions intrinsic to some particular group's identity, to be handed down by each generation to the next within the group for ever (see Mead 1938: 177). Rather, they were treated as luxury goods and were produced or acquired in the first place to move along lines of communication between groups. Often, a village seeking to purchase a new dance first had to sell its current dance to obtain the necessary funds: '[Village A] may be making advance payments to [village B] for the Midep complex, while [village B] is trying to collect enough to buy the Shené complex from [village C]. The pigs paid for the Midep become part of the purchase price for the Shené' (Mead 1938: 334). The interdependent, chain-like structure of these transactions recalls some of Melanesian prestige economies I discussed in Chapter 3. Indeed, the commerce in dance complexes was, I suggest, a prestige economy, with its key valuables being cultural forms. Each community in the system was in effect continuously exchanging – to use Bourdieu's (1990: 128, 135) terminology – its symbolic capital for the economic capital of its inland partners, and then doing the opposite with its partners towards the sea.

Some other Melanesian societies too seem to have quite literally produced culture for export, as a commodity intended from the very start for trafficking with outsiders; in effect, they were groups specialised in the production and export of culture (see Harrison 1987). Larcom (1982) provides an example in her discussion of the Mewun people of what is now the state of Vanuatu, and of their use of the Melanesian pidgin term *kastom* ('tradition'). Until the 1980s, the Mewun employed this term to refer to a complex of ideas, dating back to the precolonial period, having to do with the treatment of cultural forms as transactable commodities; *kastom* at that time referred to:

> knowledge and its manifestations, sold and exchanged from district to district. Many cultural items today enshrined as past tradition (*kastom*) had been purchased from neighbouring districts such as Seniang or Laus for appropriate kinds and numbers of tusked boars. Such transactions included songs, spells, dances, ceremonies and the right to make certain kinds of sculptured objects. For example, Mewun sold an important men's grading dance-step to Seniang; they also purchased from Seniang the *likan*, a dance which was part of women's *nimangi*, a hierarchy of grades. The rights to funerary figures called *rhambaramb* were purchased by Laus from Seniang. (Larcom 1982: 333, footnotes omitted)

The precolonial Mewun seem to have defined themselves, not through the possession of a fixed ensemble of reified cultural traits, but through the joint activity of collectively producing and disbursing such traits. They did not seem to use cultural practices to commemorate history or continuity with the past (see Connerton 1989), but rather to create social and political relationships in the present through prestations of rights in newly invented songs, dances, ceremonies and other expressive forms. The details of these symbolic goods were kept secret from the intended recipients until the rights in them were transferred, because the very act of revealing the dances, ceremonies and so forth was their formal bestowal as property (see also Lindstrom 1990: 119); to give a performance was to give also the rights to replicate the performance.

The groups that carried out these transactions were fluid and temporary; in fact, they were created and defined by these very exchanges themselves (Larcom 1982: 333, 336; 1990: 177, 188). Social groups among the Mewun were, above all, entities that continually disbursed objectified cultural forms, held proprietary rights in these cultural products, and conducted their relations with each other through the sale and purchase of these rights. Both Larcom herself and others suggest that these were widespread features of Vanuatu societies in precolonial times (see Allen 1981; Brunton 1989: 170–71; Jolly 1992; Patterson 1981: 192). In effect, these groups sought to defeat cultural homogeneity, or keep it at bay, by endlessly generating cultural novelty.

Resisting Change

One way, then, in which a group can adapt to being imitated is by cultural overproduction. Groups in Melanesia were enabled to do this by employing models of property which defined cultures as exchange resources rather than fixed and immemorial patrimonies. But some types of social groups seem to have too much invested in their key identity symbols to be able to relinquish these easily. Harrods, for example, faced with imitation of its renowned trademark, cannot simply start calling itself something else, or adopt a new mark every time someone infringes on its existing one. Its options for change are highly constrained, and it must find other methods of countering imitation. In a sense it is trapped in its identity. It is as much owned by as it is the owner of its famous name. This is the type of situation that interests me in the remainder of this chapter: that is, situations in which two or more collectivities have unwanted cultural commonalities or similarities, and none are willing or able to give ground. A kind of competition thus arises between them for the exclusive possession or control of certain important identity symbols. This can happen when these symbols are important figures or icons from history. An ethnic group perhaps cannot always generate a new history for itself quite as readily as some can generate new styles of music or dance, or new speech idioms.

Certain kinds of identity symbols seem to be more resistant to change or manipulation than others. In some societies, religious symbols appear to be highly refractory in this way (see Bloch 1986). An important element in many ethnic, or ethnoreligious, conflicts is the contested ownership of sacred localities and places of worship, in which opposed groups claim rights to the same religious site. Inevitably, such a site has different historical and religious meanings for each group. One may claim it as a mosque, the other as a temple. But what the two groups are competing for may be identical at a certain level of abstraction: namely, the exclusive right to worship in a given historically and religiously significant location. In some quite specific respects, too, the site may have a very similar or related meaning to both sides, and what may therefore be at issue is the ownership, both of the physical site and, as it were, of key historical significations inextricably associated with it:

> Two things seem destined to signal trouble regarding sacred sites: their usurpation, their sharing. In Palestine/Israel one or both of these things has happened to two buildings: the Tomb of the Patriarchs in Hebron, and in Jerusalem, the Temple Mount (the site of the Jewish Temple, first built during the reign of Solomon) on which has stood for centuries the Mosque of Omar or Dome of the Rock ...
>
> From the Jewish point of view, then, the Temple Mount (the Temple itself was destroyed by the Romans in the first century) has been usurped ...
>
> From the Muslim point of view, the Dome of the Rock is also a holy of holies – whence Mohammed took off on his visitation to heaven. (Paine 1995: 8; see also Clarke 2000)

Paine follows Hourani (1991: 28) in noting that the building of the Dome on the Temple Mount is interpretable 'as a symbolic act placing Islam in the lineage of Abraham and dissociating it from Judaism and Christianity' (quoted in Paine 1995: 8). Some groups, in seeking to define – or redefine – themselves, seem to have tried in a similar way to wrest away from other groups key icons of myth or history and incorporate these into their own cultural legacies. A particularly clear example of this comes from Gombrich and Obeyesekere's (1988) study of Sinhalese Buddhism in Sri Lanka. They examine the processes by which the Sinhala majority has taken over the ritual practices of the Tamil (Hindu) minority, and has sought to deny the Hindu origins of these forms of devotion. This appropriation has focused on the cult of the god Kataragama, whose eponymous shrine is the most important religious centre in Sri Lanka and whose annual festival is the nation's most important ritual occasion. The Buddhist take-over of Kataragama, which began in the 1940s (Gombrich and Obeyesekere 1988: 186), involved Buddhist religious officials taking control of the shrine and, much more broadly, the incorporation into popular Sinhalese Buddhism of the particular forms of religious expression associated with the god's cult – modes of ecstatic religiosity quite alien to traditional Sinhala Buddhism, involving possession, fire-walking and spectacular forms of self-mortification (Gombrich and Obeyesekere 1988: 187). These processes were accompanied by a revision of the mythology associated with the shrine, and the development of myths which denied the Hindu origins and significance of the cult and purported 'to claim the shrine as exclusively Sinhala cultural property and to assert that its god is not Hindu but pure Buddhist' (Gombrich and Obeyesekere 1988: xii; see also pp. 411–44). Thus, in a context of continuous ethnic and religious tension since 1956, and of civil war since 1983, the Sinhalas marginalise the Tamils religiously and politically (Gombrich and Obeyesekere 1988: x, 50; see also van der Veer 1994b: 204).

In short, the most radical challenge to a group's identity comes when another community claims, not simply rights to some of its practices and traditions, but exclusive rights, and tries literally to dispossess it of key symbols of its identity. The Sinhalas, for instance, appear to be seeking, not to assimilate the Tamils culturally, but to expropriate them.

Similarly, van der Veer (1994a), in his study of the conflict brought about by Hindu religious nationalists over the Babari mosque in Ayodhya, northern India, shows that an ethnoreligious movement may deliberately appropriate and reuse elements of the traditions of a rival group so as to demonstrate power, or may lay claim to some symbol of another group's identity specifically to widen social divisions or create an opportunity or pretext for conflict (see also Bernbeck and Pollock 1996; Copley 1993). Clearly, the result of this sort of aggressive *bricolage*, of these real or perceived appropriations and counter-appropriations, can be a kind of deadly intertwining of the histories of opposed ethnic groups, which unwillingly have in common the same key symbols of the past. In this way, even groups with historically wholly unrelated cultures can find themselves sharing the same cultural icons. A case in point is the way Ayers Rock became, as we saw, an important focal point of contemporary ethnic politics in Australia, claimed as a disputed 'sacred site' both by Aborigines and by some white Australian opponents of Aboriginal land rights (Whittaker 1994).

Hence a shared symbol can become a site of struggle, even of sectarian massacres, as in the case of the Tomb of the Patriarchs in Hebron, as each side tries to force the other to relinquish it. Obviously, we have to move beyond Gluckman in trying to elucidate cases such as these. Jointly claimed ethnic heritage such as the site of the Babari mosque has no unifying significance in the relations between the two ethnic communities concerned and is purely a focal point of inter-ethnic conflict. Far from serving in some sense to constrain the conflict, it concentrates it – as Paine argues in relation to Hebron – creating a small arena in which to express it in a particularly intensified and destructive form. After 1967, the Israeli military authorities in Hebron gave Jewish settlers rights of access to the Tomb.

> From the Muslim point of view, this was zero-sum: what the Jews won – allocations of time and space inside the building – they took from the Muslims. Insofar as their position allowed, the Muslims would take retaliatory action, to which the Jews, in turn, would respond. An escalating situation evolved in which

there was mutual physical roughing-up and vandalism to sacred books of both faiths (and in the streets of Hebron: sectarian murders).

This, then, was 'sharing', against a mutually perceived background of usurpation. The semiotics of mutual offence – of mutual desecration – between these two religions under one roof is easily suggested: ceremonial use of wine by Jews, a profanity for Muslims; Muslim funeral processions inside the mosque, a profanity for Jews; Jewish heads covered, Muslims not; Muslims enter barefoot, Jews not ... so here, at the Tomb of the Patriarchs, there is a *concentration* of Jewish-Muslim antipathies: worshippers and their respective practices, usually separated, are brought, involuntarily, together. (Paine 1995: 8; footnote omitted)

Evidently, even antagonistic ethnic groups may share important religious, cultural and historical symbols, and be acutely and painfully conscious that they do so. For the reasons I have given, groups with a long history of conflict may in fact be particularly likely to have much of their history and culture in common in this way. Ethnic conflicts do not seem to arise only when 'cultural distance' (Hammell 1997: 8) exists between groups. Some conflicts quite obviously involve, in part, struggles between groups precisely to generate such distance, to disengage their cultural identities and reduce their perceived similarities – perhaps so as to justify escalating their conflict or pursuing it further (see, for instance, Conversi 1997). Their commonalities join them together like organs joining Siamese twins, representing important focuses, as Paine (1995: 8) puts it, of 'zero-sum' competition. Of course, in some alternative political and historical universe, these shared attributes might have been used to foster some form of common identity or cohesion. There is no inherent reason why they could not. Bowman (1993) shows how a variety of different Christian and Muslim sectarian communities, in parts of the Israeli-Occupied West Bank, seek to express an overarching Palestinian 'national' identity through joint use of the same religious sites. Clearly, groups can deploy the same religious symbols equally powerfully to represent themselves as united or as opposed.

Conclusion

In this chapter and the previous one, I have examined some situations in which the preservation of a distinct collective identity or of rights (such as land rights) associated with this identity, depends on a group's ability to prevent certain symbolic practices from being reproduced or appropriated by outsiders. These are circumstances of conflict over the ownership, control or possession of icons of cultural identity – conflicts which give these identities and the symbols representing them the appearance of a kind of scarce resource or limited good.

I have suggested that many of these mimetic conflicts, arising in the negotiation of collective identities, seem to cluster into four relatively distinct kinds. First, social actors may either be relatively powerful or powerless in

Summary

relation to those groups whose symbolic practices they are seeking to adopt. It is clearly not only the dominant who carry out acts of cultural appropriation: the subordinated have their own modes of cultural appropriation as well. Secondly, social actors may be seeking to appropriate inclusively the symbolic practices of others (that is, merely to share them) or to appropriate them exclusively (to expropriate them). In this way, they may be aiming to diminish or even eliminate the differences between themselves and those others – to unite with them or at least reduce the social barriers between them – or their aim may be the reverse: to create social barriers or deepen existing divisions between themselves and those from whom they are borrowing. The four prototypical situations of conflict I have identified seem to be generated by the intersection of these two axes, one concerning degrees of power and the other having to do with degrees of intended exclusion or inclusion.

The kinds of conflicts I have discussed are often clearly intertwined with what are normally called cultural property disputes (see Greenfield 1989). Ethnic groups contesting the entitlements to particular modes of dress or to specific collective memories, discourses of indigeneity or forms of religious devotion may also be contesting the possession and control of territory or of symbolically important artefacts such as monuments, religious sites, museum objects and antiquities, all of which belong very squarely in Weiner's category of inalienable possessions. These physical objects and places are, in other words, often associated with specific symbolic practices whose ownership is bound inextricably to the ownership of the territory, site or artefact itself, and struggles for the possession of these locations or objects are often fused with struggles for the control or possession of total cultural identities (see Handler 1988: 140–42).

Territory, of course, is a physical resource central to the constitution of nationalism. But it is important to remember that a national or ethnic homeland is more, to those who identify with it, than just a physical resource, a piece of real estate. The crucial ingredient of nationalism in this respect is not simply territory, but rather, as Smith shows, the sacralisation of territory – a homeland sanctified by the natural or human-made sacred places it contains, and all the national myths and rich historical memories that reference it (1986: 28, 183–90).

It is for these sorts of reasons that claims upon the sorts of material objects that are important in the definition of national or ethnic identity (such as monuments, sacred sites, museum antiquities and other cultural treasures) and claims upon practices (carnival, New Year's festivals, speech patterns indexing social status, and so forth) tend to be linked together and are contested in essentially the same way. For the symbolism of cultural identity does not seem to distinguish rigidly between cultural possessions of a physical and of an immaterial kind, as King suggests in pointing to the close interdependence between remembrance ceremonies and physical monuments:

> Remembrance ceremonies and physical memorials may appear to be quite different kinds of things. Ceremonies are composed of occasional human actions with a special place in the social calendar; memorials of state, permanent material, always

present. In two important respects, however, memorials, no matter how solid, are no less part of a pattern of human action than ceremonies. In the first place, they require constant attention to ensure their permanence. Physically, they are sustained by organizations dedicated to maintaining them ... It is organizations of this sort that give memorials their permanence, maintaining their integrity and sanctity, protecting them from desecration and enabling them to defy the attrition of time ... [Secondly, a memorial's] place in the social and ideological life of a community also depend[s] on organized action which [takes] the memorial as its focal point. (King 1999: 150–51; parentheses added, footnote omitted)

Hence in a dispute over cultural property – the controversy over Ayers Rock, for instance, or over the ownership of the Elgin Marbles – what are always at stake, I would argue, are entitlements to practices. It is just that the practices in these particular cases are patterns of management and safe keeping of material artefacts. A cultural property dispute is a conflict over the rights to carry out certain modes of action regarding some valued object. In this respect, it too is a form of mimetic conflict, but one in which the contested practices or patterns of action happen to relate to the use or custodianship of physical things.

Conclusion:
Cultural Constructions of 'Cultural Identity'

I have sought in this book to explore a way of thinking which I have called proprietary identity – a form of thought in which people represent their social identities and conceive of similarities and differences among themselves by means of symbols, and understand these symbols to be forms of property. In referring to these modes of symbolism as proprietary, I mean to suggest that they have two basic features. First, actors represent their social identities by means of symbols to which they claim exclusive entitlements of some kind, asserting rights to deny, and probably in some circumstances also to permit, specific uses of these identity markers by others. Secondly, the actors assert some degree of freedom to define their own identities without undue hindrance or interference by others.

There are undoubtedly many sorts of proprietary symbolisms. For instance, there are the totemic or heraldic emblems with which kin groups differentiate themselves in some societies based upon lineage and descent. Another proprietary symbolism, as we saw, is the system of commercial trademarks, differentiating products in the crowded and competitive identity spaces of impersonal markets.

But I have chosen to focus on the particular test case of cultural identity: that is, on proprietary symbolisms of identity consisting of objectifications of 'culture'. I have tried to show that these may be accompanied by certain anxieties concerned with the preservation of identity across time. These anxieties focus on regulating, managing or limiting in some way either (a) inflows of the culturally foreign, or (b) outflows of the culturally indigenous, or (c) both of these processes. Within this broad framework, a diversity of cultural styles of constructing cultural identity seem possible. Different concepts of 'objectification', different ways of defining what sorts of inward or outward flows are possible, between what kinds of agents and under what conditions can give rise to a variety of different modes of structuring identity space. All these are variable culturally because they follow culturally variable schemata – schemata, above all, concerned with the body, gender, personhood and property – which are largely unconscious, for the most part simply taken for granted by the actors who employ them. They are basic shared assumptions common to all the actors within a given universe of cultural 'differences', and thereby impart a common structure to their quests to differentiate themselves from one another 'culturally'.

So, for instance, we saw that élites in both Melanesia and the West draw unconsciously on their culturally and historically distinctive notions of property and personhood in constructing their images of cultural similarity and difference. Inevitably, these notions are closely intertwined with (and thus serve) the élites' own vested interests and power. In the Western cultural tradition, the principal conceptions on which élites have historically tended to draw metaphorically are images of individuals as self-sufficient creators and holders of private property. In precolonial Melanesia, the dominant images on which leaders drew were of relational persons, immanent in their social relations with one another; these relations were made manifest, above all, in those transactions of gifts and prestige goods on which the power of Melanesian leaders was commonly based. The conceptions which élites employ in representing cultural identities and differences reflect, at root, culturally specific idealisations of their own identities, and are modelled after their understandings of their relations with others, including their economic relations.

In the Western tradition, these manifest themselves in forms such as those familiar to us as 'ethnicity' and 'nationalism'. As Handler and others have argued, a central feature of these is the modelling of groups as collective 'individuals' – abstract entities that define themselves by historically producing distinctive 'cultures' and by owning them thereafter as their perpetual legacies. To Smith (1986: 216), for instance, one of the central characteristics of nationalism is that it 'makes a fetish of culture'. As Kapferer puts it, nationalism sacralises the nation's culture, making it a thing of worship (1988: 209; see also pp. 1–2). My particular focus in this book has been upon two assumptions concerning the nature of social order and conflict which seem to me to derive from these conceptions of collective individuality. They are evident both in everyday discourse and in some of the academic literature on nationalism and ethnic conflict. The first is the Durkheimian view that the sharing of a single cultural legacy, a common background of history, language, religion and so forth, is a powerful social bond generating moral cohesion and solidarity. The second, a corollary of the first, is the belief that cultural differences, or perceived differences, are divisive and play a significant role in creating, prolonging or exacerbating social conflicts.

This book has sought to explore the ideological nature of these constructs. My approach has been to try to shed light on the ways in which the sorts of assertions of cultural distinctiveness, uniqueness and individuality, undoubtedly so central to ethnicity and nationalism, are linked inextricably with other, less visible assertions concerned with the denial, forgetting and severing of felt resemblances. Certainly, a community may represent its existence, identity and distinctiveness as under threat from some Other or Others culturally alien to it. But I have tried to explore other, in a sense quite contrary, types of situations, which are nevertheless just as closely linked to ideas of collective individuality. Among these, as we saw, are contexts in which a collectivity portrays itself, or is portrayed, as endangered by ethnic Others who resemble it or who seem to identify with it too intimately. Here, similarities with outsiders, rather than differences, are the principal perceived threats to its identity.

In examining such situations I took my cue from certain shared themes in the writings of Freud, Girard, Simmel, Bateson and Blok. Their ideas help us to understand why felt resemblances between groups, and not just differences, can assume an important role in situations of conflict and can contribute to bringing such groups into conflict in the first place, as they seek to augment or enhance their identities – or, indeed, construct them – by trying to borrow or purloin elements of each other's identities. We have seen that groups can have disputes (at times, violently destructive) over their rights or claims to important symbols of identity, especially religious identity. In these situations, the sharing of a common culture or of aspects of a common cultural symbolism can be intensely divisive and contentious. Antagonistic ethnic groups often have – or may acquire as part of their conflicts – many historical and cultural commonalities, although these commonalities may be – indeed, are likely be – denied, opposed and contested. Such felt resemblances between groups, contested and conflictual in this way, can be as powerfully divisive as 'differences' and can play an important role in shaping and defining social boundaries.

The significance which these patterns of mimetic conflict have for social theory, therefore, is that they call into question two widespread assumptions evident in a variety of forms in both social science and everyday discourse: namely, that shared culture or affiliation to shared cultural symbols is a source of social cohesion, and that ethnic divisions are associated specifically with perceptions or attributions of cultural dissimilarity.

Let us first take the assumption that groups can be distinguished from one another by actual or perceived cultural differences. Certainly, as we have seen, conflicts often give rise to heightened and exaggerated perceptions or assertions of dissimilarity, and groups seeking to accentuate their social boundaries may represent themselves as separated by deeply incompatible cultures. But, as I have argued, what actually differentiates such a group from others is not its perceived distinctiveness but rather its aspirations or proprietary claims to such distinctiveness. The significance of this subtle but crucial distinction is revealed most clearly when opposed groups pursue their proprietary ambitions in regard to the same or similar 'inalienable' identity symbols, as they clearly sometimes do. Their competing and perhaps irreconcilable claims to those inalienable symbols thereby become – rather like disputes over infringements of trademarks – a key element in their own right in the broader conflict between the two sides. In other words, it seems that groups can be opposed because, in part, they have built identities, or have sought to build them, out of much the same funds of historical symbols, and perhaps have had little choice except to use these shared materials. Their cultural identities appear to them, anomalously, to overlap, and each perceives the other as an obstacle to the full expression or realisation of its own identity.

The second assumption called into question by the forms of mimetic conflict I have examined is really a corollary of the first. It is the notion that cultural commonalities, actual or perceived, are a source of social cohesion, and that shared historical or cultural symbols are a unifying force. Above all, this has been assumed to be the case with religious symbols, which have often been viewed as paramount expressions of social cohesion and of the sanctity of the bonds between members of the same group. Clearly, consciousness of shared culture does not necessarily or inherently promote cohesion, but can have wholly the opposite effect, and can indeed be deliberately exploited to generate social conflict. In ethnically divided societies, in particular, perceptions of similarity across these social divisions can have a deeply ambivalent significance, and may sometimes become the focus of destructive confrontations in which the two sides, in effect, act violently to contest and deny their resemblances. The idea that shared culture generates solidarity, like the idea that nations or ethnic groups are culturally distinct, must therefore belong to the ideological underpinnings of ethnicity and nationalism themselves, to the rhetoric by which groups seek to mobilise themselves as politically distinct entities, each through its pursuit of an ideal of an internally homogeneous and externally distinct 'culture' (see Handler 1988).

Thus, a certain folk theory of social cohesion (and thereby a folk theory also of conflict) seems to underlie ethnicity and nationalism. According to this theory, solidarity requires and arises out of cultural homogeneity: common allegiance to key symbols, and shared affiliations of language, religion, history and so forth. Of course, such notions may be effective as rhetoric, but they are highly deficient as social theory. It goes without saying that every nation or ethnic group has internal divisions of various kinds – of political party, class, gender, region and so forth. And, no matter how distinctive it may appear to be culturally, how apparently unique its heritage or history, its members – or members of some of its subgroups or factions – will acknowledge some cultural commonalities between themselves and outsiders, quite possibly including outsiders with whom they have some hostile relationship. In other words, most social conflicts – including violent ones – in practice occur between people who conceive themselves as having some common cultural allegiances.

Put rather crudely, the gap between actuality and ideology in these situations can be reduced in two alternative ways: the protagonists can either treat their conflict as the problem or they can treat their shared attributes of identity as the problem. In other words, one possible course of action is to seek to mitigate or resolve their conflict on the grounds of shared identity. This is the course which Gluckman thought was usual, with social divisions tending in the long run to be healed, or at least ameliorated, by stronger countervailing ties. There is, however, an alternative possibility: namely, that the antagonists may reconceptualise their shared identity as an anomaly, an ambiguity needing to be removed or, indeed, an opportunity to be exploited to widen their divisions further. This is the context in which perceptions of resemblance become a focus for conflict and struggles ensue as the antagonists, bound to one another unwillingly by likenesses that divide them, begin trying to generate apparent cultural dissimilarities out of their commonalities.

It may seem paradoxical and even counter-intuitive, but actors can in this way become increasingly divided and opposed to one another by their felt resemblances, perhaps just as much as by felt differences. In other words, one way in which they can act to differentiate themselves socially and politically is by entering, as it were, into demarcation disputes with each other over their shared symbols of cultural or historical identity, disputes analogous to conflicts over the ownership of trademarks and drawing on the same underlying conceptions of proprietary identity. In these cases, the Other is perceived as threatening, not so much because it appears alien, but rather because it seems in some vital respects a kind of hostile twin or double, a rival copy of the Self. In this way, ethnic boundaries can be sustained by attributions, not only of difference, but also of conflictual resemblance, or of fraught mixtures of both.

To view apparent 'difference' as a denied, muted and fractured resemblance, a mutual likeness that divides, suggests why there is relatively little variety in the ways nations and ethnic groups symbolise their identities. Far from exhibiting infinite creativity, the symbolism of ethnic and national differences seems much more like what Bernstein (1971) called a restricted code, generating mostly repetitions, parallelisms and small variations on the same themes. The point is that these recensions, which ethnicity and nationalism call 'cultural diversity', irreducible 'differences', unique 'cultural heritages' and so forth, are actually specially attenuated forms of shared identity. They are the residue of reducing or counteracting felt resemblances.

I am reminded here of an observation on surrealism by the art critic Gombrich, in an essay on art and psychoanalysis. To the art historian, the imagery which the surrealists produced (ostensibly, from the deep well-springs of the unconscious) seems quite obviously conventional and stylised, even derivative:

> [I]t is a familiar fact the eighteenth-century artist who went out to record the beauty of the English countryside was as likely as not to return from his expedition to the Lakelands with a version of Claude Lorrain's Roman Campagna, just sufficiently modified to pass as a faithful vista of a beauty spot. It is perhaps less familiar but equally true that many a young artist who sets out to record his unconscious images returns from this *descensus ad inferos* with a version of Picasso's penultimate invention just sufficiently modified to pass as self-expression ... And so the fact, for instance, that all eighteenth-century landscapes or twentieth-century dream-paintings have enough in common to allow us art historians to tell, on the whole, where and when they were made, is not due to some mysterious fluid or collective spirit that governs the modes of perception or the images of dreams but rather to the observable fact that symbols developed from a common stock will tend to have a certain family likeness. (Gombrich 1963: 34)

Such family likenesses arise because all artists, including surrealists, use the works of others as models and paradigms, whether or not they do so wholly consciously or deliberately. Of course, artists do not normally copy each other in a merely slavish way. Rather, Gombrich seems to suggest, they draw on the works of others even in defining their own difference from others.

Ethnic and national identities seem in this respect very much like surrealist dream-paintings. They tend to draw on each other for their constitutive symbolisms and to be variations on shared themes – indeed in many cases copies developed from a common stock, just sufficiently modified (in the words of Gombrich) to pass as self-expression. Yet they appear to their creators to originate autonomously, deep within themselves, or their collective selves, in profound ways unrelated to the existence of others. One should approach the understanding of 'cultural identity' in much the same spirit as the art historian, and seek to understand the role of imitation and of shared themes and conventions in the creation of ethnic and national identities, even if these are strongly denied by our respondents.

For there is actually a very real common feature here. Ethnic and national identity and Western conceptions of artistic integrity and creativity are all shaped by the same underlying culturally specific conceptions of the individual. The denial of resemblance, the systematic misrecognition of mimesis – a misrecognition itself mimetic – is a key process in the constitution of the apparent 'individuality' of the artist and of the nation or ethnic group.

It is this underlying conception of collectivities as individuals that seems, then, to have given rise to two contrary traditions in Western social thought regarding the origins of order and conflict. The major, dominant tradition is the one I referred to above, in which social cohesion is understood to rest upon commonalities among people. Here, conflict appears to arise out of dissimilarity. The other, subdominant tradition understands conflict as capable of arising, quite to the contrary, from too much likeness, and social order thus appears to require that social actors maintain a degree of mutual differentiation and distance. This is a dimension of conflict which Freud, Girard, Simmel, Bateson and Blok all recognised in their different ways. But the two traditions rest on the same underlying presupposition: they both originate in the modelling of the social actor – singular or collective – as an individual. If they contradict each other, it is because they reflect the real contradictions inherent in conceiving of society – indeed, of living in society – as if it were composed purely of individuals and the relations they come to establish with one another.

For to make this assumption must inevitably raise the problem of how such bounded, autonomous and discrete entities could come together and integrate with one another socially. It can only be by means either of their commonalities or of their differences – or, of course, both. But here is the dilemma. To favour the commonalities can make the differences and diversities that inevitably exist seem like anarchy and social fragmentation. On the other hand, to valorise diversity and difference can just as readily make the equally inevitable commonalities among these 'individuals' seem like violations of their very 'individuality'. Durkheim tried to solve the problem by imagining these two alternatives as stages in the evolution of society. The problem here, the reason why these insoluble circularities arise, clearly lies in the initial assumption: namely, that society consists of bounded individuals who have succeeded in establishing mutual relations.

These are the images of individuality that give rise to those deep and recurrent anxieties which many nationalisms seem to exhibit, and which I have sought to explore in much of this book: the pervasive fear of the possibility of the loss of cultural identity and distinctiveness, of becoming increasingly similar to others in an increasingly globalised world. This claustrophobia, with its fearful imaginings of homogeneity and blending with the Other, is a product, ultimately, of a certain conception of the person, and did not exist, at least in this heightened and pronounced form, in the culturally open and extraverted societies of precolonial Melanesia, because these societies explicitly acknowledged – indeed, went to some lengths to emphasise and valorise – the imitative foundations of their own cultural identities. Just as nationalism's tendency to deny and misrecognise its own mimetic nature is itself mimetic, so its fears of cultural standardisation are, of course, themselves culturally standardised fears. They are shared anxieties that arise from a very specific set of shared understandings about how to be diverse. A key feature of all nationalisms, clearly showing them to belong to a common global culture, is their ambivalence towards acknowledging their cultural commonalities. Because each nationalism defines its own distinctiveness by foregrounding the ways in which its heritage and history are unique in their specific contents, so nationalism taken as a whole gives full and open recognition to the creative human agency which these particularities undeniably manifest. Its blind spot is the nation form itself, which tends to appear natural, ahistorical, constructed by no human agency, invented nowhere, copied from no one. I have tried to show that the denial or misrecognition by nationalism of its own mimetic character is a constant active process, a perpetual attempt to model collective identity after an idealisation of the person as an autonomous actor – bounded, unitary, self-sufficient, discrete, owing as little as possible to others. This ideology reveals its self-contradictions particularly sharply as it takes root in the new states of the South Pacific. For here it is displacing other ways of understanding cultural identity and difference, ones which did not seek to mask or deny the inherently mimetic character of cultural identity or the inescapable embeddedness of culture in human relations of interdependence and reciprocity. It is here, perhaps, that contemporary nationalism and ethnicism show themselves most clearly to be *ideologies* of difference: ways of imagining ourselves dissimilar to one another which, in truth, have made us grow ever more alike.

Bibliography

Abadal i de Vinyals, R. d'. 1958. 'A propos du Legs Visigothique en Europe'. *Settimane di Studio del Centro Italiano di Studi sull'Alto Medioevo* 2: 541–85.

Afonso, C.A. 1998. 'Exploitable Knowledge Belongs to the Creators of it: a Debate'. *Social Anthropology* 6 (1): 119–22.

Allen, M.R. 1967. *Male Cults and Secret Initiations in Melanesia*. Melbourne: University Press.

——. 1981. 'Innovation, Inversion and Revolution as Political Tactics in West Aoba'. In M. Allen (ed.) *Vanuatu: Politics, Economics and Ritual in Island Melanesia*. Sydney: Academic Press, pp. 105–34.

Altman, J. 1989. *The Aboriginal Arts and Crafts Industry*. Canberra: Australian Government Publishing Service.

Anderson, B. 1983. *Imagined Communities: Reflections on the Origin and Spread of Nationalism*. London: Verso.

Anthias, F. and N. Yuval-Davis. 1992. *Racialised Boundaries*. London: Routledge.

Antonnen, P. (ed.). 2000. *Folklore, Heritage Politics and Ethnic Diversity: a Festschrift for Barbro Klein*. Botkryka, Sweden: Multicultural Centre.

Appadurai, A. 1981. 'The Past as a Scarce Resource'. *Man* (n.s.) 16 (2): 201–19.

——. 1986. 'Introduction: Commodities and the Politics of Value'. In A. Appadurai (ed.) *The Social Life of Things*. Cambridge: Cambridge University Press, pp. 3–63.

——. 1999. 'Dead Certainty: Ethnic Violence in the Era of Globalization'. In B. Meyer and P. Geschiere (eds) *Globalization and Identity: Dialectics of Flow and Closure*. Oxford: Blackwell, pp. 305–24.

Armstrong, J. 1982. *Nations before Nationalism*. Chapel Hill: University of North Carolina Press.

Bailey, F.G. 1970. *Stratagems and Spoils: a Social Anthropology of Politics*. Oxford: Basil Blackwell.

Balibar, E. 1988. 'Propositions on Citizenship'. *Ethics* 98 (4): 723–30.

Ball, R., A. Hargreaves, B. Marshall and A. Ridehalgh. 1995. 'French in the World: from Imperialism to Diversity'. In J. Forbes and M. Kelly (eds) *French Cultural Studies*. Oxford: Oxford University Press, pp. 264–89.

Ballard, L.M. 1998. 'Motor-cycle Dress and Undress'. In A.D. Buckley (ed.) *Symbols in Northern Ireland*. Belfast: The Institute of Irish Studies, Queen's University of Belfast, pp. 117–32.

Banton, M. 1983. *Racial and Ethnic Competition*. Cambridge: Cambridge University Press.

Barth, F. 1975. *Ritual and Knowledge among the Baktaman of New Guinea*. New Haven: Yale University Press.

——. 1987. *Cosmologies in the Making: a Generative Approach to Cultural Variation in Inner New Guinea*. Cambridge: Cambridge University Press.

——. (ed.) 1969. *Ethnic Groups and Boundaries: the Social Organisation of Cultural Difference*. Oslo: Scandinavian University Press.

Bateson, G. 1958. *Naven: a Survey of the Problems Suggested by a Composite Picture of the Culture of a New Guinea Tribe Drawn from Three Points of View*. 2nd ed. Stanford: Stanford University Press.

Baudrillard, J. 1988. 'The System of Objects'. In M. Poster (ed.) *Jean Baudrillard: Selected Writings*. Stanford: Stanford University Press, pp. 10–25.

Bauman, Z. 1992. 'Soil, Blood and Identity'. *Sociological Review* 40 (4): 675–701.

Bell, E. 1995. 'Bare-faced Robbery: Celebrities who are Used in Ads without Permission have Little Legal Comeback'. *Guardian*, Monday 24 July, p. 13.

Benedict, R. 1935. *Patterns of Culture*. London: Routledge & Kegan Paul.

Berlinerblau, J. 1999. *Heresy in the University: the Black Athena Controversy and the Responsibilities of American Intellectuals*. New Brunswick, NJ: Rutgers University Press.

Bernal, M. 1987. *Black Athena: the Afroasiatic Roots of Classical Civilization*, Vol. 1. New Brunswick, NJ: Rutgers University Press.

——. 1991. *Black Athena: the Afroasiatic Roots of Classical Civilization*, Vol. 2. New Brunswick, NJ: Rutgers University Press.

Bernbeck, R. and S. Pollock. 1996. 'Ayodhya, Archaeology, and Identity'. *Current Anthropology* 37 (1): 138–42.

Bernstein, B. 1971. *Class, Codes and Control*, Vol. 1, *Theoretical Studies Towards a Sociology of Language*. London: Routledge & Kegan Paul.

Binns, C.A.P. 1980. 'The Changing Face of Power: Revolution and Accommodation in the Development of the Soviet Ceremonial System'. *Man* (n.s.) 15 (1): 170–87.

Bloch, M. 1975. 'Property and the End of Affinity'. In M. Bloch (ed.) *Marxist Analyses and Social Anthropology*. London: Malaby Press.

——. 1986. *From Blessing to Violence: History and Ideology in the Circumcision Ritual of the Merina of Madagascar*. Cambridge: Cambridge University Press.

Blok, A. 1998. 'The Narcissism of Minor Differences'. *European Journal of Social Theory* 1 (1): 33–56.

Blommaert, J. and J. Verschueren. 1996. 'European Concepts of Nation-Building'. In E.N. Wilmsen and P. McAllister (eds) *The Politics of Difference: Ethnic Premises in a World of Power*. Chicago and London: University of Chicago Press, pp. 104–23.

Boas, F. 1921. *Ethnology of the Kwakiutl*. 35th Annual Report, 1913–1914 Washington, DC: Bureau of American Ethnology.

——. 1955 [1928]. *Primitive Art*. New York: Dover.

——. 1966. *Kwakiutl Ethnography*. Ed. H. Codere. Chicago: Chicago University Press.

Bolton, L. 1999. 'Introduction'. Special Issue on Fieldwork, Fieldworkers: Developments in Vanuatu Research. *Oceania* 70 (1): 1–8.

Bourdieu, P. 1986. *Distinction: a Social Critique of Judgements of Taste*. London: Routledge & Kegan Paul.

——. 1990. *In Other Words: Essays towards a Reflexive Sociology*. Trans. M. Adamson. Cambridge: Polity Press.

Bourdieu, P. and J.-C. Passeron. 1977. *Reproduction: in Education, Society and Culture*. London: Sage.

Bowden, R. 1983. *Yena: Art and Ceremony in a Sepik Society*. Oxford: Pitt Rivers Museum.

Bowman, G. 1993. 'Nationalizing the Sacred: Shrines and Shifting Identities in the Israeli-occupied Territories'. *Man* (n.s.) 28 (3): 431–60.

Bragge, L. 1990. 'The Japandai Migrations'. In N. Lutkehaus, C. Kaufmann, W.E. Mitchell, D. Newton, L. Osmundsen and M. Schuster (eds) *Sepik Heritage: Tradition and Change in Papua New Guinea*. Durham, NC: Carolina Academic Press, pp. 36–49.

Brown, D.M. 1955. *Nationalism in Japan: an Introductory Historical Analysis*. Berkeley and Los Angeles: University of California Press.

Brown, M.F. 1998. 'Can Culture be Copyrighted?' *Current Anthropology* 39 (2): 193–222.

Brunton, R. 1989. *The Abandoned Narcotic: Kava and Cultural Instability in Melanesia*. Cambridge: Cambridge University Press.

Buckley, A. 1989. '"We're Trying to Find our Identity": Uses of History among Ulster Protestants'. In E. Tonkin, M. McDonald and M. Chapman (eds) *History and Ethnicity*. London and New York: Routledge, pp. 183–97.

——. (ed.). 1998. *Symbols in Northern Ireland*. Belfast: Institute of Irish Studies.

Bulmer, R.N.H. 1965. 'The Kyaka of the Western Highlands'. In P. Lawrence and M.J. Meggitt (eds) *Gods, Ghosts and Men: Some Religions of Australian New Guinea and the New Hebrides*. Oxford: Oxford University Press, pp. 132–61.

Burke, P. 1969. *The Renaissance Sense of the Past*. London: Edward Arnold.

——. 1992. 'We, the People: Popular Culture and Popular Identity in Modern Europe'. In S. Lash and J. Friedman (eds) *Modernity and Identity*. Oxford: Blackwell, pp. 293–308.

Canessa, A. 2000. 'Fear and Loathing on the Kharisiri Trail: Alterity and Identity in the Andes'. *Journal of the Royal Anthropological Institute* (n.s.) 6 (4): 705–20.

Cannadine, D. 1983. 'The Context, Performance and Meaning of Ritual: the British Monarchy and the "Invention of Tradition", c. 1820–1977'. In E. Hobsbawm and T. Ranger (eds) *The Invention of Tradition*. Cambridge: Cambridge University Press, pp. 101–64.

——. 1987. 'Introduction: Divine Rites of Kings'. In D. Cannadine and S. Price (eds) *Rituals of Royalty: Power and Ceremonial in Traditional Societies*. Cambridge: Cambridge University Press, pp. 1–19.

Carrier, J.G. 1995. 'Introduction'. In J.G. Carrier (ed.) *Occidentalism: Images of the West*. Oxford: Clarendon Press, pp. 1–32.

Carter, A. 1989. *The Philosophical Foundations of Property Rights*. New York: Harvester Wheatsheaf.

Castile, G.P. 1996. 'The Commodification of Indian Identity'. *American Anthropologist* 98 (4): 743–49.

Castile, G.P. and G. Kushner (eds). 1981. *Persistent Peoples: Cultural Enclaves in Perspective*. Tucson: University of Arizona Press.

Chadwick, O. 1964. *The Reformation*. Harmondsworth: Penguin.

Chang, K.-C. 1983. *Art, Myth, and Ritual: the Path to Political Authority in Ancient China*. Cambridge, MA: Harvard University Press.

Chatterjee, P. 1986. *Nationalist Thought and the Colonial World*. London: Zed Books.

——. 1993. *The Nation and its Fragments: Colonial and Postcolonial Histories*. Princeton: Princeton University Press.

Cheater, A.P. 1986. *Social Anthropology: an Alternative Introduction*. London: Unwin Hyman.

Chippendale, C. 1990. *Who Owns Stonehenge?* London: Batsford.

Clark, J.L. 1985. From Cults to Christianity: Continuity and Change in Takuru. PhD thesis, University of Adelaide.

Clarke, R. 2000. 'Self-presentation in a Contested City: Palestinian and Israeli Political Tourism in Hebron'. *Anthropology Today* 16 (5): 12–18.

Coates, P. 1988. *The Double and the Other: Identity as Ideology in Post-Romantic Fiction*. London: Macmillan.

Codere, H. 1961. 'Kwakiutl'. In E. Spicer (ed.) *Perspectives in American Indian Culture Change*. Chicago: University of Chicago Press, pp. 431–516.

Cohen, Abner. 1974. *Two Dimensional Man*. London: Routledge & Kegan Paul.

——. 1980. 'Drama and Politics in the Development of a London Carnival'. *Man* (n.s.) 15 (1): 65–87.

——. 1993. *Masquerade Politics: Explorations in the Structure of Urban Cultural Movements*. Oxford and Providence: Berg.

Cohen, A.P. 1985. *The Symbolic Construction of Community*. London: Tavistock.

——. 1986. *Symbolising Boundaries: Identity and Diversity in British Cultures*. Manchester: Manchester University Press.

Cohen, Paul. 1963. *China and Christianity: the Missionary Movement and the Growth of Chinese Antiforeignism 1860–1870*. Cambridge, MA: Harvard University Press.

Cohen, R. 1994. *Frontiers of Identity: the British and the Others*. London and New York: Longman.

Cole, J.W., and E.R. Wolf. 1974. *The Hidden Frontier: Ecology and Ethnicity in an Alpine Valley*. New York and London: Academic Press.

Coles, J. 1991. 'Beethoven Whitewash Claim'. *Guardian*, 13 June, p. 1.

Collier, M.J. (ed). 2000. *Constituting Cultural Difference through Discourse*. London: Sage.

Comaroff, J. 1985. *Body of Power, Spirit of Resistance: the Culture and History of a South African People*. Chicago: University of Chicago Press.

Connerton, P. 1989. *How Societies Remember*. Cambridge: Cambridge University Press.

Conversi, D. 1997. *The Basques, the Catalans and Spain: Alternative Routes to Nationalist Mobilisation*. London: Hurst.

Coombe, R.J. 1997. 'The Properties of Culture and the Possession of Identity: Postcolonial Struggle and the Legal Imagination'. In B. Ziff and P.V. Rao (eds) *Borrowed Power: Essays on Cultural Appropriation*. New Brunswick, NJ: Rutgers University Press, pp. 74–96.

——. 1998. *The Cultural Life of Intellectual Properties: Authorship, Appropriation and the Law*. Durham, NC: Duke University Press.

Copley, A. 1993. 'Indian Secularism Reconsidered: from Gandhi to Ayodhya'. *Contemporary South Asia* 2 (1): 47–65.

Coser, L.A. 1956. *The Functions of Social Conflict*. London: Routledge & Kegan Paul.

Danforth, L.M. 1993. 'Competing Claims to Macedonian Identity: the Macedonian Question and the Breakup of Yugoslavia'. *Anthropology Today* 9 (4): 3–10.

Davis, E. 1994. 'The Museum and the Politics of Social Control in Modern Iraq'. In J.R. Gillis (ed.) *Commemorations: the Politics of National Identity*. Princeton: Princeton University Press, pp. 90–104.

de Lepervanche, M. 1973. 'Social Structure'. In I. Hogbin (ed.) *Anthropology in Papua New Guinea*. Melbourne: Melbourne University Press, pp. 1–60.

De Quincey, T. 1897. *Collected writings*, Vol. XI. Ed. D. Masson. London: A. & C. Black.

De Rosa, C. 1998. 'Playing Nationalism'. In A.D. Buckley (ed.) *Symbols in Northern Ireland*. Belfast: Institute of Irish Studies, pp. 99–116.

Derrida, J. 1978. *Writing and Difference*. Trans. A. Bass. London: Routledge.

De Vos, G.A. 1995. 'Ethnic Pluralism: Conflict and Accommodation'. In Lola Romanucci-Ross and George De Vos (eds) *Ethnic Identity: Creation, Conflict and Accommodation*. 3rd ed. London: Sage, pp. 106–31.

De Vos, G.A. and L. Romanucci-Ross. 1995. 'Ethnic Identity: a Psychocultural Perspective'. In Lolao Romanucci-Ross and George De Vos (eds) *Ethnic Identity: Creation, Conflict and Accommodation*. 3rd ed. London: Sage, pp. 349–79.

De Vos, G.A. and H. Wagatsuma. 1995. 'Cultural Identity and Minority Status in Japan'. In Lola Romanucci-Ross and George De Vos (eds) *Ethnic Identity: Creation, Conflict and Accommodation*. 3rd ed. London: Sage, pp. 264–97.

Dittmar, H. 1992. *The Social Psychology of Material Possessions: to Have is to Be*. Hemel Hempstead: Harvester Wheatsheaf.

Dominy, M.D. 1990. 'New Zealand's Waitangi Tribunal: Cultural Politics of an Anthropology of the High Country'. *Anthropology Today* 6 (2): 11–15.

——. 1995. 'White Settler Assertions of Native Status'. *American Ethnologist* 22 (2): 358–74.

Douglas, M. 1966. *Purity and Danger: an Analysis of Concepts of Pollution and Taboo*. London: Routledge & Kegan Paul.

——. 1993. *In the Wilderness: the Doctrine of Defilement in the Book of Numbers*. Sheffield: Society for the Study of the Old Testament.

Duara, P. 1996. 'Historicizing National Identity, c. ./ho Imagines What and When'. In S. Eley and R.G. Suny (eds) *Becoming National: a Reader*. Oxford: Oxford University Press, pp. 151–77.

Dumont, L. 1970. 'Religion, Politics, and Society in the Individualistic Universe'. *Proceedings of the Royal Anthropological Institute of Great Britain and Ireland for 1970*, pp. 31–45.

Durkheim, E. 1964 [1893]. *The Division of Labor in Society*. Trans. George Simpson. New York: Free Press.

——. 1976 [1912]. *The Elementary Forms of the Religious Life*. Trans. J.W. Swain. London: George Allen & Unwin.

Edwards, J. 1985. *Language, Society and Identity*. Oxford: Blackwell.

Eley, S. and R.G. Suny. 1996. 'Introduction: from the Moment of Social History to the Work of Cultural Representation'. In S. Eley and R.G. Suny (eds) *Becoming National: a Reader*. Oxford: Oxford University Press, pp. 3–37.

Enloe, C. 1996. 'Religion and Ethnicity'. In J. Hutchinson and A.D. Smith (eds) *Ethnicity*. Oxford: Oxford University Press, pp. 197–201.

Eriksen, T.H. 1993. *Ethnicity and Nationalism: Anthropological Perspectives*. London: Pluto Press.

Errington, F. 1974. *Karavar: Masks and Power in a Melanesian Ritual*. Ithaca and London: Cornell University Press.

Errington, F. and D.B. Gewertz. 1986. 'The Confluence of Powers: Entropy and Importation among the Chambri'. *Oceania* 57 (2): 99–113.

Evans-Pritchard, E.E. 1940. *The Political System of the Anuak of the Anglo-Egyptian Sudan*. London: Percy Lund, Humphries.

Evenson, S.L. and D.J. Trayte. 1999. 'Dress and Interaction in Contending Cultures: Eastern Dakota and Euroamericans in Nineteenth Century Minnesota'. In L.B. Arthur (ed.) *Religion, Dress and the Body*. Oxford: Berg, pp. 95–116.

Fabian, J. 1983. *Time and the Other*. New York: Columbia University Press.

Featherstone, M. (ed.). 1990. *Global Culture: Nationalism, Globalism and Modernity*. London: Sage.

Feil, D.K. 1984. *Ways of Exchange*. St Lucia: University of Queensland Press.

———. 1987. *The Evolution of Highland Papua New Guinea societies*. Cambridge: Cambridge University Press.

Firth, R. 1973. *Symbols: Public and Private*. London: Allen & Unwin.

Fischer, J.L. 1958. 'Social Influences in the Choice of a Linguistic Variant'. *Word* 14: 47–56.

Forbes, J. 1995. 'Popular Culture and Cultural Politics'. In J. Forbes and M. Kelly (eds) *French Cultural Studies*. Oxford: Oxford University Press, pp.232–63.

Forbes, J. and M. Kelly (eds). 1995. *French Cultural Studies*. Oxford: Oxford University Press.

Ford, A. 1996. 'Whose Move is This?' *The Times*, Tuesday 30 July, p. 33.

Forge, A. 1966. 'Art and Environment in the Sepik'. *Proceedings of the Royal Anthropological Institute* 1965: 23–31.

———. 1972. 'The Golden Fleece'. *Man* (n.s.) 7: 527–40.

———. 1990. 'The Power of Culture and the Culture of Power'. In N. Lutkehaus, C. Kaufmann, W.E. Mitchell, D. Newton, L. Osmundsen and M. Schuster (eds) *Sepik Heritage: Tradition and Change in Papua New Guinea*. Durham, NC: Carolina Academic Press, pp. 160–70.

Forsythe, Diana. 1989. 'German Identity and the Problems of History'. In E. Tonkin, M. McDonald and M. Chapman (eds) *History and Ethnicity*. London and New York: Routledge, pp. 137–56.

Fortes, M. 1969. *Kinship and the Social Order*. London: Routledge & Kegan Paul.

———. 1987. *Religion, Morality and the Person*. Cambridge: Cambridge University Press.

Fortes, M. and E.E. Evans-Pritchard (eds). 1940. *African Political Systems*. London: Oxford University Press.

Foster, R.J. 1992. 'Commoditization and the Emergence of Kastom as a Cultural Category: a New Ireland Case in Comparative Perspective'. *Oceania* 62 (4): 284–94.

———. 1995a. 'Introduction: the Work of Nation Making'. In R.J. Foster (ed.) *Nation Making: Emergent Identities in Postcolonial Melanesia*. Ann Arbor: University of Michigan Press, pp. 1–30.

———. 1995b. 'Print Advertisements and Nation Making in Metropolitan Papua New Guinea'. In R.J. Foster (ed.) *Nation Making: Emergent Identities in Postcolonial Melanesia*. Ann Arbor: University of Michigan Press, pp. 151–81.

———. (ed.) 1995c. *Nation Making: Emergent Identities in Postcolonial Melanesia*. Ann Arbor: University of Michigan Press.

Fox, R.G. 1990. 'Hindu Nationalism in the Making, or the Rise of the Hindian'. In R.G. Fox (ed.) *Nationalist Ideologies and the Production of National Cultures*. Washington, DC: American Anthropological Association, pp. 63–80.

Frazer, G.J. 1967 [1911]. *The Golden Bough: a Study in Magic and Religion*. Abridged ed. London: Macmillan.

Freud, S. 1930. *Civilization and its Discontents*. London: Hogarth Press for the Institute of Psycho-analysis.

——. 1945 [1921]. *Group Psychology and the Analysis of the Ego*. London: Hogarth Press for the Institute of Psycho-analysis.

——. 1957 [1910]. *Five Lectures on Psycho-analysis, Leonardo da Vinci and Other Works*. London: Hogarth Press for the Institute of Psycho-analysis.

——. 1964 [1937–39]. *Moses and Monotheism, An Outline of Psycho-analysis, and Other Works*. London: Hogarth Press for the Institute of Psycho-analysis.

Friedman, J. 1992. 'The Past in the Future: History and the Politics of Identity'. *American Anthropologist* 94: 837–59.

——. 1994. *Cultural Identity and Global Process*. London: Sage.

Frith, S. 1996. 'Music and Identity'. In S. Hall and P. du Gay (eds) *Questions of Cultural Identity*. London: Sage, pp. 108–27.

Fustel de Coulanges, N.D. 1963 [1864]. *The Ancient City*. New York: Doubleday.

Gajek, E. 1990. 'Christmas under the Third Reich'. *Anthropology Today* 6 (4): 3–9.

Gambetta, D. 1991. '"In the Beginning was the Word...". The Symbols of the Mafia'. *Archives Européennes de Sociologie* 32 (1): 53–80.

Gefou-Madianou, D. 1999. 'Cultural Polyphony and Identity Formation: Negotiating Tradition in Attica'. *American Ethnologist* 26 (2): 412–39.

Gellner, E. 1983. *Nations and Nationalism*. Oxford: Basil Blackwell.

Gewertz, D.B. 1983. *Sepik River Societies: a Historical Ethnography of the Chambri and their Neighbors*. New Haven and London: Yale University Press.

——. (ed.). 1988. *Myths of Matriarchy Reconsidered*. Sydney: Oceania Monographs.

Girard, R. 1965. '"Triangular" Desire'. In R. Girard, *Deceit, Desire and the Novel*. Trans. Yvonne Freccero. Baltimore and London: Johns Hopkins University Press, pp. 1–52.

——. 1977. *Violence and the Sacred*. Trans. Patrick Gregory. Baltimore and London: Johns Hopkins University Press.

——. 1978. *'To Double Business Bound': Essays on Literature, Mimesis and Anthropology*. Baltimore and London: Johns Hopkins University Press.

Gluckman, M. 1977. *Politics, Law and Ritual in Tribal Society*. Oxford: Blackwell.

Goffman, E. 1968. 'The Inmate World'. In C. Gordon and K.J. Gergen (eds) *The Self in Social Interaction*, Vol 1: *Classic and Contemporary Perspectives*. New York: Wiley, pp. 267–74.

Goldman, I. 1975. *The Mouth of Heaven: an Introduction to Kwakiutl Religious Thought*. New York: Wiley.

Gombrich, E.H. 1963. 'Psycho-analysis and the History of Art'. In E.H. Gombrich *Meditations on a Hobby Horse, and Other Essays on the Theory of Art*. Oxford: Phaidon, pp. 30–44.

Gombrich, R. and G. Obeyesekere. 1988. *Buddhism Transformed*. Princeton, NJ: Princeton University Press.

Goody, J. 1962. *Death, Property and the Ancestors*. London: Tavistock.

Gorman, F.J.E. 1981. 'The Persistent Identity of the Mohave Indians, 1859–1965'. In G.P. Castile and G. Kushner (eds) *Persistent Peoples: Cultural Enclaves in Perspective*. Tucson: University of Arizona Press, pp. 43–68.

Graybill, B. and L.B. Arthur. 1999. 'The Social Control of Women's Bodies in Two Mennonite Communities'. In L.B. Arthur (ed.) *Religion, Dress and the Body*. Oxford: Berg, pp. 9–30.

Green, V.H.H. 1964. *Luther and the Reformation*. London: Methuen.

Greenfield, Jeanette. 1989. *The Return of Cultural Treasures*. Cambridge: Cambridge University Press.

Grossberg, L. 1996. 'Identity and Cultural Studies – Is That All There Is?' In S. Hall and P. du Gay (eds) *Questions of Cultural Identity*. London: Sage, pp. 87–107.

Guardian. 1996. 'The High Cost of Name-dropping: Imitation can Turn Out to Be the Costliest form of Flattery'. *Guardian*, Friday 9 August, p. 14.

Gupta, A. and J. Ferguson. 1992. *Culture, Power, Place: Explorations in Critical Anthropology*. Durham, NC: Duke University Press.

Hall, S. 1989. 'Ethnicity: Identity and Difference'. *Radical America* 23 (4): 9–20.

——. 1993. 'Culture, Community, Nation'. *Cultural Studies* 7 (3): 349–63.

——. 1996. 'Introduction: Who Needs Identity?' In S. Hall and P. du Gay (eds) *Questions of Cultural Identity*. London: Sage, pp. 1–17.

Hall, S. and P. du Gay. (eds). 1996. *Questions of Cultural Identity*. London: Sage.

Hall, S. and T. Jefferson (eds). 1976. *Resistance through Rituals: Youth Subcultures in Post-war Britain*. London: Hutchinson.

Hamerton-Kelly, R.G. (ed.). 1987. *Violent Origins: Walter Burkert, René Girard and Jonathan Z. Smith on Ritual Killing and Cultural Formation*. Stanford: Stanford University Press.

Hammell, E.A. 1997. 'Ethnicity and Politics: Yugoslav Lessons for Home'. *Anthropology Today* 13 (3): 5–9.

Handler, R. 1988. *Nationalism and the Politics of Culture in Quebec*. Madison: University of Wisconsin Press.

Hannerz, U. 1992. *Cultural Complexity: Studies in the Social Organization of Meaning*. New York: Columbia University Press.

Hanson, A. 1991. 'The Making of the Maori: Cultural Invention and its Logic'. *American Anthropologist* 91: 890–902.

Harris, R. 1972. *Prejudice and Tolerance in Ulster: a Study of Neighbours and 'Strangers' in a Border Community*. Manchester: Manchester University Press.

Harrison, S.J. 1987. 'Cultural Efflorescence and Political Evolution on the Sepik River'. *American Ethnologist* 14 (3): 491–507.

——. 1990. *Stealing People's Names: History and Politics in a Sepik River Cosmology*. Cambridge: Cambridge University Press.

——. 1992. 'Ritual as Intellectual Property'. *Man* (n.s.) 27 (2): 225–44.

——. 1993a. 'The Commerce of Cultures in Melanesia'. *Man* (n.s.) 28(1): 139–58.

——. 1993b. *The Mask of War: Violence, Ritual and the Self in Melanesia*. Manchester: Manchester University Press.

——. 1995a. 'Four Types of Symbolic Conflict'. *Journal of the Royal Anthropological Institute* (n.s.) 1 (2): 255–72.

——. 1995b. 'Anthropological Perspectives on the Management of Knowledge'. *Anthropology Today* 11 (5): 10–14.

——. 1999a. 'Cultural Boundaries'. *Anthropology Today* 15 (5): 10–13.

——. 1999b. 'Identity as a Scarce Resource'. *Social Anthropology* 7 (3): 239–51.

——. 2002. 'The Politics of Resemblance: Ethnicity, Trademarks, Headhunting'. *Journal of the Royal Anthropological Institute* 8 (2): 211–32.

——. 2003. 'Cultural Difference as Denied Resemblance: Rethinking Ethnicity and Nationalism'. *Comparative Studies in Society and History* 15 (2): 343–61.

Hart, J. 1997. 'Translating and Resisting Empire: Cultural Appropriation and Postcolonial Studies'. In B. Ziff and P.V. Rao (eds) *Borrowed Power: Essays on Cultural Appropriation*. New Brunswick, NJ: Rutgers University Press, pp. 137–68.

Hastrup, K. 1995. *A Passage to Anthropology: Between Experience and Theory*. London: Routledge.

Hebdige, D. 1979. *Subculture: the Meaning of Style*. London: Methuen.

Heiberg, M. 1980. 'Basques, Anti-Basques, and the Moral Community'. In R.D. Grillo (ed.) *'Nation' and 'State' in Europe: Anthropological Perspectives*. London: Academic Press, pp. 45–60.

Hendry, J. and C.W. Watson (eds). 2001. *An Anthropology of Indirect Communication*. New York and London: Routledge.

Henshall, K.G. 1999. *A History of Japan*. London: Macmillan.

Herzfeld, M. 1987. *Anthropology through the Looking-glass: Critical Ethnography in the Margins of Europe*. Cambridge: Cambridge University Press.

———. 1995. 'Hellenism and Occidentalism: the Permutations of Performance in Greek Bourgeois Identity'. In J.G. Carrier (ed.) *Occidentalism: Images of the West*. Oxford: Clarendon Press, pp. 218–33.

Hetherington, K. 1998. *Expressions of Identity: Space, Performance, Politics*. London: Sage.

Hitti, P.K. 1928. *The Origins of the Druze People and Religion*. New York: Columbia University Press.

Hobsbawm, E. 1983. 'Mass-Producing Traditions: Europe 1870–1914'. In E. Hobsbawm and T. Ranger (eds) *The Invention of Tradition*. Cambridge: Cambridge University Press, pp. 263–308.

Hobsbawm, E. and T. Ranger (eds). 1983. *The Invention of Tradition*. Cambridge: Cambridge University Press.

Hogbin, I. 1970. *The Island of Menstruating Men: Religion in Wogeo, New Guinea*. Scranton, London and Toronto: Chandler.

Horowitz, D.L. 1975. 'Ethnic Identity'. In N. Glazer and D.P. Moynihan (eds) *Ethnicity: Theory and Experience*. Cambridge, MA: Harvard University Press, pp. 111–40.

———. 1985. *Ethnic Groups in Conflict*. Berkeley and Los Angeles: University of California Press.

Hostetler, J. 1968. *Amish Society*. Baltimore and London: Johns Hopkins Press.

Hourani, A. 1991. *A History of the Arab Peoples*. London: Faber & Faber.

Hughes, P. 1957. *The Reformation*. London: Burns and Oates.

Hughes-Freeland, F. and M.M. Crain (eds). 1998. *Recasting Ritual: Performance, Media, Identity*. London: Routledge.

Hutton, Will. 1995. 'A Spirit that Moved'. *Guardian*, Wednesday 4 October, p. 19.

Isaacs, H.R. 1975. 'Basic Group Identity: the Idols of the Tribe'. In N. Glazer and D.P. Moynihan (eds) *Ethnicity: Theory and Experience*. Cambridge, MA: Harvard University Press, pp. 29–52.

Iteanu, A. 1983. *La Ronde des Échanges*. Paris: Maison de Sciences de l'Homme.

Jackson, J.E. 1995. 'Culture, Genuine and Spurious: the Politics of Indianness in the Vaupés, Colombia'. *American Ethnologist* 22 (1): 3–27.

Jacobson-Widding, Anita. 1983a. 'Introduction'. In Anita Jacobson-Widding (ed.) *Identity: Personal and Socio-cultural*. Atlantic Highlands, NJ: Humanities Press, pp. 13–34.

———. 1983b. 'Body and Power: Symbolic Demarcations of Separate Identity'. In Anita Jacobson-Widding (ed.) *Identity: Personal and Socio-cultural*. Atlantic Highlands, NJ: Humanities Press, pp. 371–88.

———. (ed.). 1983c. *Identity: Personal and Socio-cultural*. Atlantic Highlands, NJ: Humanities Press.

Jakubowska, L. 1990. 'Political Drama in Poland: the Use of National Symbols'. *Anthropology Today* 6 (4): 10–13.

James, G.G.M. 1954. *The Stolen Legacy*. New York: Philosophical Library.

Jarman, N. 1998. 'Painting Landscapes: the Place of Murals in the Symbolic Construction of Urban Space'. In A. Buckley (ed.) *Symbols in Northern Ireland*. Belfast: Institute of Irish Studies, pp. 81–98.

———. 1999. 'Commemorating 1916, Celebrating Difference: Parading and Painting in Belfast'. In A. Forty and S. Küchler (eds) *The Art of Forgetting*. Oxford and New York: Berg, pp. 171–96.

Jenkins, R. 1997. *Rethinking Ethnicity: Arguments and Explorations*. London: Sage.

Jolly, M. 1991. 'Soaring Hawks and Grounded Persons: the Politics of Rank and Gender in North Vanuatu'. In M. Godelier and M. Strathern (eds) *Big Men and Great Men: Personifications of Power in Melanesia*. Cambridge: Cambridge University Press, pp. 48–80.

———. 1992. 'Specters of Inauthenticity'. *The Contemporary Pacific* 4 (1): 49–70.

Jolly, M. and N. Thomas. 1992a. 'Introduction'. *Oceania* (Special Issue on the Politics of Tradition in the Pacific) 62 (4): 241–48.

Jolly, M. and N. Thomas (eds). 1992b. 'The Politics of Tradition in the Pacific'. *Oceania* (Special Issue) 62 (4).

Kahn, M. 1986. *Always Hungry, Never Greedy*. Cambridge: Cambridge University Press.

Kandiyoti, D. 1996. 'Women, Ethnicity and Nationalism'. In J. Hutchinson and A.D. Smith (eds) *Ethnicity*. Oxford: Oxford University Press, pp. 311–16.

Kapferer, B. 1988. *Legends of People, Myths of State: Violence, Intolerance, and Political Culture in Sri Lanka and Australia*. Washington, DC: Smithsonian Institution Press.

Keen, I. 1994. *Knowledge and Secrecy in an Aboriginal Religion: Yolngu of Northeast Arnhem Land*. Oxford: Clarendon.

Keesing, R.M. 1982. *Kwaio Religion*. New York: Columbia University Press.

———. 1993. 'Kastom Re-examined'. In G.M. White and L. Lindstrom (eds) *Custom Today. Anthropological Forum* (Special Issue) 6 (4): 587–96.

Keesing, R.M. and R. Tonkinson (eds). 1982. 'Reinventing Traditional Culture: the Politics of Kastom in Island Melanesia'. *Mankind* (Special Issue) 13 (4).

Kelly, R.C. 1976. 'Witchcraft and Sexual Relations: an Exploration in the Social and Semantic Implications of the Structure of Belief'. In P. Brown and G. Buchbinder (eds) *Man and Woman in the New Guinea Highlands*. Washington, DC: American Anthropological Association, pp. 36–53.

Kempf, W. 1994. 'Ritual, Power and Colonial Domination: Male Initiation among the Ngaing of Papua New Guinea'. In C. Stewart and R. Shaw (eds) *Syncretism/Anti-syncretism: the Politics of Religious Synthesis*. London: Routledge, pp. 108–26.

Kertzer, D.I. 1988. *Ritual, Politics and Power*. New Haven and London: Yale University Press.

Kiberd, D. 1989. 'Irish Literature and Irish History'. In R.F. Foster (ed.) *The Oxford Illustrated History of Ireland*. Oxford: Oxford University Press, pp. 275–338.

King, A. 1999. 'Remembering and Forgetting in the Public Memorials of the Great War'. In A. Forty and S. Küchler (eds) *The Art of Forgetting*. Oxford, New York: Berg, pp. 147–70.

Kinross, Lord. 1964. *Atatürk: the Rebirth of a Nation*. London: Weidenfeld & Nicolson.

Knauft, B.M. 1985a. *Good Company and Violence: Sorcery and Social Action in a Lowland New Guinea Society*. Berkeley: University of California Press.

——. 1985b. 'Ritual Form and Permutation in New Guinea: Implications of Symbolic Process for Socio-political Evolution'. *American Ethnologist* 12: 321–40.

Kooijman, S. 1959. *The Art of Lake Sentani*. New York: Museum of Primitive Art.

Kopytoff, I. 1986. 'The Cultural Biography of Things: Commoditization as Process'. In A. Appadurai (ed.) *The Social Life of Things: Commodities in Cultural Perspective*. Cambridge: Cambridge University Press, pp. 64–91.

Krohn-Hansen, C. 2001. 'A Tomb for Columbus in Santo Domingo: Political Cosmology, Population and Racial Frontiers'. *Social Anthropology* 9 (2): 165–92.

Küchler, S. 1987. 'Malangan: Art and Memory in a Melanesian Society'. *Man* (n.s.) 22 (2): 238–55.

——. 1988. 'Malangan: Objects, Sacrifice and the Production of Memory'. *American Ethnologist* 15 (4): 625–37.

Kuhrt, A. 1987. 'Usurpation, Conquest and Ceremonial: from Babylon to Persia'. In D. Cannadine and S. Price (eds) *Rituals of Royalty: Power and Ceremonial in Traditional Societies*. Cambridge: Cambridge University Press, pp. 20–55.

Kuper, A. 1988. *The Invention of Primitive Society: Transformations of an Illusion*. London and New York: Routledge.

Kuper, H. 1973. 'Costume and Identity'. *Comparative Studies in Society and History* 15 (3): 348–67.

Lane, C. 1981. *The Rites of Rulers*. Cambridge: Cambridge University Press.

——. 1984. 'Legitimacy and Power in the Soviet Union through Socialist Ritual'. *British Journal of Political Science* 14(2): 207–14.

Langness, L.L. 1973. 'Traditional Political Organization'. In I. Hogbin (ed.) *Anthropology in Papua New Guinea*. Melbourne: Melbourne University Press, pp. 142–73.

Laqueur, T.W. 1994. 'Memory and Naming in the Great War'. In J.R. Gillis (ed.) *Commemorations: the Politics of National Identity*. Princeton: Princeton University Press, pp. 150–67.

Larcom, J. 1982. 'The Invention of Convention'. In R.M. Keesing and R. Tonkinson (eds.) Reinventing Traditional Culture: the Politics of Kastom in Island Melanesia. *Mankind* (Special Issue) 13 (4): 330–37.

——. 1990. 'Custom by Decree: Legitimation Crisis in Vanuatu'. In J. Linnekin and L. Poyer (eds) *Cultural Identity and Ethnicity in the Pacific*. Honolulu: University of Hawaii Press, pp. 175–90.

La Rue, H. 1994. 'Music, Literature and Etiquette: Musical Instruments and Social Identity from Castiglione to Austen'. In M. Stokes (ed.) *Ethnicity, Identity and Music: the Musical Construction of Place*. Oxford and Providence: Berg, pp. 189–206.

Lash, S. and J. Friedman. 1992. 'Introduction: Subjectivity and Modernity's Other'. In S. Lash and J. Friedman (eds) *Modernity and Identity*. Oxford: Blackwell, pp. 1–30.

Lawrence, H.R. and D. Niles (eds). 2001. *Traditionalism and Modernity in the Music and Dance of Oceania*. Sydney: Syndey University Press.

Lawrence, P. 1964. *Road Belong Cargo: a Study of the Cargo Movement in the Southern Madang District New Guinea*. Melbourne: Melbourne University Press.

——. 1965. 'The Ngaing of the Rai coast'. In P. Lawrence and M.J. Meggitt (eds) *Gods, Ghosts and Men: some Religions of Australian New Guinea and the New Hebrides*. Oxford: Oxford University Press, pp. 198–223.

Lawrence, P. and M.J. Meggitt. 1965. *Gods, Ghosts and Men: some Religions of Australian New Guinea and the New Hebrides*. Oxford: Oxford University Press.

Leach, E.R. 1954. *Political systems of highland Burma*. London: Athlone Press.

——. 1964. 'Anthropological Aspects of Language: Animal Categories and Verbal Abuse'. In E.H. Lenneberg (ed.) *New Directions in the Study of Language*. Cambridge, MA: MIT Press, pp. 28–63.

Lebovics, H. 1994. 'Creating the Authentic France: Struggles over French Identity in the First Half of the Twentieth Century'. In J.R. Gillis (ed.) *Commemorations: the Politics of National Identity*. Princeton: Princeton University Press, pp. 239–57.

Lederman, R. 1986. *What Gifts Engender: Social Relations and Politics in Mendi, Highland Papua New Guinea*. Cambridge: Cambridge University Press.

Lefkowitz, M. 1996. *Not Out of Africa: How Afrocentrism Became an Excuse to Teach Myth as History*. New York: Basic Books.

Leone, M.P. 1981. 'Mormon "Peculiarity": Recapitulation of Subordination'. In G.P. Castile and G. Kushner (eds) *Persistent Peoples: Cultural Enclaves in Perspective*. Tucson: University of Arizona Press, pp. 78–85.

Levine, Stephen. 1990. 'Cultural Politics in New Zealand: Responses to Michele Dominy'. *Anthropology Today* 6 (3): 4–6.

Lévi-Strauss, C. 1969. *The Elementary Structures of Kinship*. Trans. J.H. Bell, J.R. von Sturmer and R. Needham. London: Eyre & Spottiswoode.

——. 1973. *Totemism*. Trans. R. Needham. Harmondsworth: Penguin.

Lindenbaum, S. 1984. 'Variations on a Sociosexual Theme in Melanesia'. In G.H. Herdt (ed.) *Ritualized Homosexuality in Melanesia*. Berkeley: University of California Press, pp. 337–61.

Lindstrom, L. 1985. 'Personal Names and Social Reproduction on Tanna, Vanuatu'. *Journal of the Polynesian Society* 94: 27–45.

——. 1990. *Knowledge and Power in a South Pacific Society*. Washington and London: Smithsonian Institution Press.

Linnekin, J. 1990. 'The Politics of Culture in the Pacific'. In J. Linnekin and L. Poyer (eds), *Cultural Identity and Ethnicity in the Pacific*. Honolulu: University of Hawaii Press, pp. 149–73.

——. 1992. 'On the Theory and Politics of Cultural Construction in the Pacific'. *Oceania* 62 (4): 249–63.

Linnekin, J. and L. Poyer. 1990a. 'Introduction'. In J. Linnekin and L. Poyer (eds) *Cultural Identity and Ethnicity in the Pacific*. Honolulu: University of Hawaii Press, pp. 1–16.

Linnekin, J. and L. Poyer (eds.). 1990b. *Cultural Identity and Ethnicity in the Pacific*. Honolulu: University of Hawaii Press.

Linton, R. 1943. 'Nativistic Movements'. *American Anthropologist* 45: 230–40.

LiPuma, E. 1995. 'The Formation of Nation-states and National Cultures in Oceania'. In R.J. Foster (ed.) *Nation Making: Emergent Identities in Postcolonial Melanesia*. Ann Arbor: University of Michigan Press, pp. 33–68.

——. 1997. 'History, Identity and Encompassment: Nation-making in the Solomon Islands'. *Identities* 4 (2): 213–44.

——. 1998. 'Modernity and Forms of Personhood in Melanesia'. In M. Lambek and A. Strathern (eds) *Bodies and Persons: Comparative Perspectives from Africa and Melanesia*. Cambridge: Cambridge University Press, pp. 53–79.

Lowenthal, D. 1994. 'Identity, Heritage, and History'. In J.R. Gillis (ed.) *Commemorations: the Politics of National Identity*. Princeton: Princeton University Press, pp. 41–57.

McArthur, M. 1971. 'Men and Spirits in the Kunimaipa Valley'. In L.R. Hiatt and C. Jayawardena (eds) *Anthropology in Oceania: Essays Presented to Ian Hogbin*. Sydney: Angus and Robertson, pp. 155–90.

McAuley, J.W. and J. McCormack. 1990. 'The Hound of Ulster and the Re-writing of Irish History'. *Études Irlandaises* 15 (2): 149–64.

McGrath, A.E. 1988. *Reformation Thought: an Introduction*. Oxford: Basil Blackwell.

McGrory, D. and D. Kennedy. 1998. 'Diana's Face "Belongs to the World"'. *The Times*, Saturday 4 July, p. 1.

McIvor, G. 1995. 'Squabbling Santas Poles Apart on Site of Father Christmas's Home'. *Guardian*, Tuesday 18 July, p. 9.

Macfie, A.L. 1994. *Atatürk*. London and New York: Longman.

Mach, Z. 1994. 'National Anthems: the Case of Chopin as a National Composer'. In M. Stokes (ed.) *Ethnicity, Identity and Music: the Musical Construction of Place*. Oxford: Berg, pp. 61–70

Macpherson, C.B. 1962. *The Political Theory of Possessive Individualism: Hobbes to Locke*. Oxford: Oxford University Press.

Maddock, K. 1998. 'The Dubious Pleasures of Commitment'. *Anthropology Today* 15 (5): 1–2.

Mair, L. 1962. *Primitive Government: a Study of Traditional Political Systems in Eastern Africa*. London: The Scholar Press.

——. 1976. *Witchcraft*. New York and Toronto: McGraw-Hill.

Malinowski, B. 1922. *Argonauts of the Western Pacific*. New York: Dutton.

——. 1935. *Coral Gardens and their Magic*, Vol. 1. London: George Allen & Unwin.

——. 1948. 'Myth in Primitive Psychology'. In B. Malinowski *Magic, Science and Religion, and Other Essays*. New York: Free Press, pp. 93–148.

Mango, A. 1999. *Atatürk*. London: John Murray.

Marcus, G.E. and M.J. Fischer (eds). 1986. *Anthropology as Cultural Critique: an Experimental Moment in the Human Sciences*. Chicago and London: University of Chicago Press.

Marwick, M.G. 1964. 'Witchcraft as a Social Strain-gauge'. *Australian Journal of Science* 26: 263–68.

Mauss, M. 1925. 'Essai sur le don: forme et raison de l'échange dans les sociétés archaïques'. *Année Sociologique* (n.s.) 1: 30–186.

Mead, M. 1935. *Sex and Temperament in Three Primitive Societies*. New York: William Morrow.

——. 1938. *The Mountain Arapesh*, Part 1: *an Importing Culture*. New York: American Museum of Natural History.

——. 1975 [1956]. *New Lives for Old: Cultural Transformation – Manus, 1928–1953*. New York: William Morrow.

Meyer, B. 1994. 'Beyond Syncretism: Translation and Diabolization in the Appropriation of Protestantism in Africa'. In C. Stewart and R. Shaw (eds)

Syncretism/Anti-syncretism: the Politics of Religious Synthesis. London: Routledge, pp. 45–68.

Meyer, B. and P. Geschiere (eds). 1999. *Globalization and Identity: Dialectics of Flow and Closure*. Oxford: Blackwell.

Miller, D. 1987. *Material Culture and Mass Consumption*. Oxford: Blackwell.

Mills, C.W. 1970. *The Sociological Imagination*. Harmondsworth: Penguin.

Modjeska, N. 1991. 'Post-Ipomoean Modernism: the Duna Example'. In M. Godelier and M. Strathern (eds) *Big Men and Great Men: Personifications of Power in Melanesia*. Cambridge: Cambridge University Press, pp. 234–55.

Morauta, L. 1973. 'Traditional Polity in Madang'. *Oceania* 44 (2): 127–55.

Morley, D. and K. Robins. 1990. 'No Place like *Heimat*: Images of Home(land) in European Culture'. *New Formations* 12: 1–23.

Morphy, H. 1991. *Ancestral Connections: Art and an Aboriginal System of Knowledge*. Chicago and London: University of Chicago Press.

Morris-Suzuki, T. 1998. *Re-inventing Japan: Time, Space, Nation*. New York and London: M.E. Sharpe.

Nadel-Klein, J. 1991. 'Reweaving the Fringe: Localism, Tradition and Representation in British Ethnography'. *American Ethnologist* 18 (3): 500–17.

Nairn, T. 1996. 'Scotland and Europe'. In S. Eley and R.G. Suny (eds) *Becoming National: a Reader*. Oxford: Oxford University Press, pp. 79–105. (Reprinted from *New Left Review*, 1974, Vol. 83: 57–82).

Neumann, K. 1992. *Not the Way it Really Was: Constructing the Tolai Past*. Honolulu: University of Hawaii Press.

Nederveen Pieterse, J. 1996. 'Varieties of Ethnic Politics and Ethnic Discourse'. In E.N. Wilmsen and P. McAllister (eds) *The Politics of Difference: Ethnic Premises in a World of Power*. Chicago and London: University of Chicago Press, pp. 25–44.

Newton, N.J. 1997. 'Memory and Misrepresentation: Representing Crazy Horse in Tribal Court'. In B. Ziff and P.V. Rao (eds) *Borrowed Power: Essays on Cultural Appropriation*. New Brunswick, NJ: Rutgers University Press, pp. 195–224.

Nic Craith, M. 2002. *Plural Identities, Singular Narratives: the Case of Northern Ireland*. New York and Oxford: Berghahn Press.

Nicholls, D. 1979. *From Dessalines to Duvalier: Race, Colour and National Independence in Haiti*. London: Macmillan.

Norton, R. 1993. 'Culture and identity in the South Pacific'. *Man* (n.s.), 28 (4): 741–60.

O'Donnell, M. 1981. *A New Introduction to Sociology*. Walton-on-Thames: Nelson.

Ohnuki-Tierney, Emiko. 1995. 'Structure, Event and Historical Metaphor: Rice and Identities in Japanese History'. *Journal of the Royal Anthropological Institute* (n.s.) 1 (2): 227–54.

——. 2001. 'Historicization of the Culture Concept'. *History and Anthropology*, 12 (3): 213–54.

——. 2002. *Kamikaze, Cherry Blossoms, and Nationalisms: the Militarization of Aesthetics in Japanese History*. Chicago and London: University of Chicago Press.

Oliver, D. 1955. *A Solomon Island Society*. Boston: Beacon Press.

Oosterval, G. 1961. *People of the Tor: a Cultural-Anthropological Study on the Tribes of the Tor Territory (Northern Netherlands New-Guinea)*. Assen: Van Gorkum.

Otto, T. 1991. The Politics of Tradition in Baluan: Social Change and the Construction of the Past in a Manus Society. PhD Thesis, Australian National University (reproduced by the Centre for Pacific Studies, University of Nijmegen).

———. 1992. 'The Ways of *Kastom*: Tradition as Category and Practice in a Manus Village'. *Oceania* 62 (4): 264–83.

Paine, R. 1989. 'Israel: Jewish Identity and Competition over "Tradition"'. In E. Tonkin, M. McDonald and M. Chapman (eds) *History and Ethnicity*. London and New York: Routledge, pp. 121–36.

———. 1995. 'Behind the Hebron Massacre, 1994'. *Anthropology Today* 11 (1): 8–15.

Pareto, V. 1935. *The Mind and Society*. New York: Harcourt Brace.

Parkin, F. 1979. *Marxism and Class Theory: a Bourgeois Critique*. London: Tavistock.

Parsons, T. 1975. 'Some Theoretical Considerations on the Nature and Trends of Change of Ethnicity'. In N. Glazer and D.P. Moynihan (eds) *Ethnicity: Theory and Experience*. Cambridge, MA: Harvard University Press, pp. 53–83.

Patterson, M. 1981. 'Slings and Arrows: Rituals of Status Acquisition in North Ambrym'. In M.R. Allen (ed.) *Vanuatu: Politic ̄conomics and Ritual in Island Melanesia*. Sydney: Academic Press, pp. 189–236.

Penrose, J. 1993. 'Reification in the Name of Change: the Impact of Nationalism on Social Constructions of Nation, People and Place in Scotland and the United Kingdom'. In P.J. Jackson and J. Penrose (eds) *Constructions of Race, Place and Nation*. London: University College London Press, pp. 27–49.

Perrin, N. 1979. *Giving up the Gun: Japan's Reversion to the Sword, 1543–1879*. Boston: David Godine.

Piehler, G.K. 1994. 'The War Dead and the Gold Star: American Commemoration of the First World War'. In J.R. Gillis (ed.) *Commemorations: the Politics of National Identity*. Princeton: Princeton University Press, pp. 168–85.

Posey, D. 1990. 'Intellectual Property Rights and Just Compensation for Indigenous Knowledge'. *Anthropology Today* 6 (4): 13–16.

Powell, H.A. 1967. 'Competitive Leadership in Trobriand Political Organisation'. In R. Cohen and J. Middleton (eds) *Comparative Political Systems*. New York: Natural History Press, pp. 155–92.

Radcliffe-Brown, A.R. 1951. 'The Comparative Method in Social Anthropology'. *Journal of the Royal Anthropological Institute* 81: 15–22.

———. 1952. 'Religion and society'. In A.R. Radcliffe-Brown *Structure and Function in Primitive Society*. London: Cohen & West, pp. 153–77.

Rank, O. 1971. *The Double: a Psychoanalytic Study*. New York: New American Library.

Renan, E. 1996 [1882]. 'What is a Nation?' In S. Eley and R.G. Suny (eds) *Becoming National: a Reader*. Oxford: Oxford University Press, pp. 42–55.

Rhodes, T. 1998. 'Pop Greats Take on the Pretenders'. *The Times*, Tuesday 26 May, p. 3.

Robbins, K. 1996. 'Interrupting Identities: Turkey/Europe'. In S. Hall and P. du Gay (eds) *Questions of Cultural Identity*. London: Sage, pp. 61–86.

Robertson Smith, W. 1889. *Lectures on the Religion of Semites*. Edinburgh: Black.

Rogers, R. 1970. *A Psychoanalytic Study of the Double in Literature*. Detroit: Wayne State University Press

Rohatynskyi, M. 1997. 'Culture, Secrets and Ömie History: a Consideration of the Politics of Cultural Identity'. *American Ethnologist* 24 (2): 438–56.

Rohner, R.P. and E.C. Rohner. 1970. *The Kwakiutl: Indians of British Columbia*. New York: Holt, Rinehart & Winston.

Roosens, E. 1989. *Creating Ethnicity: the Processes of Ethnogenesis*. London: Sage.

Root, D. 1996. *Cannibal Culture: Art, Appropriation and the Commodification of Difference*. Boulder: Westview.

Rosin, P. and C. Nemeroff. 1990. 'The Laws of Sympathetic Magic: a Psychological Analysis of Similarity and Contagion'. In J.W. Stigler, R.A. Shweder and G. Herdt (eds) *Cultural Psychology: Essays on Comparative Human Development*. Cambridge: Cambridge University Press, pp. 205–32.

Rowlands, M. 1994. 'The Politics of Identity in Archeology'. In G.C. Bond and A. Gilliam (eds) *Social Construction of the Past: Representation as Power*. London and New York: Routledge, pp. 129–43.

Rubinstein, R.L. 1981. 'Knowledge and Political Process on Malo'. In M.R. Allen (ed.) *Vanuatu: Politics, Economics and Ritual in Island Melanesia*. Sydney: Academic Press, pp. 135–72.

Rush, S. and F. Reeve. 2000. 'They Think It's All Over – It Isn't Yet'. *The Times*, Tuesday 8 February, p. 3.

Ryan, D.J. 1961. Gift exchange in the Mendi valley. PhD thesis, University of Sydney.

Said, E.W. 1978. *Orientalism*. London and Henley: Routledge & Kegan Paul.

Sax, W.S. 1998. 'The Hall of Mirrors: Orientalism, Anthropology, and the Other. *American Anthropologist* 100 (2): 292–301.

Schieffelin, E.L. 1976. *The Sorrow of the Lonely and the Burning of the Dancers*. St Lucia: University of Queensland Press.

Schwartz, T. 1973. 'Cult and Context: the Paranoid Ethos in Melanesia'. *Ethos* 1 (2): 153–74.

——. 1975. 'Cultural Totemism: Ethnic Identity, Primitive and Modern'. In G. De Vos and L. Romanucci-Ross (eds) *Ethnic Identity*. 1st ed. Palo Alto: Mayfield, pp. 106–31.

Seeger, A. 1987. *Why Suyá Sing: a Musical Anthropology of an Amazonian People*. Cambridge: Cambridge University Press.

Sharp, J. 1996. 'Ethnogenesis and Ethnic Mobilization: a Comparative Perspective on a South African Dilemma'. In E.N. Wilmsen and P. McAllister (eds) *The Politics of Difference: Ethnic Premises in a World of Power*. Chicago and London: University of Chicago Press, pp. 85–103.

Sheriff, R.E. 1999. 'The Theft of Carnaval: National Spectacle and Racial Politics in Rio de Janeiro'. *Cultural Anthropology* 14 (1): 3–28.

Sibley, D. 1995. *Geographies of Exclusion: Society and Difference in the West*. London and New York: Routledge.

Simmel, G. 1950. *The Sociology of Georg Simmel*. Trans. K.H. Wolff. New York: Free Press.

——. 1955. *Conflict, and The Web of Group-affiliations*. Trans. K.H. Wolff and R. Bendix. New York: Free Press.

——. 1971. *Georg Simmel on Individuality and Social Forms: Selected Writings*. Ed. D.N. Levine. Chicago and London: University of Chicago Press.

Simpson, M. 1994. 'St Pat "was a Prod": Ian Paisley Jnr's Startling Claim'. *Belfast Telegraph* Thursday 17 March, p. 6.

Slezkine, Y. 1996. 'The USSR as a Communal Apartment, or How a Socialist State Promoted Ethnic Particularism'. In G. Eley and R.G. Suny (eds) *Becoming National: a Reader*. New York and Oxford: Oxford University Press, pp. 203–38.

Smith, A.D. 1986. *The Ethnic Origin of Nations*. Oxford: Basil Blackwell.
——. 1996. 'Chosen Peoples'. In J. Hutchinson and A.D. Smith (eds) *Ethnicity*. Oxford: Oxford University Press, pp. 189–96.

Spicer, Edward H. 1971. 'Persistent Cultural Systems: a Comparative Study of Identity Systems that can Adapt to Contrasting Environments'. *Science* 174 (4011): 795–800.

Srinivas, M.N. 1952. *Religion and Society among the Coorgs of South India*. Oxford: Clarendon Press.

Steiner, G. 1975. *After Babel: Aspects of Language and Translation*. Oxford: Oxford University Press.

Stewart, C. 1994. 'Syncretism as a Dimension of Nationalist Discourse in Modern Greece'. In C. Stewart and R. Shaw (eds) *Syncretism/Anti-syncretism: the Politics of Religious Synthesis*. London: Routledge, pp. 127–44.
——. 1998. 'Who Owns the Rotonda? Church vs. State in Greece'. *Anthropology Today* 14 (5): 3–9.

Stewart, J. 1986. 'Patronage and Control in the Trinidad Carnival'. In V.W. Turner and E.M. Bruner (eds) *The Anthropology of Experience*. Urbana and Chicago: University of Illinois Press, pp. 289–315.

Stiling, M. 1980. *Famous Brand Names, Emblems and Trade-marks*. Newton Abbot: David & Charles.

Stolke, V. 1995. 'Talking Culture: New Boundaries, New Rhetorics of Exclusion in Europe'. *Current Anthropology* 36 (1): 1–24.

Strathern, A.J. 1971. *The Rope of Moka: Big-men and Ceremonial Exchange in Mount Hagen, New Guinea*. Cambridge: Cambridge University Press.

Strathern, M. 1980. 'No Nature, No Culture: the Hagen Case'. In C. MacCormack and M. Strathern (eds) *Nature, Culture and Gender*. Cambridge: Cambridge University Press, pp. 174–222.
——. 1985. 'Kinship and Economy: Constitutive Orders of a Provisional Kind'. *American Ethnologist* 12 (2): 191–209.
——. 1988. *The Gender of the Gift: Problems with Women and Problems with Society in Melanesia*. Berkeley, Los Angeles and London: University of California Press.

Suwa, J. 2001. 'Ownership and Authenticity of Indigenous and Modern Music in Papua New Guinea'. In H.R. Lawrence and D. Niles (eds) *Traditionalism and Modernity in the Music and Dance of Oceania*. Sydney: Sydney University Press, pp. 91–102.

Taussig, M. 1993. *Mimesis and Alterity: a Particular History of the Senses*. London and New York: Routledge.

The Times Diary. 1999. 'Clark of Words'. *The Times*, Thursday 15 April, p. 22.

Thomas, N. 1992. 'The Inversion of Tradition'. *American Ethnologist* 19 (2): 213–32.

Todorow, Tzvetan. 1984. *The Conquest of America: the Question of the Other*. Trans. Richard Howard. New York: Harper & Row.

Tomlinson, J. 1991. *Cultural Imperialism: a Critical Introduction*. London and Washington: Pinter.

Trotter, D.A. 1993. 'The French Language since 1945'. In M. Cook (ed.) *French Culture since 1945*. London: Longman, pp. 269–88.

Trudgill, P. 1974. *Sociolinguistics: an Introduction*. Harmondsworth: Penguin.

Turton, D. 1997. *War and Ethnicity*. New York: University of Rochester.

Tuzin, D.F. 1976. *The Ilahita Arapesh: Dimensions of Unity*. Berkeley: University of California Press.

———. 1990. 'Fighting for their Lives: the Problem of Cultural Authenticity in Today's Sepik'. In N. Lutkehaus, C. Kaufmann, W.E. Mitchell, D. Newton, L. Osmundsen and M. Schuster (eds) *Sepik Heritage: Tradition and Change in Papua New Guinea*. Durham, NC: Carolina Academic Press, pp. 364–69.

Uberoi, J.P.S. 1962. *Politics of the Kula Ring*. Manchester: Manchester University Press.

van Baal, J. 1966. *Dema: Description and Analysis of Marind-Anim Culture (South New Guinea)*. The Hague: Martinus Nijhoff.

van der Veer, P. 1994a. *Religious Nationalism: Hindus and Moslems in India*. Berkeley: University of California Press.

———. 1994b. 'Syncretism, Multiculturalism and the Discourse of Tolerance'. In C. Stewart and R. Shaw (eds) *Syncretism/Anti-syncretism: the Politics of Religious Synthesis*. London: Routledge, pp. 196–211.

Veblen, T. 1934 [1899]. *The Theory of the Leisure Class*. New York: Modern Library.

Verdery, K. 1990. 'The Production and Defence of "the Romanian Nation", 1900 to World War II'. In R.G. Fox (ed.) *Nationalist Ideologies and the Production of National Cultures*. Washington, DC: American Anthropological Association, pp. 81–111.

Vicedom, G. and H. Tischner. 1943–48. *Die Mbowamb*. 3 vols. Hamburg: Cram, de Gruyter.

Wagner, R. 1967. *The Curse of Souw: Principles of Daribi Clan Definition and Alliance in New Guinea*. Chicago and London: University of Chicago Press.

———. 1975. *The Invention of Culture*. Englewood Cliffs: Prentice-Hall.

Walker, M. 1991. 'MGM Sees Red over Homosexual Pink Panthers'. *Guardian*, Tuesday 28 May, p. 18.

———. 1992. 'Church Leaders Warn Bush that God is not a Republican'. *Guardian*, Monday 31 August, 1992, p. 1.

Walker, N. 1995. 'A Watchdog for the Copycats: Supermarket Brands Packaged Like the Top Sellers are Under Scrutiny'. *Independent*, Tuesday 31 October, p. 11.

Watson, J. 1990. 'Other People do Other Things: Lamarckian Identities in Kainantu Subdistrict, Papua New Guinea'. In J. Linnekin and L. Poyer (eds) *Cultural Identity and Ethnicity in the Pacific*. Honolulu: University of Hawaii Press, pp. 17–41.

Weber, M. 1930. *The Protestant Ethic and the Spirit of Capitalism*. Trans. T. Parsons. London: Allen & Unwin.

Weiner, A.B. 1977. *Women of Value, Men of Renown*. St Lucia: University of Queensland Press.

———. 1992. *Inalienable Possessions: the Paradox of Keeping-while-giving*. Berkeley: University of California Press.

Westney, D.E. 1987. *Imitation and Innovation: the Transfer of Western Organisational Patterns to Meiji Japan*. Cambridge, MA, and London: Harvard University Press.

Whitehead, A. 1983. 'Men and Women, Kinship and Property: some General Issues'. In R. Hirschon (ed.) *Women and Property, Women as Property*. London: Croom Helm, pp. 176–92.

Whittaker, E. 1994. 'Public Discourse on Sacredness: the Transfer of Ayers Rock to Aboriginal Ownership'. *American Ethnologist* 21 (2): 310–34.

Wilkinson, G.N. 1978. 'Carving a Social Message: the Malanggans of Tabar (Papua New Guinea)'. In M. Greehalgh and V. Megaw (eds) *Art in Society*. London: Duckworth, pp. 227–42.

Williams, F.E. 1940. *Drama of Orokolo: the Social and Ceremonial Life of the Elema*. Oxford: Clarendon Press.

Wilmsen, E.N. and P. McAllister (eds). 1996. *The Politics of Difference: Ethnic Premises in a World of Power*. Chicago and London: University of Chicago Press.

Wilson, M. 1951. 'Witch Beliefs and Social Structure'. *American Journal of Sociology* 56: 307–13.

Wolf, E. 1982. *Europe and the People without History*. Berkeley: University of California Press.

Wolfe, P.1991. 'On being Woken Up: the Dreamtime in Anthropology and in Australian Settler Culture'. *Comparative Studies in Society and History* 33 (2): 197–224.

Wright, S. 1998. 'The Politicization of "Culture"'. *Anthropology Today* 14 (1): 7–15.

Yang, M. 1996. 'Tradition, Travelling Theory, Anthropology and the Discourse of Modernity in China'. In H.L. Moore (ed.) *The Future of Anthropological Knowledge*. London and New York: Routledge, pp. 93–114.

Yoruk, Z.F. 1997. 'Turkish Identity from Genesis to the Day of Judgement'. In Kathryn Dean (ed.) *Politics and the Ends of Identity*. Aldershot: Ashgate, pp. 103–34.

Young, M.W. 1971. *Fighting with Food*. Cambridge: Cambridge University Press.

Zegwaard, G.A. 1968. 'Headhunting Practices of the Asmat of Netherlands New Guinea'. In A.P. Vayda (ed.) *Peoples and Cultures of the Pacific*. New York: Natural History Press, pp. 421–50.

Ziff, B. and P.V. Rao (eds). 1997. *Borrowed Power: Essays on Cultural Appropriation*. New Brunswick, NJ: Rutgers University Press.

Index